Black Political History

FROM THE ARCH OF SAFETY INTO THE MOUTH OF THE LION

Ken Raymond

ISBN 978-1-0980-4543-2 (paperback)
ISBN 978-1-0980-4845-7 (hardcover)
ISBN 978-1-0980-4544-9 (digital)

Christian Faith Publishing, Inc.
832 Park Avenue
Meadville, PA 16335
www.christianfaithpublishing.com

Printed in the United States of America

Dedication

I'd like to dedicate this book to two individuals that stood behind me as I researched, wrote, revised, edited, and struggled to create the best single source of black political historic information for the public. They were both looking over my shoulders as I hunched over my keyboard day and night.

Looking over my right should was the Lord Himself. It was the Lord Himself that first inspired me to create this volume. He led me to resource materials that helped fill gaps of knowledge to help make this book complete, He strengthened me and kept me encouraged throughout the entire writing process.

Looking over my left shoulder was my fiancé Vertie Moore. Vertie always kept me encouraged and always reminded me that history books for the modern era are long overdue—especially in the black community.

Thank you to you both....

Preface

To say that the journey toward political, social, and economic equality, for black American's, was replete and laden hardships, deadly traps and snares would be a profound understatement.

Since the end of the Civil War, the path has been marked with major victories and heart-breaking setbacks. Frederick Douglass, one of the most prominent figures in black history, bore witness to many of these events himself.

Born a slave, Douglass knew first-hand how much blacks suffered under bondage. And as an abolitionist, a political spokesman, and successful businessman, he saw how former slaves made political choices and organized quickly to secure freedom for themselves and their children. And their political choices led them directly to the Republican Party.

And today, the lives of African Americans are a largely the result of the political choices made during the 1930's and 1960's. And, for better or for worse, a significant majority of America's black community has committed itself to the Democrat Party and is reaping the results of their decision.

Were these decisions foreseen by Frederick Douglass? Douglass was many things, but could he possibly have been a prophet?

Perhaps he was. Because Douglass, along with several other well-known African Americans during his day, accurately predicted the condition of 21st century black America.

In **Black Political History: From the Arch of Safety into the Mouth of the Lion**, we track the political journey of black Americans since the end of the Civil War. We witness their glorious victories despite overwhelming odds. We join them in their disappointment as proven and faithful allies appear to falter in the face of growing violence.

We watched in stunned disbelief as many black American's turned to a deadly foreign enemy for support. And we cheer as many black Americans decide to take control of their future themselves.

This book also enlightens the reader about the first black congressmen elected and their epic battle to pass the Civil Rights Act of 1875. And it also answers questions such as:

- What was the Civil Rights Act of 1875?
- Why did black Americans leave the Republican Party and join the Democrats?
- Will blacks ever return to the GOP?
- Who was the first black man to appear on a national presidential ticket?
- What was the Civil Rights Act of 1957?
- Why did the NAACP join with the Democrats after fighting them for so long?
- What was the Big Switch?
- What was Nixon's Southern Strategy?

Additionally, this book teaches important historic events that are not taught in schools and never addressed during Black History Month. It also helps African Americans better understand themselves and provides greater insight into the black culture.

And this book shows that what Frederick Douglass referred to as "the Mouth of the Lion" is truly an accurate description of the condition of black America today.

Contents

Chapter 1: 1865–1875
From the Plantation Fields to Congress

Months before Confederate General Robert E. Lee surrendered his troops to General Ulysses S. Grant at Appomattox Court House, the American people started to take great strides toward the lofty belief of its founders that "*all men are created equal.*"

No one thought this day would come, certainly not the slaves themselves, but the American people were about to pass judgment on the institution of slavery and decide whether they wanted it to continue. It was an institution that completely devalued human life, separated families, and led to a war that ultimately cost both the North and South millions of dollars. The South's "peculiar institution" also caused nearly two million people lose their lives at the hands of their own countrymen.

Confederate Vice President
Alexander H. Stephens

But many of the leaders of the Confederacy believed that the preservation of slavery was worth that and more.

Most notably among them was Alexander Hamilton Stephens, vice president of the Confederacy. In a speech given in Savannah, Georgia, on March 21, 1861, Vice President Stephens said, "*The South's new government is founded upon the exactly opposite ideas of the found-*

ing fathers: its cornerstone rests upon the great truth that the Negro is not equal to the white man; and subordination to the superior race is his natural and moral condition."[1]

The Confederate vice president's position on the issue was very clear. But the American people were about to weigh in on the subject. Since the nation's founding, only the wealthy and the powerful were deemed worthy to address the issue. But after years of controversy, debate, division and war among themselves, the individual states were about to decide the fate of the most important issue of the day once and for all.

Judgment came from Congress in the form of the Thirteenth Amendment to the US Constitution, which permanently bans slavery in America. By January 31, 1865, the amendment passed both houses of the Republican-controlled Congress and was signed by President Abraham Lincoln. And during the month of February, the other states would speak and, one way or another, end the slavery debate in America forever.

The honor of casting the first votes, for or against the Thirteenth Amendment, went to the state of Illinois on February 1. The "*Land of Lincoln*" eagerly voted to adopt the Thirteenth Amendment. The question then went to the state of Rhode Island, which happily voted to end the institution.

Two months before General Lee, an example of dignity and honor to his men, sat proudly on his white horse before the Union forces at Appomattox Courthouse, his own home state of Virginia voted to adopt the Thirteenth Amendment on February 9, 1865.

General Robert E. Lee

---

[1]   https:teachingamericanhistory.org/library/document/cornerstone-speech

Did the general know about it on that day? Did General Lee know that the foundation of the new government, the new nation that he and his men sacrificed everything for was being surrendered by his home state and the other southern states?

No one will ever know if news ever reached General Lee before he surrendered. And no one will ever know if the news of the other Southern states' support of the Thirteenth Amendment ever reached the ears of the Confederate soldiers who stood with him.

If they heard, we can only speculate that their feelings, at best, would be mixed. Some, likely, rejoiced to see the end of an extremely divisive issue that literally tore their nation apart. Others, perhaps, lamented and mourned the loss the cornerstone spoken and upheld by Vice President Stephens.

But despite it all, slavery came crashing down. One state after another declared it to be a cancer that was destroying our country. And one state after another declared that it must be removed before America decomposed any further.

Three hundred and nine days after the bill passed Congress, two-thirds of the country in Northern, Midwestern, and Southern states condemned slavery to death never to rise again.

The Fourteenth Amendment

Although the American people adopted the Thirteenth Amendment with relative ease, the Fourteenth Amendment was met with much greater resistance.

The amendment, which provided citizenship and equal protection under the law to former slaves, was first proposed in Congress on June 13, 1866. And just as the Democratic Party fought against the Thirteenth Amendment, they fought harder to derail the passage of the Fourteenth Amendment.

It was, however, much easier for them to fight against Fourteenth Amendment because many Americans could not accept the idea of former slaves, or the children of former slaves, being considered equal in social, political, or economic standing with themselves—even if they did agree that slavery had to end.

It took over two years for the Fourteenth Amendment to be adopted. In 1866, it was rejected by the people of Texas, North Carolina, and South Carolina. But the people of the Tar Heel State apparently had a change of heart and voted to support the amendment on July 4, 1868, followed by South Carolina on July 9, with Texas coming aboard on February 18, 1870.

But acceptance of the Fourteenth and Fifteenth Amendments did not come without resistance from the South and a lot of arm-twisting from the Republican-controlled federal government and the courts.

A perfect example is the events that took place in Georgia. On September 12, 1868, Democrats in the Georgia General Assembly expelled 23 black Republicans from office and replaced them with white Democrats.

The Democrats argued that blacks did not have the constitutional right to hold public office within their state. But the constitution they referred to was adopted when the state was still a part of the Confederacy.

During a moment of extreme arrogance, the Democrats agreed to allow the black Republicans to convince them why they should legally be allowed to hold office under the Constitution of the Confederate States, which was still the legitimate governing document in their minds.

State Senator Tunis George Campbell Sr. accepted their challenge. Campbell, who was also a minister, spoke on the floor of the Senate for eight days and respectfully yet boldly reminded his Democrat colleagues that the Confederacy had lost the war and its constitution was no

Tunis Campbell

longer valid. This was something the Democrats likely believed Tunis did not have the nerve to do, but he did.

Tunis also argued several points of law, the federal Constitution, and quoted several scriptures from the Bible, which they all claimed to honor.

During the first few days, the Democrats ignored Campbell and considered his speech as light entertainment. But as Campbell persisted, the Democrats became angry. They responded with clamor, tumult, and did everything they could to intimidate him.

Throughout his time on the floor, Democrat representatives displayed their weapons or even pointed guns at him to disrupt his speech. Senator Campbell wrote about the experience in his autobiography.

"Upon the question of my eligibility to office, I was compelled to stand alone for eight days on the floor of the Senate, contending for the rights of the colored members to hold their seats; and at different times when I was speaking I could see Democrat members with their hands on the butts of their pistols with their teeth hard together and using threatening gestures at me."[2]

No one could have made a better case for the black members of the Georgia legislature, but that did not matter. The staunch guardians of the old Confederacy were determined to uphold its obsolete principles and forced the black members to leave.

In response, Senator Campbell developed a very bold plan. Campbell and the other expelled black representatives went to Washington to request that the US Senate refuse to seat the two senators from Georgia, Joshua Hill and H.M.V. Miller, until the Georgia General Assembly restored the black representatives to their positions.

Campbell and his delegation met with Senators Charles Sumner and E.D. Morgan. They explained the situation in Georgia, and Sumner and Morgan agreed that Georgia should not be represented

---

[2] Tunis G. Campbell, The Sufferings of the Rev. T.G. Campbell and his Family in Georgia (Washington: Enterprise Publishing Company, 1877): P. 13.

in the US Senate until its black representatives were restored to their seats.

When Congress convened, the senate leadership did not seat Hill and Miller. Furthermore, the leadership of the House of Representatives echoed the Senate's resolve, refusing to seat Georgia's congressional delegation.

Campbell successfully delayed the Georgia's readmission into the Union. He, and the other black representatives, then took their case to the state supreme court. And because Georgia lacked representation in the US House or Senate, the state reverted back to its previous status as a military district.

Georgia's temporary loss of its statehood had the full support of Republican Governor Rufus Bullock. Bullock was routinely defied, harassed, and undermined by former confederates and saw the situation as an opportunity deal a decisive blow to his opponents.

As a military district, the Territory of Georgia was placed under the complete control of the US military under the command of General Alfred H. Terry.

During the fall of 1869, Georgia's State Supreme Court ruled that blacks were eligible to hold office. Campbell, and the other black representatives were free to return to their legislative seats, but Governor Bullock was not satisfied. Governor Bullock did not want any more trouble from the Democrats, knowing they would give him than he could handle in the future. So, he consulted with General Terry and they came up with a plan of their own. Bullock and Terry decided to use the full power and legal authority of the general's position to change the Georgia legislature before the state was admitted back into the Union.

The plan is known historically as Terry's Purge in which General Terry cleansed the state legislature of nearly all Democrats. And under the Reconstruction laws, he had the authority to carry it out. Not only did the black Republican representatives return to the state General Assembly, but they were joined by more white Republicans, which replaced the unseated Democrats.

And with a Republican super majority, the Georgia legislature ratified the Fourteenth and Fifteenth Amendments to the

Constitution. The Fourteenth Amendment, formerly ratified on July 28, 1868, made 3.1 million former slaves American citizens.

The Fifteenth Amendment

Through much opposition and struggle, the Republican Party, with the support of the American people, bestowed personal freedom and citizenship to millions who only knew hardship, oppression, and poverty.

But the Party of Lincoln saw that for the former slaves to truly protect themselves, their children, and their freedom, they needed another constitutional weapon.

On February 26, 1869, the Fifteenth Amendment was proposed in Congress. The amendment granted former slaves the right to vote. The amendment passed the House of Representatives 144 to 44 with almost 100 percent support from Republicans. The Democrats either voted against the amendment or abstained.

Nineteenth-century illustration of blacks casting ballots.

The states of North Carolina, South Carolina, Louisiana, and Arkansas were among the first to vote in favor of the Fifteenth Amendment in March 1869. Texas joined them and gave the proposal the final support it needed.

Who could have foreseen the day in which the people of six Southern states, states that had provided massive numbers of volunteers for the Confederate Army, would also provide the votes needed to institutionalize the right of blacks to vote? But they did, and the Fifteenth Amendment was formerly ratified by the end of March 1870.

The Arch of Safety

The reconstruction of the South was well under way, and the newly freed slaves took full advantage of their new status as citizens as they organized themselves politically.

With the hardship and pain of slavery fresh in their minds, they knew they had to learn the political process and become a part of it if they were going to keep freedom for themselves and their children.

When it was time to choose their party affiliation, the choice was obvious. Nearly 100 percent of the 3.1 million former slaves registered as Republican.

The Republican Party was the obvious choice. It was the Republican Party that consisted of committed abolitionists such as Senator Charles Sumner, Congressman Thaddeus Stevens, Senator Henry Wilson, and Senator Lyman Trumbull—figures who had fought and sacrificed for black freedom since the party's creation in 1854.

Frederick Douglass, a Republican himself, strongly encouraged the former slaves to add their strength to the Republican Party. Douglass expressed his thoughts about the Republicans many times and in different ways.

Even in the wake of the Compromise of 1877, Douglass strongly urged former slaves to continue their support of the Republican Party.

That unfortunate bargain left many Republican supporters so angry and disappointed that Douglass

Frederick Douglass, an ardent supporter of the Republican Party.

found himself playing the role of peacekeeper among the Republican faithful.

During the 1888 elections, Republican nominee Benjamin Harris faced incumbent Democratic President Grover Cleveland. Southern support for Republicans was on shaky ground and, despite the Democrat's history and obvious hostility towards former slaves, some Democrats aggressively pursued blacks for their political support.

It was within this political environment in which Douglass responded to the concerns of local activists in Petersburg, Virginia, about congressional candidate John Mercer Langston, as well as the entire Republican ticket, in a letter written in August of that year.

In that letter, Douglass wrote, *"I recognize the Republican Party as the sheet anchor of the colored man's political hopes and his arch of safety."* [3]

There he also talked about the complexity of navigating through the treacherous waters of American politics. It is likely that Douglass had the Compromise of 1877 in mind. He explained that although the choices made could be difficult to accept, *"the Republican Party is the ship, and all else is the sea."* [4]

The sacrifices made during the Civil War and the passage of the Thirteenth, Fourteenth, and Fifteenth Amendments to the Constitution left no doubt in Douglass's mind about who the true political allies of blacks were.

Congressman Robert Brown Elliott

---

[3] Library of Congress, The Frederick Douglass Papers, https://www.loc.gov/resource/mfd.07005/?sp=1

[4] Library of Congress, The Frederick Douglass Papers, https://www.loc.gov/resource/mfd.07005/?sp=1

And because the Republicans had proved themselves as true friends, and because former slaves were encouraged by people like Frederick Douglass, black Americans throughout the South organized and established Republican organizations at the state and county levels within each Southern state.

On September 4, 1867, former slave Abraham Galloway gave the opening address at the founding convention of the North Carolina Republican Party in Raleigh. Galloway was among 20 black republicans elected to serve as state representatives.

These events, which were completely unforeseeable, were repeated throughout the former Confederacy. In South Carolina, Georgia, Louisiana, Texas, Virginia, Arkansas, Alabama, and other parts of the South, former slaves gathered in cities, held conventions, and created Republican Party organizations. No one knew that former slaves would, so aggressively, launch themselves into the world of politics like this. But they did—and they did it for their own survival.

To say that white Southerners were alarmed would be an understatement. Many of them still had difficulty accepting the loss of the Civil War, and the quick, dramatic change of Southern society. But now they were faced with the reality of either sharing the responsibility of government or being governed by a race of people they deemed inferior.

From their perspective, it was probably a living nightmare. From birth, they were taught that blacks were like animals and had to be controlled. And a lifetime of teaching and tradition does not fade away so quickly.

But from the perspective of blacks, it was a dream come true. They were free, with the political power to establish their freedom and chart their own futures.

Among the first things they believed they had to do was secure political power for themselves. And with the help of Republicans, Quakers, and Abolitionists from the North and the Midwest (commonly referred to as carpetbaggers by Southerners), that's exactly what they did.

For example, former slave Jefferson Long was one of the founders of the Georgia Republican Party; John Adams Hyman, also a slave, cofounded the North Carolina Republican Party. Robert C. De Large and Robert Brown Elliott were founders of the South Carolina Republican Party; former slave Benjamin Sterling Turner was one of the founders of the Alabama Republican Party.

Many of these founders were elected to Congress including Robert Brown Elliott, Benjamin Sterling Turner, and Jefferson Franklin Long.

Violent Response by Democrats

After losing the Civil War and watching their fellow Southerners vote to support the Thirteenth, Fourteenth, and Fifteenth Amendments, active members of the Democratic Party could not bear to live and work side by side with people they truly believed to be less than human. And it was even more difficult for them think of their new neighbors as fellow citizens equal to them.

As a result, the Ku Klux Klan (KKK) was formed, whose mission was to enforce white supremacy and support the Democratic Party agenda at all costs!

The Klan's agenda was to return the South to Democrat control, force white Republicans to leave the South, and return Southern society to a pre-Civil War condition as much as possible.

It started by targeting white Republican state legislators throughout the South. With their faces concealed with various types of masks, Klan members rode from house to house and dragged white Republican lawmakers from their beds to shoot them down or to lynch them.

The Klan also terrorized former slaves by

Congressman Joseph Hayne Rainey

23

burning their property and threatening their lives. But unlike their white Republican victims, the Klan demanded that blacks vote for the Democratic Party under threat of violence.

Republican Congressman Joseph Hayne Rainey delivered a speech on the floor of the House of Representatives describing an incident in which a white Republican state senator, John Winsmith, was forcibly removed from his home and shot down by Klan members.[5]

Senator Winsmith lived to testify before a congressional committee, which convened in January of 1871. For several weeks, the committee heard testimony from dozens of witnesses and examined evidence of Klan atrocities throughout the South.

After all the testimony was heard and evidence presented, Congress published a thirteen-volume report entitled, "Report of the Joint Select Committee Appointed to Inquire into the Affairs of the Late Insurrectionary States" After the report was made public, it was used garner support for action and to persuade the president to become involved.[6]

This illustration, appearing in Harpers Weekly on October 21, 1876, shows former slaves forced to vote for Democrat at gunpoint, which occurred throughout the South.

State law enforcement officials refused to protect former slaves and white Republicans because many of them were members of the Democratic Party themselves. The situation left victims of Klan violence with no protection.

Republican Congressmen Samuel Shellabarger and Benjamin Franklin Butler sponsored a bill that became known as the Ku Klux Klan Act of 1871. The bill authorized the federal government to

---

5   Congressional Globe: Debates and Proceedings 42nd Congress 1st Session. https://www.memory.loc.gov/cgi-bin/query

6   http://www.paperlessarchives.com/kkk_1871_testimony.html

send troops into Southern states to help protect black and white Republicans from the Klan.[7]

Congressman Raincy was one of three black Republican congressmen to deliver speeches on the floor of the House in favor of the bill. The others were Robert Brown Elliott and Robert C. De Large. Both were from South Carolina, and De Large was a former slave.

The bill passed and was signed into law by Republican President Ulysses S. Grant on April 20, 1871. Nevertheless, for unknown reason, the military response was delayed until President Grant finally dispatched troops on October 18, 1871.

The Violence Gets Worse

Grant's use of the military did not dissuade radical Democrats or the various paramilitary organizations that supported them. Chaos reigned in the South, and the possibility of death and violence became a part of daily life for former slaves; white Republicans from the north, also known as "*carpetbaggers*"; and white Republicans in the South, also known as "*scalawags*."

Elections during the Reconstruction Era were plagued with voter intimidation, suppression, and fraud throughout the South. It was no secret that Democrats constantly tried to stop blacks from voting during every election through acts of intimidation and violence. And in most cases, the fraud and intimidation during elections was caused by the Democrats.

When confronted about their attempts at voter suppression, the Democrats hurled charges of fraud and intimidations at Republicans. As a result, chaos dominated during the election season. And the disputed local and statewide election results throughout Louisiana in 1872 led to violence and the death of many blacks across the state.

Because neither Republicans or Democrats accepted the other's claim of victory, the impasse led to dual governments. In Louisiana's

---

[7] Congressional Globe: 42nd Congress 1st Session. http://memory.loc.gov/cgi-bin/ampage?collId=llhb&fileName=042/llhb042.db&recNum=1163

Grant Parish, both sides fought for control over the courthouse in Colfax, near the Red River.

The Republicans claimed the offices of sheriff and judge for candidates Dan Shaw and R.C. Register, while the Democrats claimed that those positions had been won by Christopher Columbus Nash and Alfonse Cazabat.

With the help of a black militia unit, the Republicans gained control of the courthouse building and began to appoint deputies. For weeks, Democrat supporters threatened to uproot the Republican carpetbaggers and kill their black militia until finally, they fulfilled their threats.

And on Easter Sunday, April 13, 1873, about 150 armed Democrat supporters gathered at the courthouse and attacked. The attackers forced the black militia into the courthouse, and they set the building on fire.[8]

The destruction of the courthouse was not part of their plan. Enraged by the loss of the courthouse, the

Colfax Massacre Illustration

white militants turned their anger toward a crowd a of blacks nearby and slaughtered them.

The event became known as the Colfax Massacre, and over 200 blacks were killed.

US Attorney James Beckwith indicted the members of the white militia, but only three were convicted.

One of the worst acts of sedition swept from American history books occurred on September 14, 1874, in New Orleans, Louisiana.

It was on that day when a Democratic Paramilitary Group, known as the Crescent City White League, attacked the Louisiana State House with over 1,500 armed men, overthrowing the elected

---

[8] 64parishes.org/entry/Colfax-Massacre

state government.[9] A fierce battle erupted in the streets of New Orleans that ended with the death many Republican supporters and former slaves. The incident became known as the Battle of Liberty Place.

And once again, confusion over the election results of 1872 gave birth to violence. During that year, US Republican Senator William Kellogg faced Democrat John McEnery for the governor's office. Unfortunately, voter intimidation and fraud prevailed throughout the election just as it had across the South during the Reconstruction Era.

The state elections commission referred the entire matter to the federal court, and the court ruled in favor of Senator Kellogg.

GOVERNOR KELLOGG.

Governor William Kellogg

The Democrats, and their supporters, did not like the court's decision and openly defied Governor Kellogg and the entire state government. They first responded by creating an alternative government that met in the Odd Fellows Hall in New Orleans.

The inability to collect funds and garner statewide support caused the illegitimate government to wither away by the spring of 1873. But McEnery, who was determined to unseat Kellogg and overthrow the state government, organized many militia groups from rural counties across the state between the summer of 1873 and 1874.

The militia groups consisted mainly of former Confederate soldiers who were still angry about losing the war. McEnery was easily

---

[9] NewOrleanshistorical.org

able to keep their hatred and bitterness alive with a relentless propaganda campaign against Governor Kellogg and the black Republican state lawmakers.

They characterized the Republican government as "tyrannical" and inspired fear into the minds of the people about being governed by black representatives.

The White League's leadership met in exclusive "white only" clubs to make their plans, only allowing trusted former Confederate soldiers to attend. This made it very difficult for the police to keep track of their activities. In mid-September of 1874, a White League spy told the New Orleans Police Commissioner, Algernon Sidney Badger, that the league just received a large shipment of weapons.

On September 13, 1874, the league called a public meeting at the intersection of Canal Street and Royal Street. About 5,000 people gathered, and the meeting organizers made speeches and hurled outlandish accusations at the governor, calling for his resignation.

Governor Kellogg was likely informed about the league's arms shipment. So, when he saw them gathered in the street, he knew that McEnery and the White League were about to launch an attack. The governor fled and took refuge in State Custom House before the fighting started. But before he left, Kellogg placed Police Commissioner Badger and former Confederate General James Longstreet in charge of defending the government.

As the meeting continued, militia members marched through the city's present-day Central Business District, snipers were positioned on rooftops, and barricades were erected in strategic places.

The intense fighting completely overwhelmed the city's police. Longstreet, who had only a handful of black regiments, kept his men out of the fighting. According to some historians, it is likely that Longstreet had little confidence in his men, so ordered them to remain at the state house.

That left Badger and his police force alone to fight the militia. Although armed with a cannon and Gatling guns, the police force fell to McEnery's militia.

The White League controlled the city within a few hours and inaugurated John McEnery as governor of Louisiana and Davidson B. Penn as lieutenant governor.

Before the attack, the league cut the city's telegraph wires in an attempt to sever communication with the rest of the country until the militia was firmly entrenched. But apparently, they missed a few lines because news of the attack reached Washington, DC very quickly.

JOHN F. M'ENERY.

John McEnery

When President Grant was informed of the insurrection, he was enraged and quickly dispatched federal troops. The troops defeated and scattered the White League and their militia forces. The league held Louisiana's state government for three days before President Grant restored Governor Kellogg and the other state officials to their positions.

The Civil Rights Act of 1875

As the number of assaults and murders—and the intimidation of black Americans—increased, it became evident that the leadership of the Democratic Party, in Southern states, had no intention of honoring the rights granted to the newly freed slaves by the Fourteenth and Fifteenth Amendments to the Constitution.

And many believed that the Democratic Party, if possible, would overturn the Thirteenth Amendment and place black Americans back into slavery—if they could.

But other Southerners, those who supported the amendments, confronted the Democrat leaders about the completely inhumane and barbaric methods they used. They were truly shocked to see many of their friends and neighbors attempt to overrule Constitutional authority in the South with the use of terrorist tactics.

And somehow, perhaps because of prejudices about Northerners and blacks, the Democrats were able to deceive many of their fellow Southerners into believing they had to resort to violence because of a Northern plan to "Africanize" the South. Southerners sympathetic to blacks were told that Republicans wanted to make Southern states more like the continent of Africa to gain political power for themselves and to suppress the rights of Southern whites.[10]

Some Southerners did not believe such an outrageous charge. Nonetheless, they were often eventually intimidated into silence and submission to the Democratic Party's agenda.

In 1870, the US Republican Senator from Massachusetts Charles Sumner decided to deal with the problem with additional legislation. Senator Sumner proposed Senate Bill 18, which later became known as the Civil Rights Act of 1875. The bill would end segregation in the South and grant equal access and equal treatment to blacks in public places.[11]

The bill languished in committee for years, and, during that time, Senator Sumner's health sharply declined. Republican Senator George F. Edmunds, from Vermont, and Republican Congressman Benjamin Franklin Butler continued to move Sumner's bill through Congress. Unfortunately, Senator Sumner died on March 11, 1874, shortly after the bill made it to the House floor.

The Original Black Caucus

The debate over the Civil Rights Act began in December of 1873 and continued for about 14 months. The reason for the length of time for debate is unclear, but it seems likely that the Democrats were able to delay a final vote after they gained seats in Congress in 1874.

---

[10] George Henry White: An Even Chance in the Race of Life. By Benjamin R. Justesen, Louisiana State University Press. 2001 P. 432

[11] Congressional Globe, 1833-1873: 41st Congress, 2nd Session. History of Bills and Resolutions. http://memory.loc.gov/cgi-bin/query/r?ammem/hlaw:@field(DOCID+@lit(cg0896))

Although the bill was introduced and moved through Congress primarily by Senator Edmunds and Congressman Butler, they believed it seemed appropriate to hand off the next phase of the process to their black Republican colleagues.

Edmunds and Butler knew those in the caucus very well and worked with them on several pieces of legislation. Not only were they confident that the men could lead the debate, but they believed it was a great opportunity to show the world that blacks were fit and capable of representing voters in Congress.

The First Black Members of the U.S. Congress

Therefore, Congressmen Joseph Hayne Rainey, Alonzo Jacob Ransier, Robert Brown Elliott, Josiah Thomas Walls, Richard Harvey Cain, James T. Rapier, and John Roy Lynch led the charge on behalf of the bill's passage. Only Congressmen Walls and Lynch were former slaves, but all of them were well acquainted with the humiliation and indignities that blacks were forced to endure.

The black congressmen endured overwhelming persecution from the media, and the KKK, throughout the time the bill was being considered. But they were steadfastly willing to suffer additional harassment for the chance to prove that blacks belonged in the House of Representatives.

Unlike other congressional debates, including the debate on the KKK Act, the Civil Rights Act garnered a great deal of attention from the national media and drew hundreds of curious spectators, black and white, to the public gallery.

Many among the white onlookers and the media expected to see the black congressmen make public fools of themselves. They believed the black congressmen were intellectually inferior, incompetent, and slow-witted. They expected to see the men completely humiliated during the formal, public debate with some of the wealthiest, most well-educated, and highly esteemed members of Congress, who also happened to be former slave owners. And many of them hoped the debate would prove once and for all that blacks did not belong in politics.

Most of the black attendees, however, were present for the opposite reasons. They wanted to show their support for the black Republican congressmen and the Civil Rights Bill, while some had doubts in the congressmen's public speaking abilities.

Congressman Rainey was the first take the floor of the House on December 10, 1873. Rainey and Ransier each delivered three speeches, Congressman Cain boldly spoke four times, Congressman Rapier added two speeches, and Elliott, Walls, and Lynch each spoke once.

Illustration of the Civil Rights Act debate

For months, the black congressmen debated the merits and morality of the bill against former slave owners such as Democratic Congressmen John Robbins, from North Carolina, and Joseph Whitehead.

One after another, they engaged the Democrat opposition with eloquence, passion, honor, dignity, and humor. They also articulated points and counterpoints of the law and court rulings, citing Constitutional principles that supported their positions.

The black congressman more than held their own against the Democrat's congressional elite. And many in the gallery completely underestimated the abilities of black congressmen to express themselves intelligently and with clarity. Like many in America during that time, unfortunately, Southern whites were taught that blacks were more like animals—and they expected to see something to support their long-held beliefs.

But they saw for themselves that everything they believed was a grievous error.

As surprised as the white members of the gallery were, none were more shocked than the Democratic congressmen themselves. Congressman Robbins was reduced to making a futile attempt to persuade everyone that the passage of the bill would somehow cause white people, throughout the South, to die![12]

Congressman Cain injected humor into his speeches throughout the debate. And Cain could not resist providing a snarky response to the outrageous claim that the Civil Rights Act would somehow inflict death on white Southerners. When Cain replied to the Gentleman from North Carolina, the entire House Chamber as well as the gallery filled with laughter and applause at the expense of Congressman Robbins.

The black Republican congressmen had successfully turned the tables. And it was the wealthy, well-educated Democrat elite that was humiliated before the media and the American public. The news spread quickly among black Americans about how seven of their own had successfully engaged the proudest among the Democrat aristocracy in an intellectual battle—and emerged victorious.

Congressman Richard
Harvey Cain

The black congressmen were congratulated by their Republican colleagues for their outstanding and eloquent display of knowledge of the Constitution and the law. And on February 5, 1875, the Civil Rights Act passed the House of Representatives 162–99. On March 1, 1875, President Ulysses S. Grant signed the bill into law.

---

[12] Congressional Record, House of Representatives, 43rd Congress, 2nd Session. Page 34 of 202. http://memory.loc.gov/cgi-bin/ampage?collId=llcr&fileName=005/llcr005.db&recNum=35

Chapter 2: 1876–1883
Democrats Grow More Violent and Republicans Compromise

With the passing of the Civil Rights Act of 1875, the black congressmen earned tremendous respect for themselves from many who believed, only months earlier, that blacks were too feebleminded to do anything more than manual labor, much less serve in Congress.

But just as the Democratic Party refused to respect the Thirteenth, Fourteenth, and Fifteenth Amendments to the Constitution, it, likewise, refused to honor the passage of the Civil Rights Act of 1875.

Senator Matthew Calbraith Butler

The determined Democrats and their supporters did not submit to any law that conflicted with their desire to restore the South to the way it was before the Civil War. And they made it clear that they would resort to any cruel method and conceivable means—including violence and oppression—to achieve their goals.

On July 8, 1876, Democratic Senator Matthew Calbraith Butler led a violent mob that killed many blacks and displaced them from their homes in Hamburg, South Carolina. Butler provoked the fight by first demanding that the people of Hamburg—who were mainly former slaves—stop their Fourth of July parade so that he and his men could pass.

In an attempt to preserve peace with the former Confederates, the town officials suspended the parade to allow Senator Butler and his men to ride through. Senator Butler, however, did not come to Hamburg for a peaceful celebration of the Fourth of July.

When it became obvious that disruption of their celebration wasn't going to provoke the town's officials to fight, Senator Butler then demanded that the town's law enforcement surrender their weapons. When they refused, Butler, who arrived with hundreds of armed men, ordered them to attack the town. Many of the town's residents were killed and others fled.

Between November of 1876 and March of 1877, the people of South Carolina witnessed one the most outrageous political spectacles in history when both Democrat and Republican officeholders, and office seekers, laid siege on the state capitol building, with both sides demanding that the other side surrender its seats.

This incident began when Wade Hampton appeared to have won the race for governor of South Carolina that year. But South Carolina's bipartisan electoral commission discovered massive voter fraud in Laurens and Edgefield counties, where it appeared that more white voters had voted then actually lived there.

Following the commission's findings, President Grant recognized incumbent Republican Governor Daniel Chamberlain as the winner in his race against Democrat candidate Wade Hampton.

Despite the findings of the commission, Hampton led hundreds of armed men to the statehouse in Columbia and declared himself the new governor of South Carolina. Hampton's men greatly outnumbered the federal troops present. And although they stood between Hampton's mob and the members of the state legislature, the commander of the federal troops, General Thomas H. Ruger, did not order his men to fire for fear of being slaughtered.

Chaos in Columbia

The people of South Carolina were completely stunned by what happened next. The Hampton supporters marched into the state capitol, elected a Democrat Speaker of the House, W.H. Wallace, and seated the new legislators in the presence of the current legislators and Republican Speaker E.W.M. Mackey.

Both sides demanded that the other vacate its seats, both sides threatened violence, and neither side allowed the other to conduct business. Additionally, neither side left the capitol building for fear it would not be able to return.[13]

The Compromise of 1877

The same disputes surrounding elections that produced chaos in South Carolina clouded the outcome of the presidential election as well. In the contest for president, Republican candidate Rutherford B. Hayes faced Democrat candidate Samuel Tilden, with neither candidate having won the necessary 185 electoral college votes to take the presidency. Tilden won 184, and Hayes finished with 166.

Republican leaders not only disputed the election results from South Carolina, but those from Florida and Louisiana as well. The situation in Washington, DC, quickly began to resemble the events in Columbia when both Democrat and Republican electors, from all three states, reported to Washington, DC, to cast their votes with the rest of the Electoral College.

Absent a constitutional method to resolve the dispute, the House and Senate created a 15-member Electoral Commission and charged them with resolving the problem.[14]

The commission was made up of five house members, five senators, and five Supreme Court justices. Eight of the commission members were Republicans and seven were Democrats.

---

[13] Dray, Philip "Capitol Men: The Epic Story of Reconstruction Through the lives of the first Black Congressmen. Boston, New York, Mariner Books and Houghton Mifflin Company P. 263-269

[14] www.rbhayes.org/hayes/frequentlyaskedquestions

Throughout the month of February of 1877, the commission members held hearings and ultimately decided to award the electoral votes from all three of the disputed states to Rutherford Hayes.

The Senate confirmation process was very long and contentious, but, in the end, the disputed electoral college votes were awarded to Hayes. Or, at least, that was the public version of events during that time.

Many historians, however, believe that the decision in Haye's favor was not made by the Electoral Commission, but by the Republican and Democrat leaders who met in the in Wormley's Hotel, in Washington, DC, during the month of February.

Although the Democrats certainly wanted to win the White House, they always cared much more about gaining full control of the Southern states. They wanted Southerners to live their own lives, create their own laws, and to restore a pre-Civil War society in the South.

President Rutherford Hayes

Published reports indicate that Democrats used the presidential impasse to achieve what they could not acquire with an army of Confederate soldiers. The not-so-secret deal is known as the Compromise of 1877.

According to newspaper reports, the Democrats agreed to acquire enough congressional support to give Hayes the presidency. And in return, Hayes would end Reconstruction, withdraw federal troops, and support Democrat control over Southern states. This version of events has survived the passage of time, rather than Haye's victory being attributed to the resolution of the congressional Electoral Commission.

Regardless, the Republican representatives at the meeting knew what this meant for blacks in the South. And the Lincoln Republicans, the faction that proudly identified with Abraham Lincoln and believed that the fight for freedom was the morally right thing to do, knew that not only would the Democrats violently deny blacks the right to vote, but blacks would become the focus of Democrat rage and hostility for the foreseeable future.

Although some of the Republicans immediately refused the offer, some paused to consider it. National sentiments regarding race relations gave life to a possible agreement with the Democrats. After decades of tension with the South and four years of war, the American people had grown weary of the constant battle over race relations with the South. And although it was the Abolitionist and the Republican Parties that forged the path to freedom for slaves, a significant number of moderate Republicans wanted to abandon the race issue, which was the most controversial issue of their day. We shall refer to them as the Rutherford Hayes Republicans.

The Democrats presented them with the opportunity to do just that. And thus, black civil rights, along with blacks' quality of life, became a political bargaining chip.

Reportedly, the Republicans countered the Democrat offer. Among other things, the Republicans wanted the Democrats to agree to respect the rights of blacks to vote. They also wanted Southern law enforcement authorities to protect blacks from the Klan, and they wanted the Southern courts to honor the newly passed Constitutional rights of freed slaves. The Democrats accepted the offer and Rutherford Hayes became the nineteenth president of the United States.

One of his first acts as president was to withdraw federal troops from Southern states and declare that the Era of Reconstruction had ended. Blacks throughout the South felt deeply betrayed, especially because they risked their lives to vote for Hayes. Additionally, the federal troops that provided security against Klan violence was now gone.

But Democrat leaders praised Hayes for this act, and President Hayes was well received, by white Southerners, whenever he visited the South.

The media, however, severely criticized Hayes for the agreement. Some went as far to say that Hayes had made a deal with the devil.

For example, on September 29, 1877, *The Weekly Louisianan*—a black newspaper—published the following: *"Why does the South receive a Republican president so enthusiastically? Is it because they look upon him as a convert to certain political ideas heretofore held by them and for which they have fought so pertinaciously for these many years? At every Democrat gathering and in every Democrat newspaper we find the Democrats showering the president with praise based solely on the ground that he has abandoned some of the cardinal principles of Republicanism and adopted the cardinal principles of the Democrats in their place."*[15]

President Hayes and his supporters vehemently denied reports that any deal was struck with the Democrats, insisting that his victory was entirely the result of the decision made by the 15-member Electoral Commission. But questions about the compromise followed and haunted him throughout his presidency.

Either version of events reflects badly on Hayes. Hayes knew about the situation in the South as well as anyone else. He knew that blacks were terribly oppressed. Their homes were being destroyed, their rights were being trampled upon, and they lived in a state of constant fear.

If students of history accept Hayes's account of events, then he simply didn't care about protecting the voting rights and general safety of black Americans. He only cared about securing the support of white Democrats and turned a blind eye and a deaf ear to blacks.

At the same time, if the presidency of Rutherford Hayes was the result of an arrangement made at Wormley's Hotel and he trusted the Democrats to keep their word and honor the Constitution, then he was very foolish. The price of Hayes's foolishness was the lives of many blacks for decades to come.

---

[15] https://chroniclingamerica.loc.gov

The South Partially Regresses to Pre-Civil War Society

If President Hayes truly believed that the Democrats would honor the voting rights of freed slaves, then the Democrats did not waste any time proving how naïve he was for trusting them.

From the Southern Democrat perspective, regional pride was not the only reason to restore the pre-Civil War society. The loss of life caused by the war left the black population with much greater numbers than the white population throughout the South. And the Democrats knew that having a president willing to look the other way was not enough to regain control of Southern governments.

The Democrats had to control of the growth of the black population as well as black votes. And if they couldn't control the vote, they had to suppress it. And no method was too harsh, too lethal, or too cruel. They terrorized blacks with violence, threats, and intimidation, and used various forms of legal trickery to confuse them about the voting process or created reasons to disqualify their votes.

Lynching became a common event throughout the South, which was used to control not only the growth of the black population but also who they voted for. Militant Democrats and their supporters in the KKK threatened to kill blacks and destroy their homes and churches if Democrat candidates did not win in their voting districts.

Between 1877 and 1950, there were about 3,100 incidents of lynching, with over 3,800 people killed. About 84 percent of them were black, and 16 percent of them where white Republicans.[16]

These acts of savagery and barbarism drew harsh criticism from the North and Midwest. Blacks in those parts of the country lived in relative freedom and were also free to vote. In response to criticisms from their countrymen, Southern Democrats developed other ways to achieve their goals while mitigating the severity of judgment against them from their fellow Americans and the media.

---

[16] E.M. Beck, Judge Lynch Denied: Combating Mob Violence in the American South, 1877-1950, North Carolina, University of North Carolina Press, 2015, p. 117

To give the impression that the rights of black Americans were being respected, Southern governments passed state laws that allowed blacks to vote, but only if certain conditions were met. And the conditions were in areas in which the Democrats knew the former slaves were vulnerable.

Literacy tests, poll taxes, confusing voter regulations, and other laws were established to completely disenfranchise black voters. Some literacy tests required black voters to read random sections of the US Constitution and explain their meaning to the satisfaction of election officials.

But a significant number of white Southerners were also illiterate. So, the Democrats passed a law that became known as "the grandfather exemption," which allowed whites to bypass the literacy tests.

The grandfather clause declared that any voter whose father or grandfather could vote on or before 1867 was illegible to vote and exempt from literacy tests and other regulations.

This clearly made voting impossible for former slaves because the Fifteenth Amendment was not proposed in Congress until 1869. And many of them still could not read and were not provided a formal education.

Congressman Thomas
Ezekiel Miller

Poll taxes were an economic barrier that most Southern blacks could not overcome. It required voters to pay a fee that was far out of reach to the former slaves.

One of the most confusing voter regulations was created in South Carolina and became known as the "the Eight Box Ballot Law." The law required different ballot boxes for each contest. The size of each box also had to meet different regulations, and each box required a different paper ballot.

The measurements and layout of the ballots themselves were also heavily regulated.

If the ballot boxes or the ballots themselves did not comply with the regulations, the votes were declared illegal and therefore disqualified.

In 1888, black Republican Thomas Ezekiel Miller ran for Congress in South Carolina against incumbent Democrat William Elliott. Congressman Elliott was declared the winner, at first, with 54 percent of the vote.

But Miller challenged the election results. Miller appeared before the House Committee on Elections and provided evidence that South Carolina's strict regulations were not fairly applied, which had cost him the election. The committee also heard the case of John Mercer Langston, a black Republican that ran for Congress in Virginia.[17]

On September 23, 1890, both cases went to the full House of Representatives and both Miller and Langston were seated in Congress.

Southern blacks had to struggle much harder to hold onto what remained of their political rights after the Compromise of 1877. And their road to the polls became much more dangerous as a result.

In October of 1883, black political rights took another severe blow. The US Supreme Court heard arguments from five cases grouped as one that challenged the Civil Rights Act of 1875. The members of the high court were Chief Justice Morrison Waite, and associate Justices Samuel F. Miller, Stephen J. Field, Joseph P. Bradley, William B. Woods, Stanley Matthews, Horace Gray, Samuel Blatchford, and John M. Harlan.

The Court ruled 8-1 that the Civil Rights Act of 1875 was unconstitutional. Justice Harlan was the dissenting justice. In his dissent Justice Harlan wrote: *"Today it is the colored race which is denied by corporations and individuals wielding public authority, rights fundamental in their freedom and citizenship. At some future time, it may be that some other race will fall under the ban of race discrimination. But if*

---

[17] www.history.house.gov/People/Listing/M/MILLER,-Thomas-Ezekiel-(M000757)/

the constitutional amendments be enforced according to the intent with which, as I conceive, they were adopted, there cannot be, in this republic, any class of human beings in practical subjection to another class with power in the latter to dole out to the former just such privileges as they may choose to grant."[18]

The ruling absolutely devasted southern blacks. The victory of the black Republican congressmen over the white Democrat congressmen was a source of great inspiration to them. They saw former slaves engage former slave owners in an intellectual battle and the former slaves prevailed. The entire country saw it, read about it or were told about it.

Southern blacks talked about it, among themselves, for years. The achievement strengthened, emboldened, and uplifted them tremendously. It made them feel good about themselves in a way they never felt before.

But now their victory was taken from them by the Supreme Court and the hope they drew from it was crushed. And in the minds of most white Americans, the victory of the black republican congressmen never happened. And as time passed, American's black community stopped talking their historic victory in the US House of Representatives. And future generations were robbed of any inspiration the event may have provided.

Frederick Douglass responded to the Court's ruling during a Civil Rights Mass Meeting at Lincoln Hall in Washington, D.C. on October 22, 1883. He believed that the wise thing to do was to remain calm so he spoke with a respectful, yet sorrowful, tone to a meeting hall filled with civil rights supporters that expected to hear the same fiery indignation they've heard come from him in the past.

During his speech Douglass said, "*Few events in our national history have surpassed this event in magnitude, importance, and moral significance. This event has swept over this land like a moral cyclone leaving moral devastation in its wake. The Court's decision has inflicted a heavy calamity upon millions of people of this country and left them*

---

[18] Civil Rights Cases, 109 U.S. 3 (1883)https://supreme.justia.com/cases/federal/
us/109/3/

naked and defenseless against the action of a malignant, vulgar, and pitiless prejudice."[19]

The Court's ruling made it much easier for the southern political class to pass segregation laws throughout the South. The great strides made toward racial equality were quickly being erased. And because Southern society appeared to be rapidly regressing, Frederick Douglass demanded Republican lawmakers to continue their fight on behalf of black Americans—especially black Civil War veterans.

"When your army was melting away before the fire and pestilence of rebellion, when your star-spangled banner trailed in the dust heavy with blood, you called the Negro. And he came 200,000 strong," Douglass said during the National Republican Convention in Chicago in 1888. *"Let us remember that these brave black men are now stripped of their right to vote. Do not leave them to wade through blood to the ballot box. Make their pathway to the ballot box as smooth and safe as that of any class of citizens."* [20]

But the architects of the Compromise of 1877 still held the reigns Republican Party. Southern blacks were able to support a small number of black representatives at every level. But those numbers had become even smaller because of Democrat violence and oppression.

Another Supreme Court ruling that further trampled on the rights of blacks occurred after the passage of the 1890 Louisiana Separate Car Act. The law required separate cars for blacks and whites on railroads.

The Separate Car Act was challenged by Homer Plessy and the Committee of Citizens. Plessy, who was mixed race, was arrested when he refused to leave a railroad car for whites only. Plessy sued and the case became known as *Plessy vs. Ferguson*.

When the case went before the US Supreme Court, the court ruled that Louisiana had the right to segregate its citizens. The ruling was in direct conflict with the Fourteenth Amendment, but, apparently, that did not matter at the time.

---

[19] Edited by Philip S. Foner, Frederick Douglass: Selected Speeches and Writings, Chicago, Illinois, Lawrence Hill Books, P. 685

[20] Edited by Philip S. Foner, Frederick Douglass: Selected Speeches and Writings, Chicago, Illinois, Lawrence Hill Books, P. 724

Chapter 3: 1883–1922
The Era of Black Disenfranchisement Begins

The two Supreme Court rulings emboldened Democrats to institutionalize segregation and racism in the South. In November of 1890, delegates of the Mississippi Constitutional Convention adopted a new state constitution that effectively denied blacks the right to vote. And within the next few years, Democrats in South Carolina, Louisiana, Florida, Alabama, and Texas all adopted new state constitutions that denied blacks the right to vote.

Congressman Alfred Moore Waddell

Other southern states did not go as far as to change their constitutions, but they did pass more state laws that stripped blacks of their voting rights. North Carolina Democrats, for example, changed the state's constitution to deny the right to vote only to those who were illiterate, which disproportionately affected blacks.

Still, a significant number of blacks could read, and that number was growing. These individuals bravely proceeded to risk their lives to exercise their right to vote.

This led to one of the most horrific and barbaric acts of political violence in American history, which took the lives of about 300 blacks in Wilmington, North Carolina in 1898.

The incident began after the successful election of black Republicans to the Wilmington City Council. Shortly afterward, a group of white supremacists complained about articles published in a black newspaper. The group confronted the newspaper editor, Alex Manly, and demanded that he close his business and leave Wilmington.

The complaint, however, was merely a pretense to help justify what the Democrats were about to do. Before the group complained to Manly, a small army of white supremacists were already gathered just outside of Wilmington. And they didn't try to create any further justification for themselves, because immediately after Manly refused to leave the city, about 2,000 heavily armed men attacked the local government, killed approximately 300 black people, destroyed their businesses, displaced others from their homes, and overthrew the newly elected local government.

The attack was led by Democratic Congressman Alfred Moore Waddell. Congressman Waddell then appointed the city's new mayor and city council. Neither Waddell nor any of the attackers were indicted by local or state officials.[21]

And despite the precedent set by President Grant in Louisiana in 1874, the federal government did not get involved. Just as North Carolina's state law enforcement authorities ignored the pleas of its black citizens in Wilmington, Republican President William McKinley turned a blind eye as well as a deaf ear to them and there were federal indictments either.

Clearly this unspeakable atrocity can be laid at the feet at the Democrat Party in North Carolina during that time. But the silence and inaction of the Hayes-Republicans also made them complicit in this horrific bloodbath.

By the early 1900s racism, voter disenfranchisement, and segregation became enshrined within state constitutions and state laws throughout the South. Southerners were greatly criticized by Republican members of Congress as well as by many of their countrymen in the North and the Midwest for their cruel treatment of blacks and their total disregard for the US Constitution.

---

[21] https://northcarolinahistory.org/encyclopedia/alfred-moore-waddell-1834-1912/

In most cases, the southern response was to claim that they did honor the Constitution and the constitutional rights of blacks to vote—but only if they could successfully navigate themselves through a confusing network of voting regulations that also baffled many white voters.

But during a rare moment of complete honestly, South Carolina Democratic Senator Benjamin Tillman admitted that the Democratic Party purposely intended to strip blacks of their Fourteenth and Fifteenth Amendment rights. Senator Tillman made the confession during a speech on the floor of the US Senate on March 23, 1900.

"As white men we are not sorry for it, and we do not propose to apologize for anything," Tillman said. *"We took the government from them in 1876, and if no other senator will acknowledge it, more is the pity. We had the state constitutional conventions…with the purpose of disenfranchising as many of them as we could under the 14th and 15th Amendments.*

"We never believed him to be the equal to the white man…I would to God the last one of them was in Africa and that none of them had ever been brought to our shores."[22]

Senator Benjamin Tillman

Because the number of black voters shrank dramatically at the end of the nineteenth century, the number of black representatives also dwindled. Black Republican Congressman George Henry White from North Carolina was one of the last to serve.

---

[22] Benjamin Tillman, Speech: Their Own Hot-Headedness, Washington, D.C., http://historymatters.gmu.edu/d/55

At the end of his congressional career, White found himself standing with only a few remaining Lincoln-Republicans that wanted to continue the fight for blacks in the South. By this time, the strength of Republican resolve to fight for blacks was almost non-existent. Led by the cowardly and politically ambitious Hayes-Republican faction, which outnumbered the Lincoln-Republicans, the Republican Party distanced itself from racial issues as much as possible. Congressman White and the few Lincoln-Republicans tried to help southern blacks whenever they could.

A perfect example is the effort made during the Census of 1900. On December 20, 1900, the House Committee on the Census passed a reapportionment bill, for members of Congress, based on the census information. But Republican Congressman Edgar D. Crumpacker, from Indiana, strongly denounced the committees report because many citizens within southern states were disenfranchised.

Congressman Edgar D. Crumpacker

"The language of the Constitution is clear, direct, and mandatory, and it leaves no discretion in Congress. In Louisiana, Mississippi, North Carolina, and South Carolina a significant number of residents are deprived of their right to vote," Crumpacker argued. *"If the Negro is not entitled to the protection of political laws, under what laws is he entitled protection? "Congress must act as a counter prevailing force to the injustices and the tendencies of the South. And in so doing help both races.*[23]

When the reapportionment bill came to the floor of the House, Crumpacker offered an amendment to reduce the number of congressional representatives, from the South, according to the number of citizens those states recognized

---

[23] Richard B. Sherman, The Republican Party and Black America from McKinley to Hoover 1896-1933, Charlottesville, 1973, P.18

as voters. If the amendment passed, Louisiana would've lost three of their seven representatives, Mississippi would lose three of its seven, South Carolina would lose two out of their six, and North Carolina would lose three from their nine.

Predictably, the Democrats railed against the amendment and denounced it in the strongest possible terms. Congressman Crumpacker became a target of Democrat hatred and contempt throughout the debate. Congressman White, however, was more than happy to endure the slings and arrows alongside Crumpacker.

"If we are unworthy of suffrage and if it is necessary to maintaining white supremacy, then you ought to have the benefit only of those who are allowed to vote," White said.[24]

Crumpacker and White were joined by Ohio Republican Congressman Charles H. Grosvenor, and a Democrat Congressman from Massachusetts John F. Fitzgerald. But the most shocking and eye-opening aspect of the effort was the passive attitude embraced by the House republicans. Out of 196 members only Crumpacker, White, and Grosvenor publicly supported the amendment. And the amendment was defeated 136-94.

Congressman George Henry White

Before the fight over the census, Congressman White introduced a bill that would make lynching a federal crime., but the bill didn't have enough support in committee. White perhaps believed that the 1900 US Census presented his best, and only opportunity, to help Southern blacks. So, on January 29, 1901, he delivered his farewell address to the House of Representatives.

"Now, Mr. Chairman, before concluding my remarks I want to

---

[24] Congressional Record: The Proceedings and Debates of the 55th Congress, 3rd Session. Volume XXXII, Washington, D.C. P. 1125

submit a brief recipe for the solution of the so-called American negro problem. He asks no special favors, but simply demands that he be given the same chance for existence, for earning a livelihood, for raising himself in the scales of manhood and womanhood that are accorded to kindred nationalities.

"This, Mr. Chairman, is perhaps the Negroes' temporary farewell to the American Congress; but let me say, Phoenix-like he will rise up some day and come again. These parting words are on behalf of an outraged, heart-broken, bruised, and bleeding, but God-fearing people, faithful, industrious, loyal people, rising people, full of potential force. And the only apology that I have to make for the earnestness with which I have spoken is that I am pleading for the life, the liberty, the future happiness, and manhood suffrage for one-eighth of the entire population of the United States," Congressman White said.[25]

Moderate Republican Leadership Avoids Controversy

Republican Senator Thomas C. Platt from New York supported the effort to reduce number of white supremacist Democrats and believed the reasoning was sound. On December 7, 1904, Senator Platt made an attempt himself, and introduced a bill that would reduce the number of Democratic congressmen in reapportionment bills in the future.

Platt's effort was met with stern denunciation from Democrats and apathy from the moderate Republican leadership, like Crumpacker, and his bill never emerged from the committee.

The Lincoln-Republicans, such as Crumpacker and Platt, were completely marginalized during the first

Senator Thomas C. Platt

---

[25] Benjamin R. Justesen: George Henry White, An Even Chance in Race of Life; Bertram Wyatt-Brown, Editor; Louisiana State University Press, 2001

half of the 20th century. During that time, GOP moderates, such as Presidents James A. Garfield, Chester A. Arthur, William McKinley, Theodore "Teddy" Roosevelt, and William H. Taft, were firmly entrenched within congressional and party leadership positions.

There were several reasons why the Hayes-Republicans continued to lead the GOP to turn their backs on black America. For one thing, civil rights was not a popular issue to mainstream America back then. And, unfortunately, that helped the Democrats get away with many injustices against blacks. The issue was considered a very low priority and secondary just as the people to whom it benefitted were considered secondary. And the moderate Republicans didn't want the party to stray outside what America deemed to be popular into what was unpopular.

Furthermore, the moderate Republicans earnestly sought the approval of white Southern Democrats because they viewed their position as strategic. Many of them believed they needed the approval of southern voters to break the Democrat's hold on the South. They hoped that by moderating the party's historic stance on civil rights, they'd get more favorable coverage from the media which would translate into gaining power within southern states. And once they won key positions within the South, they could help its black citizens.

But their strategy had a clear an obvious flaw. While they remained silent on civil rights and ingratiated themselves to southern Democrats, their inaction emboldened white supremacists toward more anarchy and bloodshed against the people the Republicans claimed they wanted to protect. Which led many Republican supporters to believe that the Hayes-Republicans weren't executing a strategy at all. But they were motivated by ambition and paralyzed by fear.

As the Hayes-Republicans weakened the party's position on racial equality, they maintained that the GOP was still the best place for blacks and Republicans would, one day, restore their political rights in the South. For decades, they promised to continue to be their champions for the cause of freedom, but those promises weren't worth the breath it took to speak them.

The moderates believed Southern blacks could be pacified with high profile, showcase appointments of prominent blacks to federal positions. President Hayes, for example, quickly appointed Frederick Douglass to the position of Marshall of the District of Columbia. No doubt President Hayes incorrectly believed that seeing one of their own people working at the highest level of the federal government was a fair exchange for blacks' voting rights.

The Republican presidents that followed President Hayes dealt with black Americans in the same manner. Among their highest priorities was to avoid all controversial issues for the sake of political gain. And nothing was more controversial than voting rights for Southern blacks.

Some Republicans like Senator Platt were ready to take up the cause of freedom once again, just like their nineteenth century predecessors. But time and time again, they ran into opposition from their own party as well as from the Democrats.

The lynching of blacks was rampant throughout the South.

The Rise of the NAACP

In the absence of any effective change, political representation, and civil rights progress in America, a fledging anti-discrimination organization began to take shape in New York to fill the void. The group intended to address Democrat oppression through court challenges and public protests. The organization eventually became known as the National Association for the Advancement of Colored People—the NAACP.

The NAACP's first major challenge came quickly in the form of a lawsuit. On October 17, 1913, attorneys for the NAACP argued the case of *Guinn v. United States* before the US Supreme Court.

The case challenged the constitutionality of the grandfather clause in Oklahoma and six Southern state constitutions.

On June 21, 1915, the US Supreme Court ruled that the grandfather clause was unconstitutional and compelled Oklahoma, Maryland, Alabama, Louisiana, North Carolina, Georgia, and Virginia to change their state constitutions.

In the aftermath of the court decision, Democrat lawmakers created new ways to disenfranchise blacks. Most Southern states adopted grandfather clauses based on voter registration that declared that anyone not registered to vote in 1915, with a few exceptions, was not illegible to vote. The Supreme Court eventually struck down those laws as well.

As the NAACP began to fight in court rooms across the country, lynching and unfettered mob violence against blacks became national political issues. More and more stories were published about how Southern law enforcement, rather than granting blacks due process through the legal system, chose to throw them into the waiting hands of bloodthirsty, angry mobs.

Southern blacks lived in a state of constant fear knowing that it only took a false accusation from a white person to get themselves and their family members killed. Between 1885 and 1915, about 2,850 people were lynched throughout the South.[26]

In 1916, the NAACP launched a nationwide anti-lynching campaign. The organization began by collecting as much information as possible about every reported lynching throughout the South— including information about local Democrat elected officials and law enforcement officials. The organization raised money, educated the public, and ran national ad campaigns to publicly shame and expose Democrat public officials. The ads also publicly condemned Democrat public officials who were complicit in lynching because of their indifference to and support of mob violence.

Several years of relentless and continuous bombardment of ads finally compelled Democratic President Woodrow Wilson to finally to make a public statement about lynching. On July 26, 1918,

---

[26] https://www.naacp.org/wp-content/uploads/2016/04/NAACP_anti_lynch.pdf

President Wilson publicly condemned the act of lynching in the South.[27]

"I therefore very earnestly and solemnly beg that all the governors of all the States, the law officers of every community, and above all, the men and women of every community in the United States, all who revere America and wish to keep her name without stain or reproach will cooperate, not passively, but actively, and watchfully make an end to this disgraceful evil," Wilson said.

This was a major achievement considering that fact that President Wilson was a supporter of the Ku Klux Klan and only a few years earlier, on March 21, 1915, he dramatically increased Klan membership nationwide when he allowed a special screening of *The Birth of a Nation* at the White House.

The Dyer Anti-Lynching Bill

Congressman Leonidas Dyer

The Birth of a Nation is a feature film that glorified the Klan and its members as heroic saviors of the South while depicting all blacks as evil, dim-witted animals who lurked in the shadows waiting to prey upon unsuspecting Southern white women. The film is pure racist propaganda that features the Klan in a favorable light and black men as monsters. The film completely misinformed and deceived the American public about everyday life among black Americans for the pur-

---

[27] New York Times, July 27, 1918

pose of drawing support for segregation and Jim Crow laws from the rest of the country.

As the NAACP continued the pressure, the conscious of the nation was stirred and deeply troubled. And the moderate Hayes Republicans found themselves in a very awkward position because it was their indifference that had helped the situation grow to this point.

But the NAACP's anti-lynching campaign reignited the Lincoln Republicans and inspired them to take up the cause of freedom with less resistance from within their party.

On April 8, 1918, Republican Congressman Leonidas C. Dyer from Missouri introduced an anti-lynching bill that made the death of any US citizen by mob violence a federal crime, while anyone who was a part of the mob would be charged with murder.

The county in which the crime took place would forfeit $5,000 to $10,000 to family members of the victims. Additionally, any law enforcement official who failed to seriously protect black residents from lynching would face imprisonment.

The NAACP was relentless in its campaign to educate the public during the next few years. And on January 26, 1922, the US House of Representatives passed the Dyer Anti-Lynching Bill 231–119. The bill was supported by 223 Republicans and eight Democrats. It was opposed by 116 Democrats and only three Republicans.

The NAACP knew it was too early to celebrate the victory because now the organization was faced with the task of getting the bill through the Senate. And that would be much more difficult.

Although the Republicans held a 60–36 majority, many were moderate Republicans and it was an election year. And, as always the moderates wanted to avoid difficult and controversial issues at all costs.

The NAACP intensified its media campaign, hoping to put pressure on the moderate Republicans. Congressman Dyer also joined the NAACP's effort to educate the public by traveling across the country and making speeches on the subject. And the mounting pressure finally compelled Republican President Warren Harding to add his voice to the cause. During his first address to Congress, on April 12, 1921, President Harding made it clear that he wanted Congress, particularly the Republicans, to put an end to lynching in America.

"*Congress ought to wipe the stain of barbaric lynching from the banners of our free and representative democracy,*" President Harding said.

The nation's largest newspapers published ads throughout the country that focused harsh criticism and stern condemnation upon the South. On November 23, 1922, *The Evening Star* published this ad: "*The shame of America. Did you know that the United States is the only country on Earth where human beings are burned at the stake? Between 1918 and 1921, 28 people were burned by American mobs and the lynchers go unpunished!*" [28]

The efforts of the NAACP and Congressman Dyer did penetrate some parts of the South and yielded some fruit. Anti-lynching sentiments gained considerable ground in Georgia where state and local authorities indicted 22 people involved in lynching in 1922. Among them, 15 were tried and four were convicted. [29]

But the Democratic Party stood firmly united against Dyer's bill. They argued that the bill completely undermined the police authority and judicial system of the Southern states and was, therefore, unconstitutional.

And although the NAACP's media campaign was very effective, racist propaganda had taken hold of the minds of Americans, in the North and South, long before the NAACP even existed.

The Reconstruction Era not only added over 3 million new Americans to the population, it also gave birth to a continuous flow of severe judgment and criticism about them.

Newly freed slaves were first condemned as ignorant children who required constant oversight and supervision. That assessment

---

[28] The Evening Star, November 23, 1922, page 34; https://chroniclingamerica.loc. gov/lccn/sn83045462/1922-11-23/ed-1/seq-4/#date1=1922&index=0&row s=20&words=LYNCH+lynched+Lynching+lynching+LYNCHING+lynch-ings&searchType=basic&sequence=0&state=&date2=1922&proxtext=lynch-ing&y=17&x=22&dateFilterType=yearRange&page=1

[29] The Broad Ax, November 25, 1922

evolved into the belief that blacks, especially black men, were nothing but vicious animals who had to be treated accordingly. Throughout the Reconstruction Era and well into the twentieth century, the Democrats claimed that black men could not control themselves and were lurking around every corner waiting to attack white women. The Democrats clothed the monstrous act of lynching in the gleaming, glorious armor of chivalry. And the act of lynching, therefore, became a badge of honor for all Southern gentlemen who held the virtue of Southern women in high regard.

Congressman Thomas Sisson

The NAACP hoped to uproot these beliefs from the minds of Americans in a very short period.

During the anti-lynching debate, the Democrats turned to their long-standing racist propaganda, and one of their newest disinformation tools, *The Birth of a Nation*, to defend and justify the acts of lynching. And it became clear that lynching was stilled considered just as chivalrous in 1922 as it was in 1877.

"*I deplore lynching,*" said Democratic Congressman Thomas Sisson from Mississippi. "*But as long as the black fiends put one hand on white women, they are going to be treated that w*ay."[30]

A clear example of how white supremacist propaganda completely twisted the minds of southerners is the brutal murder of Emmitt Till in Sisson's home state of Mississippi. Till was a 14-year old black young man, from Chicago, that was visiting family members in Money, Mississippi during the summer of 1955.

On August 28th, he went into a grocery store to buy candy. Later, the store's clerk Carolyn Bryant, a white woman, alleged that the 14-year old flirted with her, grabbed her arm, and made lewd comments towards her. [31]

---

[30] Alexandria Gazette, January 26, 1922
[31] https://www.history.com/this-day-in-history/the-death-of-emmett-till

Bryant's husband and the store's owner, Roy Bryant, was told about the allegation. Roy Bryant, along with other family members, found Till and forced him into their car. After beating him throughout the night, they took him to a toolshed behind the Tallahatchie River.

Emmitt Till was accused of flirting with a white woman and brutally murdered.

Till's body was found three days later completely disfigured. He was naked, shot multiple times, beaten, one eye gouged out, tied to a cotton-gin fan with barbed wire and laying in the river. And on September 23, 1955, an all-white jury found the attackers "not guilty."

Years later in the book entitled, *The Blood of Emmitt Till,* by Tim Tyson, Carolyn Bryant completely recanted her story and confessed that Till never touched her, threatened her, or harassed her in anyway. *"Nothing that boy did could ever do could justify what happened to him,"* Carolyn Bryant said.

The irony of the white supremacist propaganda is even more staggering when we consider the fact that many white slave owners raped and sexually assaulted black women during the era of American slavery without fear of punishment or prosecution. And whether they realized it or not, Democrat Congressmen such as Thomas Sisson only reminded the public about the terrible abuse suffered by black women by their slave masters. This historical fact was known by Sisson and the other Democrats in Congress and likely something they preferred not to not talk about, but their arrogance completely blinded them to it for decades.

On election day, November 7, 1922, the Republicans lost seats in both chambers, but still held onto the majority. The GOP lost seven seats in the US Senate shrinking its majority from 53 to 42, and lost 76 in the House.

The NAACP's media campaign was not enough to root out the negative beliefs of blacks in the minds of all Americans. And it was not enough to send much needed help to the US Senate.

Senator Pat Harrison

Emboldened by their electoral gains, the Democrats dug in their heels even deeper against the anti-lynching bill. And on December 2, 1922, Democratic Senator Pat Harrison led the filibuster against the bill. One by one the Democrats went to the Senate floor to speak against the bill and stopped any other business in the Senate from moving forward.

Although the Republicans maintained their majority, it became clear that the situation was more a battle of wills than a battle of numbers. And the fate of the bill would be determined by the group that held the greatest desire for victory.

The Republicans declared that they wanted to end the practice of lynching and save the lives of black Americans. But how strong was their commitment to save their lives? Black southerners were certainly depending upon the strength of Republican resolve to rescue them from angry mobs.

And the Democrats falsely claimed they wanted to save the lives of white women, while in truth they wanted to continue their oppression of Southern blacks with impunity. How strong was their commitment to keep their iron boot on the necks of black Americans?

As the fight continued, the Republican senators, who were already discouraged because of their loss of seven seats saw that the Democrats were united in their determination to defeat the bill. It became clear that their collective pride wouldn't allow them to admit they were wrong. And they'd allow all business of the federal government to grind to a halt before admitting that, once again, the South was on a destructive path. Evidently, the Democrats' desire for victory was very strong.

On December 4, 1922, the Republican senators caucused to discuss the situation. All of them were well informed about lynching. They had followed the NAACP's campaign very closely, and they knew about the horrors and atrocities committed against blacks. But unfortunately, their hardships were not enough to strengthen the already weakened Republican resolve. The Democrats glared at the Republicans with hardened faces and equally hardened hearts for two days, hoping to intimidate the majority into giving up on their cause.

Eventually the Republicans surrendered the battle of wills and voted to abandon the Dyer Anti-Lynching Bill.

After the historic defeat, Republican Senate Majority Leader Henry Cabot Lodge made the following statement: *Of course Republicans feel very strongly about that the bill should become law. But the situation before us is this: Under the rules of the Senate the Democrats, who are filibustering, could keep filibustering indefinitely and there is no doubt in our minds that they will do so. An attempt to change the rules would only shift the filibuster to other subjects. We cannot pass the bill in*

Senator Henry Cabot Lodge

this Congress and, therefore, we had to choose between giving up the whole session to a protracted filibuster or going ahead with the regular business of the session—which includes farm legislation, shipping, and appropriation bills. The conference very reluctantly decided to set aside the Dyer Bill and go on with the business of the session."[32]

---

[32] Alexandria Gazette, January 26, 1922

NAACP Executive Secretary James Weldon Johnson did not restrain his anger and disappointment. During the months and years to follow, at every interview and press conference, Johnson laid the defeat of the Dyer Anti-Lynching Bill at the feet of the Republican Party: "*The colored people will not be deceived by appearances. They see and they know that the actual fight was made by the Democrats against the bill rather than the Republicans on its behalf. The Democrats roared like a lion and the Republicans laid down like a scared possum.*"[33]

The Aftermath

It was very difficult for Southern blacks to accept Senator Lodge's justification for the defeat of the bill—especially because Republicans held the majority in the Senate, and the bill's passage was a matter of life or death.

Clearly the Democrats cared nothing about the lives of Southern blacks. That much was known by all. They celebrated their victory and congratulated themselves for standing firm on the practice of lynching.

But surely the Party of Lincoln and the heirs to the Abolitionist cause would place greater value on human life than on any other issue before the Senate. Surely the Republicans would fight for the sanctity, dignity, and preservation of life just as their predecessors had fought during the Civil War. Surely the sanctity of life was more important than any farm bill, appropriations bill, or any other pending legislation.

Sadly, the moderate Republicans were in control of the Senate and they did not hold this view. The moderates preferred to not address the issue at all but had just been dragged into the fight by the NAACP and the Lincoln Republicans.

The Hayes Republicans continued to share the beliefs of President Rutherford Hayes, which meant avoiding controversy at all cost. They chose to hide behind Senate rules rather than fight for the lives of Southern blacks.

---

[33] The Richmond Planet, December 16, 1922

As a result, a great feeling of despair and hopelessness swept through the minds and hearts of blacks. To many, the defeat of the anti-lynching bill was a very clear expression of indifference and apathy from the federal government and from both political parties. And the bill's defeat also represented de facto approval of the lawless practice of lynching.

Southern blacks made no distinction between the Lincoln Republicans and the Hayes Republicans. Their faith in the party of Lincoln was shaken to its core. To them, all Republicans had failed—all of them were cowards and now blacks had no representation in the federal government just as they had no representation in the Southern governments.

Perhaps the moderate Republicans believed they were free to abandon the anti-lynching bill because blacks throughout the rest of the country still supported them. And certainly Southern blacks would continue to support them because they had nowhere else to go. They could not turn to the Democrats because the Democrats literally sought justification and the legal right to kill Negroes.

In the next chapter, we will see that blacks did have a political alternative, and many exercised it. And that alternative eventually led America's black citizens to a very dangerous place.

Unfortunately, moderate Republicans believed they could ignore the needs of blacks and still enjoy their support. The next decade would prove them wrong. Southern blacks knew the Democrats wanted to continue acts of lynching and that they could not expect any help from the Republicans. So, they turned to themselves for a remedy.

Chapter 4: 1922–1930

The Great Black Migration

Hundreds of thousands of blacks fled to the North after congressional Democrats defeated the Republican anti-lynching bill.

Just before the NAACP began its anti-lynching campaign in 1916, momentum for a mass exodus from Southern states began to grow. Black families began to leave the South to free themselves from Democrat oppression. Some could not travel too far for long. They could only move north by going town to town. But slowly and quietly, they moved themselves beyond the Democrats' reach.

The numbers were not impressive in the beginning. About several hundred black families began moving from thirteen Southern states, barely drawing any attention.

But by 1918, about 450,000 blacks had moved from Southern states into Northern cities.[34]

Between 1920 and 1930, about 260,000 blacks left Georgia, about 204,300 left South Carolina, about 80,700 left Alabama, and approximately 68,700 fled Mississippi.[35]

---

[34] Richard B. Sherman, The Republican Party and Black America: From McKinley to Hoover 1896–1933, Charlottesville, The University Press of Virginia, 1973, p. 125

[35] Social Science History, Vol. 14, Stewart E. Tonlay and E.M. Beck, Black Flight: Lethal Violence and the Great Migration, 1900-1930, Cambridge University

At the time, there is much disagreement about what caused the migration. A significant number of researchers believed that the reason was entirely economic, and that racial oppression had nothing to do with it.

But the fact that nearly 100 percent of the travelers were members of the same race left very little room to doubt about the primary reason for the exodus. Eventually the American public agreed that the sole reason for such a massive abandonment of the South had more to do with institutionalized hostility rather than with economics.

Add to this the fact that only a small number of black families were trickling out of the South before the NAACP began its information campaign about lynching. But during the campaign, the trickle became waves. And when the anti-lynching bill failed, blacks left the South in even greater waves.

Southern cities and towns were being depopulated at an alarming rate. By the end of 1922, another half million black Americans fled the South and another half million by 1928.

They went to the urban areas of New York, Chicago, Cleveland, Philadelphia, Detroit, Pittsburgh, and Boston. They also went west to Seattle, Washington, and Portland, Oregon.[36]

The exodus continued for decades, and their departure turned into a very effective political weapon. The loss of such a large labor force nearly crippled the South's economy.[37] And the loss of residents threatened to reduce the number of Democrats in Congress.

Robbed of their right to freedom of speech, stripped of their right to vote, and either oppressed or ignored by their representatives in Congress, many Southern blacks used the last weapon that remained in their political arsenal—their freedom to move, the freedom to reestablish themselves someplace that might not have been perfect, but was noticeably better than where they came from.

Press, 1990, p. 347-370

[36] Arizona and the West Vol. 23 No. 2, Quintard Taylor, The Great Migration: The Afro-American Communities of Seattle and Portland during the 1940's, Journal of the Southwest, p. 109-126

[37] Alferdteen Harrison, Black Exodus: The Great Migration from the American South, University Press of Mississippi, 1991

The use of this weapon yielded limited results. There were still significant numbers of blacks living in cities and towns in Southern states. They remained in the South, either by choice, the inability to relocate, or to remain close to their families.

Black Americans had completely lost faith in their representative republic and their constitutional democracy. The lofty idea of all men being created equal and all men treated equally under the law, as expressed in the US Constitution, meant nothing if the men charged with upholding those principles were either pure evil or useless cowards.

With no hope in sight for a better future for themselves and their children, America's black community began to turn to and seriously consider an alternative form of government and an alternate form of economics—Communism and Socialism.

Blacks Seduced by Communists

The 1930s were a very significant time in black political history. But unfortunately, the events of this time are not taught or even mentioned during Black History Month.

It was clear that neither major political party would defend the Constitutional rights of the black community. And although the principles of the Constitution were grand and noble, it seemed as if the promises offered to blacks would never be fulfilled.

For that reason, a significant number of black American's decided to rally under the Communist flag.

Communist ideology began to grow in America's largest cities in the North, Midwest, and

Foreign and Domestic Communists embrace black America.

Western states between the late 1890's and the early 1920s. It was not uncommon for someone to walk down any street in America and be given a pamphlet or a flyer extending an invitation to a meeting of their local Communist Party.

And as more blacks arrived from the Southern states, Communist Party activists greeted them warmly.

The Communist Party represented something completely new to black Americans. They were familiar the both the Republican and Democrat parties. But they knew little to nothing about the Communist Party, which they believed may be a viable alternative.

Local Communist Party organizations were mixed raced, but they were mainly white. And they expressed sincere outrage at the treatment of blacks in America, especially in the South. As the black population in American cities grew, the more local Communist groups spoke out against discrimination and the Jim Crow laws.

One section of New York City became the focal point for Communist recruitment activity—Harlem.

Why Harlem? Why not Boston, Chicago, Pittsburg, Los Angeles, Philadelphia, or any of the other cities southern blacks migrated?

Because Harlem was the cultural capital of Black America. During the early 20th century, especially between 1920 and 1940, the Harlem Renaissance shaped, molded, and set the tone for popular black culture in America.

In fact, Harlem's influence was very similar to how Hollywood and the television and movie industries shape popular culture in America today. Just as television shows and movies attempt to mold and shape political ideas and opinions of the general public with outspoken characters such as Julia Sugarbaker from the show *Designing Women* or even through animated characters such as Brian from *Family Guy*, likewise the stage actors in theater productions, Harlem's poetry and book writers, dancers, comedians, and various performers and entertainers held great influence over Black America during the early 20th century.

A very large segment of black America followed the thoughts and opinions of Harlem's entertainment industry leaders, intellectuals, and politicians on the most important issues of their time. And whatever was embraced by New York's black elite virtually guaranteed support from much of black America.

And the Communist Party knew that.

Among Harlem's royalty who openly embraced either the Communist Party or Socialist ideology were Cyril Briggs, James W. Ford, Richard Morris, Benjamin Davis Jr., A. Philip Randolph, Solomon Harper, Paul Robeson, W.E.B. Dubois, and Grace Campbell.

W. E. B Dubois

Briggs and Morris were two of the most influential black American Communists. Briggs worked as an editor for the *Amsterdam News* and later owned his own newspaper, *The Crusader*. Briggs, who was also a militant nationalist, wrote columns and editorials that encouraged blacks to form alliances with radical forces. He insisted that it was impossible for blacks to live in peace and prosperity in America under its current form. And the only way prosperity would be achieved was to overthrow American capitalism and establish an economy based on Socialism.[38]

Morris, known for being an excellent speaker, traveled across the country speaking to large crowds of blacks about joining the Communist Party.

Briggs's columns were reprinted in black newspapers throughout the country. And his writings provided those who had lost faith in America's constitutional republic an alternative to consider.

The national movement to recruit American blacks into the Communist Party was financed and supported by Communist International, which was also known as Comintern.

---

[38] Mark Nasion, Communists in Harlem During the Depression. Chicago, University of Illinois Press, 2005, P. 6

Comintern, based in Moscow, was an association of national Communist parties founded in 1915 by Vladimir Lenin. The organization played a major role in the Russian Federation's foreign policy and its goal was to establish Communist governments and create Socialist economies throughout the world.

Comintern sent representatives into nations worldwide to speak and recruit groups of people that were oppressed and disenfranchised from the mainstream of society. They trained them, financed them, and sent them out to recruit more of their own countrymen to the Communist movement.

Comintern used the legitimate grievances of black Americans to gain a stronger foothold in America. It saw the potential to greatly increase its numbers in the United States by making civil rights issues a top priority.

In Russia, the success of the Bolshevik Revolution was largely due to support from disenfranchised minorities throughout the Russian Empire. And although most blacks rejected the idea of a violent, militant, Bolshevik-style revolution, many adopted the concept of the government taxation of money and resources from some individuals to redistribute to others.

That ideology is alive and well in much of black America today.

By 1930, Communist International brought black leaders from Harlem and throughout America to Russia for inten-

NY City Councilman
Benjamin Davis Jr.

sive ideological training. The black American visitors saw integrated Russian schools, integrated neighborhoods, and peace and prosperity among blacks, Asians, non-Europeans, and Soviet nationals.[39]

The Russians told their visitors they had completely overcome age-old divisions through the adoption of the Communist philoso-

---

[39] Mark Nasion, Communists in Harlem During the Depression. Chicago, University of Illinois Press, 2005, P. 11

phy. And they were confident that the same could happen in America with the help of America's black community.

The Russians also told their visitors they would help them fight for the concerns of black America, they promised to fight vigorously at their side, and they promised to finance their efforts.

The black Communists returned to America very excited and convinced they found what they were searching for and that the Communist Party held the answers to their societal problems.

Benjamin Davis Jr., a black American lawyer and New York City councilman, published a 15-page booklet, "*The Negro People and the Communist Party*," to reach out to all black Americans and invite them to join the Communist Party.

In his publication, Davis wrote that he became a Communist because of what he experienced in America's judicial system. Davis also said that he believed that the Communist Party was the new party of freedom.

"The job of emancipation that Lincoln left incomplete is the job I want to complete now. I feel it can be completed only through the use of the new Party of Emancipation, the new Party of Douglass and Abolitionists—the Communist Party. So, I joined the Communist Party determined to secure the full benefits of membership..."[40]

Davis called all black Americans to unite under the hammer and sickle, convinced that Communism was the key to peace, prosperity, and justice.

"The Communist Party is the party of the American workers Negro and White. The Negro-haters long ago tried to scare the southern white workers away from the Communist Party by calling it the "Negro Party." But it is not only the party of the American workers but of all races, creeds, and colors. The Communist Party is proud to be known as the party of the Negro people and seeks ever to be worthy of that name."[41]

---

[40] Benjamin Davis Jr., The Negro People and the Communist Party, New York, p. 4
[41] Benjamin Davis Jr., The Negro People and the Communist Party, New York, p. 13-14

But Harlem's political and social elite had no idea what they were getting themselves, and leading other blacks, into. They were the blind leading the blind into a ditch.

James W. Ford nominated for vice president of the United States.

American blacks, including the so-called elite, were not educated in world history or world events. They did not study the horrors, the anarchy, and the mass executions of the Bolshevik Revolution, the abomination and Godlessness of Communism that sprang from it, or the dangers of Socialism.

They did not see what was going on beyond America's shores and had no idea that they were being used by the Communists like many other disenfranchised groups around the world.

But the Communist Movement within black America was not united. Some agreed with militant nationalist activists, such as Cyril Briggs, who believed that the only way Blacks could live in peace was to violently overthrow the United States government.

Others believed such action was impossible. But they did believe that Socialism was the only way blacks could prosper in America, so they worked to transform the United States into a Socialist republic. The two groups often clashed with each other as they recruited more and more blacks to their side.

In 1928, Comintern declared that Black Americans should have a country for themselves on the North American continent, free from the oppression and dictates of the federal government.

They proposed that the states of Louisiana, Alabama, Mississippi, Georgia, and North and South Carolina should be given to or "acquired" by blacks so they could live in peace and prosperity under a Communist government. A directive was issued from

Moscow that all American Communist organizations were to help achieve this goal.[42]

The directive created confusion and great concern among many black Communists. Those among them who only wanted a Socialist form of government had no desire to be a part of militant uprising that had no hope of success.

Only a very small number of militant black Communists were willing to try, but their voices were quickly suppressed by their colleagues. The militant black Communists remained silent until the 1960s.

And despite their disagreements, neither side wanted to return to a region of the country they had just abandoned, which many blacks were still trying to leave. But they also did not want to lose their financial support from Moscow.

James Ford, the first black man to run on a presidential ticket in the 20th century.

Additionally, the directive called for the national segregation of blacks and whites, which was in direct conflict with the effort of the American Communists to desegregate public institutions.

To make matters worse, the continuous talk of overthrowing the federal government and forming a Communist country from six Southern states drew considerable attention from J. Edgar Hoover and the Bureau of Investigation, now known as the FBI.

Because the Communist Party sold itself as a civil rights organization, the FBI not only watched groups that openly identified as Communist but kept close track of all civil rights organizations. The federal government also watched civil rights groups that wanted nothing to do with the Communist agenda.

---

[42] http://socialistworker.org/2012/06/15/self-determination-and-the-black-belt

The Communist Party experienced tremendous growth and great support from the black community during the Great Depression of the 1930s. During that time, American unemployment jumped from 8.8 percent to 25.2 percent in just a few years.

But in the black community, unemployment remained between 40 percent to 55 percent in cities like Boston, Pittsburg, Chicago, Detroit, Philadelphia, and New York.

To take full advantage of the crisis, the Communist Party organized multiple protests in America's largest cities. It demanded unemployment relief for black Americans and more public housing. In New York, about 50,000 demonstrators gathered in Union Square and protested the loss of jobs, food shortages, and crime in the city.

The protests in each city led more blacks to join the Communist Party. In Birmingham, Alabama, the local organization grew to about 1,000 members.

Most of the protests turned violent and white Communists struggled alongside blacks whenever police arrived with riot gear, batons, and tear gas. Three blacks were killed when a protest turned into a riot in Chicago in 1931.

Riots and demonstrations continued throughout the Depression era. And during the entire period, white Communists showed solidarity and support for the black community.

To garner even more support, the Communist Party USA nominated James W. Ford, a black man from New York City, as vice president of the United States during three election cycles. Ford ran on the Communist Party ticket with William Z. Foster in 1932, and with Earl Browder in 1936 and 1940.

James Ford was the first black man to run on a presidential ticket in the 20th century. But because of his commitment to the Communist Party, no one ever heard about him.

Ford attended several Communist meetings throughout the world as a representative of American Communists. In the spring of 1928, he attended of the Red International Labor Unions in Moscow and during the summer he attended a meeting of Communist International in Hamburg, Germany, as a delegate of the American Communist Party.

Black Americans had certainly seen former slaves and free blacks rise within the ranks of the Republican Party to become local and state public officials and even congressmen. But they had never seen white people express enough trust and confidence in black men to nominate one to the extremely high-profile position of nominee for vice president of the United States.

There is no doubt the gesture from the Communists made a profound and lasting impression upon black Americans. It is likely that they believed that if the Communists trusted them, then they could trust the Communists.

Chapter 5: 1930–1945
Political Change and a Convergence of Events

An unforeseeable and completely unexpected merging of three world events during the 1930s left a long-lasting mark on blacks Americans. And those events initiated a change of direction of black politics for generations.

The Depression

The first event was the Depression itself. No segment of American society suffered from the brutal pain, hardships and indignities like America's black community. Throughout the country's largest cities, black families were being evicted, forced to live in the streets, beg for food for their children, and suffer unspeakable indignities.

And with black unemployment between 40 and 55 percent, their situation was desperate to say the least.

The Seduction

The second event was black Americans' introduction to Communism and their seduction by Socialism. Local Communist organizations were already trying to reach the hearts and minds of some Americans by proclaiming the benefits of joining and support-ing unions and union workers.

As urban areas throughout the country began to fill with black migrants from the South, local Communists and Socialists proclaimed themselves to be the champions of civil rights to draw the new arrivals into the fold.

They said everything the black community wanted to hear. They said that they were in favor of black voting rights, and equality under the law. They told blacks that the only way they could have this for themselves and their children was under a Communist form of government and an economy based upon Socialism.

By the mid-1930s many blacks heard what the Communists had to say about how their lives would be much better if they lived in a Socialist republic. Many black celebrities and politicians spoke at great length before large crowds about what they had seen when they visited Moscow.

And they persuaded many blacks to abandon the Republican party.

But while most blacks rejected the idea of a violent overthrow of the US government, which the Communists were advocating, many were convinced that they only way to prosper was if the government intervened, confiscated everything, and distributed everything equally—which is the primary aspect of Socialism.

The New Deal

President Franklin D. Roosevelt

The third event was executed by Democratic President Franklin Roosevelt, whose Depression-era policies helped initiate a change in the direction of black politics.

As part of President Roosevelt's New Deal, the Roosevelt Administration created the Federal Emergency Relief Administration (FERA).

FERA literally put food on the table of many black Americans as they struggled through the

Depression. FERA also issued loans to states to create unskilled jobs in state and local governments.

About 52.2 percent of black families, and only 13.3 percent of white families, in Northern cities were completely dependent upon the federal government for food throughout the Depression. Within states that bordered the South, 51.8 percent of black families and only 10.4 percent of white families received assistance.

And within Southern cities, 33.7 percent of black families received government assistance and only 11.4 percent of white families.[43]

Because blacks did not see any other possible source of provision, they were profoundly grateful. Their gratitude caused them to overlook the fact that President Roosevelt was the current leader of the political party that had lynched and cruelly oppressed them for centuries.

Prior to Democratic President Roosevelt's election in 1932, virtually all blacks voted Republican. And since the days of Abraham Lincoln, the Republican Party knew that black voters would support them at the polls. And many blacks continued to support Republicans even after their half-hearted attempted to pass the Dyer Anti-Lynching Bill.

But after the implementation of the New Deal, which for many blacks ended the uncertainty about where their next meal would come from, President Roosevelt won reelection in 1936, with about 71 percent of the black vote![44]

Oddly enough, the Democrats did not have a change of heart about blacks. President Roosevelt supported racial segregation and disenfranchisement of the black vote in the South. He was also silent on lynching and continued the policy of segregation throughout the federal government established by President Woodrow Wilson. President Roosevelt also supported racial segregation in the military during World War II.

---

[43] https://trumanlibrary.org/civilrights/srights4.htm#139
[44] https://www.factcheck.org/2008/04/blacks-and-the-democratic-party/

Moreover, President Roosevelt nominated KKK member Hugo Black to the US Supreme Court, and the Social Security Act he signed in 1935 excluded most blacks from coverage.[45]

An extensive canvass of black voters by community activists revealed a common response among them. During desperate times and the continuous uncertainty of the Depression, it was the Democrats—and the federal government—that provided a sure and certain source of food.

One precinct activist in Chicago said, *"It didn't matter that the disbursement of aid was in the hands of Democrat local officials that often severely discriminated against them. They were grateful to get something to eat, even if it was much less than what whites received."*[46]

Communist leader
Joseph Stalin

And in the minds of these grateful recipients of government largess, this was confirmation that Socialism worked. They believed that what they were told by the Communists was in fact true: The only way blacks could survive in America, in the midst of extreme discrimination, oppression, and segregation, was under a Socialist form of government.

Abandoned by the Communists

The next event that contributed to the change in direction of black politics was likely threat of World War II. During the late 1930s, Communist International abruptly stopped its aggressive pursuit to spread Socialist ideology and Communist governments.

---

[45] Bruce Bartlett, Wrong on Race: The Democratic Party's Buried Past. New York, St. Martin's Griffin, P. 119

[46] Bruce Bartlett, Wrong on Race: The Democratic Party's Buried Past. New York, St. Martin's Griffin, P. 119

As a result, the Communist Party stopped black recruitment in the United States.

Civil rights and equal treatment under the law were no longer the top priority for Communists. They let these issues fall by the wayside or placed less emphasis upon them—very much like the two major parties abandoned blacks when it suited their agenda in the United States.

A significant numbers of historians agree that the Communists abandoned black America because of the rise of Adolf Hitler and Nazi Germany. Germany's imminent attack on Russia forced the Communists to reorganize their resources to prepare for war.

By November of 1936, Nazi Germany, the Empire of Japan, and Italy formed the Anti-Comintern Pact, which was an agreement to stand and fight together against Communist aggression and the spread of Communism throughout the world.

Soviet leader Joseph Stalin knew that a great war with Germany was coming. He also knew that he would need Western allies. Therefore, Stalin could not afford to antagonize those allies anymore. He could not have his representatives within the United States offend the US government because he needed its help.

It is likely that the Russian leader called for a suspension of all foreign recruitment activity until the eminent threat of Germany passed. This meant that all of Moscow's resources, including the money used to recruit blacks in the United States, was redirected to help the Soviet Union prepare and fight during World War II.

Of course, this led to another great disappointment for black America. Blacks began to lose interest in the Communist Party little by little and had to choose, once again, between either the Republican or Democratic Party.

Their experience during the Depression, however, convinced them that although they might never enjoy full constitutional rights, the Socialist policies of the Democrats would at least put food on their tables during hard times.

President Roosevelt became the first Democratic president to enjoy a majority of the black vote since the Reconstruction era. Blacks supported Roosevelt's reelection in 1940 and again in 1944 with over 70 percent of their vote. And blacks who voted for him openly identified as Democrats.[47]

As a result of the convergence of these four events in black political history: the Depression, the introduction to Communism and Socialism, the New Deal, and World War II, the black vote changed from Republican to Democrat.

47 https://www.factcheck.org/2008/04/blacks-and-the-democratic-party

Chapter 6: 1945–1948
President Harry Truman: The Maverick Democrat

Regardless of the injustices and indignities Southern blacks suffered at the hands of Democrats, including the denial of their right to vote and discrimination in public schools and public places, President Roosevelt's New Deal policy gained their support from black Democrats in the North, the Midwest, and the West as well.

Blacks within these regions of the country also remained victims of the Depression well into the 1940s. And throughout the nation, they turned a blind eye and a deaf ear to their neighbors and family members in the South. Blacks who lived outside of

President Harry S. Truman

the South were willing to help the Democrats retain political power as long the Democrats helped feed their families.

In 1944, President Roosevelt replaced Henry Wallace as his vice president because Roosevelt wanted the support of segregationist Democrats and Wallace was a very outspoken supporter of civil rights.[48]

---

[48] Bruce Bartlett, Wrong on Race: The Democratic Party's Buried Past. New York, St. Martin's Griffin, P. 135

Roosevelt tapped Harry S. Truman, a Missouri Democrat and US Senator, to be his vice president during his unprecedented third term. Truman was from the South and, therefore, had the support of southern Democrats.

When Truman became president after the death of Franklin Roosevelt, Southern Democrats believed they had dodged a bullet by supporting Truman in place of Wallace on the Democrat ticket. They believed, as a Southern Democrat himself, Truman would support the racist policies of the South.

But the white supremacist Democrats presumed too much of Truman. And they did not bother to take a close look at his record on civil rights. Yes, President Truman was a Southern Democrat. And Democrats had been united on their racist beliefs since the beginning of slavery.

But Harry Truman was an anomaly. He was an exception to the rule. President Truman believed in the fair treatment of blacks and deviated from the Democrat's official platform of keeping blacks in complete subjugation. On the issue of civil rights, it is likely Truman was even a stronger supporter than Wallace. And Truman was elected with President Franklin Roosevelt before the Democrats realized their blunder.

Truman also supported the establishment of the Fair Employment Practices Committee, created in 1941 by President Roosevelt. The committee, which was created by executive order, aimed to investigate charges of discrimination and racism in the federal government.

But under Roosevelt, the committee was a sham. Roosevelt received over 70 percent of the black vote in 1940, so he wanted to hold onto their support while not offending the Southern Democrats. He created the committee to pacify and deceive civil rights leaders and the black community.

Under Roosevelt's administration, the committee existed only in name without doing anything of real substance. The US military—and other areas of the federal government—were completely segregated throughout World War II.

President Truman, in contrast, not only wanted the FEPC to actively investigate charges of racism, he wanted to make it a permanent government agency with the power to take action against racism. Truman also supported laws against lynching and poll taxes.[49]

Senator Richard B. Russell

On September 6, 1945, President Truman spoke in favor of making the FEPC a permanent government agency, which was a major goal of the civil rights leaders. Additionally, President Truman appointed several prominent blacks to boards, commissions, and judicial positions.

In January of 1946, New Mexico Democratic Senator Dennis Chávez—another maverick Democrat—sponsored a bill to make the FEPC a permanent government agency. Senator Chávez had the support of a majority of Republican Senators, and President Truman demanded a vote on the bill.

Five Democratic senators, John H. Overton from Louisiana, Richard B. Russell from Georgia, Millard E. Tydings from Maryland, Clyde R. Hoey from North Carolina, and Kenneth McKellar from Tennessee, led an exhaustive filibuster reminiscent of the action taken against the Dyer Anti-Lynching Bill.

But this time the Republicans did not submit to the Democrats so quickly. They had the support of a handful of Democrats, which was enough to pass the bill. But they needed two-thirds of the Senate for cloture.

The Republican Caucus was eager to allow the filibuster to continue day and night if necessary. And it appeared as if senate Democrats would follow through to prevent a vote on the bill.

---

[49] The Evening Star, April 12, 1946 p. A-16. https://chroniclingamerica.loc.gov/lccn/sn83045462/1946-04-12/ed-1/seq-16/#date1=1946&index=14&rows=20&words=FEPC&searchType=basic&sequence=0&state=&date2=1946&proxtext=FEPC&y=12&x=10&dateFilterType=yearRange&page=1

"If the opposition wants to run 24 hours a day, we are abso-100-percent-lutey ready," said Democratic Senator Theodore G. Bilbo.

During the filibuster, Democrats tried to argue that the bill would cause race riots throughout the country if it passed. Senator Russell said that the bill would force future presidents to do things they did not want to do and make the president a "lackey" of the committee.[50] They also attacked Truman as if he were a Republican and questioned his mental health and state of mind for supporting the bill.

Again the Republicans engaged the Democrats in a battle of wills. The filibuster lasted for several weeks this time. In the end, Senator Chávez was forced to remove the bill from consideration because it failed to receive the two-thirds needed for cloture.

For the first time in history, the Democrats were significantly divided on civil rights issues. And their division bore fruit for the Republicans in the form of an electoral victory during the mid-term elections in 1946.

The Republicans took complete control of both chambers of Congress that year, gaining a 51 to 45 majority in the Senate and 246 to 188 majority in the House.

Because of the providence of God, the black community found itself with a pro-civil rights president as well as a Congress favorable to civil rights—mostly because the Southern

President Truman signs an executive order to create a civil rights committee.

Democrats had not known that Harry Truman was in favor of civil rights; if they had, they would never have supported him for vice president.

Truman became the focus of outrage and anger of his fellow Democrats. And despite their bitterness, Truman made civil rights

---

[50] The Evening Star, April 12, 1946 p. A-16

the top priority on his domestic agenda. On December 5, 1946, President Truman signed an executive order to create a civil rights committee to study the effects of discrimination in America and issue a report. As the committee did its work, Truman traveled throughout the country and spoke against the Ku Klux Klan, lynching in the South, and the Jim Crow laws.

President Truman also spoke at several civil rights meetings, including the NAACP's 38th annual meeting at the Lincoln Memorial on June 29, 1947:

> *It is my deep conviction that we have reached a turning point in the long history of our country's efforts to guarantee freedom and equality to all our citizens. Recent events in the United States and abroad have made us realize that it is more important today than ever before to ensure that all Americans enjoy these rights. And when I say all Americans—I mean all Americans.*
>
> *Our immediate task is to remove the last remnants of the barriers which stand between millions of our citizens and their birthright. There is no justifiable reason for discrimination because of ancestry, or religion, or race, or color. We must not tolerate such limitations on the freedom of any of our people and on their enjoyment of the basic rights which every citizen in a truly democratic society must possess.*
>
> *We can no longer afford the luxury of a leisurely attack upon prejudice and discrimination. There is much that state and local governments can do in providing positive safeguard for civil rights. But we cannot any longer await the growth of a will to action in the slowest state or the most backward community. Our national government must show the way.*
>
> *Abraham Lincoln understood so well the ideal with you and I seek today. As this conference closes, we would do well to keep in mind his words, when he said: "If it shall please the Divine Being*

who determines the destinies of nations, this shall remain a united people, and they will humbly seek the Divine guidance, make their prolonged national existence a source of new benefits to themselves and their successors, and to all classes and conditions of mankind."[51]

The 1947 Civil Rights Committee Report

On October 29, 1947, the President's Committee on Civil Rights released its 178-page report "*To Secure These Rights*." The report not only addressed the state of race relations and civil rights of the day but also featured a comprehensive review and analysis of the nation's racial diversity. It went on to examine the country's historical efforts to improve race relations and pointed out the obstacles to progress.

Furthermore, the committee offered recommendations about how the federal, state, and local governments could correct this persistent and long-lasting problem.

Among the long list of additional topics addressed was the status of blacks within the armed forces; police brutality; voting restrictions; and discrimination in education, professional sports, and social services.

The report first pointed out the moral and economic reasons the government must protect the civil rights of all its citizens.

The pervasive gap between the principles of our founding documents and what we do is creating a kind of moral dry rot which eats away at the emotional and rational bases and

Truman Begins Military Desegregation

---

[51] The Evening Star, June 30, 1947. P. A-5

our democratic beliefs. There are times when the difference between what we preach about civil rights and what we practice is shockingly illustrated by individual outrages. As examples of moral erosion there are the consequences of suffrage limitations in the South. The fact that Negros and many whites have not been allowed to vote in some states has sapped the morality underlying universal suffrage. Many men in public and private life do not believe that those who have been kept from voting are capable of self-rule. They finally convince themselves that disfranchised people do not really have the right to vote.[52]

The committee also pointed out that America was hurting itself, economically, by not protecting the civil rights of all. The report illustrated that discrimination in employment leads to an inefficient use of America's labor force and in turn leads to less productivity, giving rise to less profits, less purchasing power, fewer home sales, and a lower standard of living for all Americans. Meanwhile, fair employment practices and the full and efficient use of all workers leads to greater efficiency, greater purchasing power, greater consumer demand, full industry production, and a higher standard of living for everyone.

One of the principal economic problems facing us and the rest of the world is achieving maximum production and continued prosperity. The loss of a huge, potential market for goods is a direct result of the economic discrimination which is practiced against many of our minority groups. A sort of vicious circle is produced. Discrimination depresses the wages and income of minority groups. As a result, their purchasing power is diminished, and markets are reduced. Reduced markets result in reduced production. This cuts down employment, which of course means lower wages and still fewer job opportunities. Rising fear, prejudice, and insecurity aggravate the very discrimination in employment which sets the vicious circle in motion.

Minority groups are not the sole victims of this economic waste; its impact is inevitably felt by the entire population. Eric Johnston, when President of the United States Chamber of Commerce, made this point

---

[52] To Secure These Rights: The Report of the President's Committee on Civil Rights. P. 139, 140

with vividness and clarity: "The withholding of jobs and business opportunities from some people does not make more jobs and business opportunities for others. Such a policy merely tends to drag down the whole economic level. You can't sell an electric refrigerator to a family that can't afford electricity. Perpetuating poverty for some merely guarantees stagnation for all. True economic progress demands that the whole nation move forward at the same time. It demands that all artificial barriers erected by ignorance and intolerance be removed. To put it in the simplest terms, we are all in business together. Intolerance

The committee recommended the prohibition of segregation on public transportation.

is a species of boycott and any business or job boycott is a cancer in the economic body of the nation. I repeat, intolerance is destructive; prejudice produces no wealth; discrimination is a fool's economy."[53]

The committee report also included a letter from Acting Secretary of State Dean Acheson in which the secretary explained how discrimination of minorities had become an albatross around the necks of state department officials and US diplomats around the world.

"The existence of discrimination against minority groups in this country has an adverse effect upon our relations with other countries. We are reminded over and over by some foreign newspapers and spokesmen, that our treatment of various minorities leaves much to be desired. While sometimes these pronouncements are exaggerated and unjustified, they all too frequently point with accuracy to some form of discrimination because of race, creed, color, or national origin. Frequently we find it next to impossible to formulate a satisfactory answer to our critics in

---

[53] To Secure These Rights: The Report of the President's Committee on Civil Rights. P. 144, 145

other countries; the gap between the things we stand for in principle and the facts of a particular situation may be too wide to be bridged. An atmosphere of suspicion and resentment in a country over the way a minority is being treated in the United States is a formidable obstacle to the development of mutual understanding and trust between the two countries. We will have better international relations when these reasons for suspicion and resentment have been removed. I think it is quite obvious that the existence of discriminations against minority groups in the United States is a handicap in our relations with other countries. The Department of State, therefore, has good reason to hope for the continued and increased effectiveness of public and private efforts to do away with these discriminations. [54]

The president's committee submitted many recommendations to protect the civil rights of minorities. Their suggestions included reorganizing the Civil Rights section of the Justice Department; establishing a special unit within the FBI to investigate civil rights violations; establishing Civil Rights Investigative Units by state and local governments; establishing a permanent Commission on Civil Rights for the White House and creating a standing Committee on Civil Rights in Congress; establishing a permanent state-level Civil Rights Commission; increasing civil rights training for local police officers; enacting by Congress of an anti-lynching law; and abolishing poll taxes by states or by Congress.

After President Truman reviewed the committee's recommendations, he sent a special message to Congress on February 2, 1948 declaring his civil rights goals. Within the message the president said:

"The protection of civil rights is the duty of every government which derives its powers from the consent of the people. This is equally true of local, state, and national governments. There is much that the states can and should do at this time to extend their protection of civil rights. Wherever the law enforcement measures of state and local governments are inadequate to discharge this primary function of government, these measures should be strengthened and improved. I recommend, therefore,

---

[54] To Secure These Rights: The Report of the President's Committee on Civil Rights. P. 146, 147

that the Congress enact legislation at this session directed toward the following specific objectives:"

1. *Establish a permanent Commission on Civil Rights, a Joint Congressional Committee on Civil Rights, and a Civil Rights Division in the Department of Justice.*
2. *Strengthen existing civil rights statutes.*
3. *Provide Federal protection against lynching.*
4. *Protect more adequately the right to vote,*
5. *Establish a Fair Employment Practice Commission to prevent unfair discrimination in employment.*
6. *Prohibit discrimination in interstate transportation facilities.*
7. *Provide home-rule and suffrage in Presidential elections for the residents of the District of Columbia.*
8. *Provide Statehood for Hawaii and Alaska and a greater measure of self-government for our island possessions.*
9. *Equalize the opportunities for residents of the United States to become naturalized citizens.*
10. *Settle the evacuation claims of Japanese Americans.*

Chapter 7: 1948–1953

Segregationist Democrats Rebel Against President Truman and the Courts

Southern Democrats were completely enraged by Truman's civil rights proposals. They were impossible, unreasonable, thick-headed, and determined to fight to keep their 19th-century social structure and traditions despite the practical, moral, and economic reasons to end discrimination in the South as clearly presented by the committee.

Even the remarks from Secretary of State Acheson about the South's oppression of blacks being the direct cause of the State Department's lack of diplomatic success failed to persuade them.

The depth of their pride would not allow them to see that the traditions their fathers and grandfathers passed along to them were wrong—and they were willing to let the entire country suffer for it.

The most brilliant and enlightened arguments from the wisest among Truman supporters were not enough to penetrate the hardened hearts and stubborn wills of the Democrats.

Not only did they promise to fight Truman's civil rights agenda, they promised to fight his nomination for another term as president all the way to the National Democratic Convention.

Truman, meanwhile, was not only willing to fight his own party, he promised to change the Democratic Party's position on the issue in the party's official platform.

Unfortunately, President Truman also fought most of the American people about the issue. A 1948 poll revealed that 94 percent of Americans were against his position on civil rights.

But regardless of the sentiments reflected in the polls and despite the Democratic Party's disgraceful history regarding civil rights, President Truman was determined to set the nation on the right course.

Still it was a path the Southern Democrats refused to take. They organized their efforts to derail Truman's civil rights agenda even if it meant losing the White House to the Republicans. South Carolina Democratic Party Chairman W.D. Baskin met with Democratic congressmen from five critical Southern states in Columbia, South Carolina, to organize a rebellion against Truman. They discussed and planned to either stop Truman from gaining the Democrat nomination for president or prevent him from winning the White House.[55]

If the national convention insists on nominating Truman or anyone else that holds similar views, the South might just go fishing on Election Day," Baskin told the media.[56]

Truman's civil rights agenda shook the Democratic Party to its foundation. The party's position on race relations had always been clearly understood since the days of slavery. At best, the Democrats believed that blacks were second-class citizens, and, at worst, they were the lowest form of humanity.

But now an obscure, little-known senator from Missouri—whose rise to the position of vice president (in their minds) was due to nothing more than good fortune, and who was then elevated even higher to the office of president not because of loyalty and faithfulness but by sheer chance—was telling them that they had been wrong about an issue in which they took great pride and that distinguished themselves from the Republicans.

Black Americans, during that time, owed the rise of President Truman to no one but God Himself. Before he became president, Harry Truman was a true Southern Democrat. And the universal norm of all Southern Democrats was to keep blacks under their feet no matter how the rest of the country felt about it.

---

[55] Evening Star, April 13, 1948. P. A-2
[56] Evening Star, July 18, 1948

Yet Truman, with his profound differences with his fellow Democrats, was able to obtain the position of US senator from right under their noses.

It truly baffles the mind when you consider how either God blinded the Democrats about Truman's true feelings, or how Truman was able to hide his position on race relations so well that Southerners sent him to Washington, DC.

And it also baffles the mind when you consider that out of all the Democrats President Roosevelt could have chosen as a running mate, he unknowingly chose one of very few nontraditional Democrats in Congress.

About half of Alabama's delegates threatened to walk out of the national convention if other delegates adopted Truman's civil rights agenda. And delegates from other Southern states threatened to do the same and throw the convention into chaos.[57]

Meanwhile, the Republicans were fully onboard and wholeheartedly supported Truman's civil rights agenda along with civil rights leaders across the country. After President Truman announced his objectives, House Republicans immediately proposed an anti-lynching bill. They were confident that this time they would get the bill passed.

Texas Gov. Dan Moody

But once again, the Senate Democrats resisted and defeated the bill. They leveraged racist and discriminatory sentiments across the country and the bill never emerged from the Senate Judiciary Committee.[58]

Despite the defeat, President Truman forged ahead with his agenda into the 1948 National Democratic Convention at the Philadelphia Convention Hall in Philadelphia, Pennsylvania. Along the way, Truman

---

[57] Evening Star, April 11, 1948
[58] New York Times, May 19, 1948

was able to pick up support for changing the Democrats' platform on civil rights.

Truman did not have any serious competition for the Democrat nomination. When the convention was called to order, feelings were mixed with clear division among the Democrats. Many did not want to support Truman, but they wanted to win the White House and Truman was going to be their nominee.

Some did support his agenda because they knew the Democrats had to change and they did not want to fight with their fellow Democrats.

Armed with the 1947 Civil Rights Committee Report, Truman and his supporters were able to convince the Platform Committee to adopt significant changes to the party's platform on civil rights. The members of the Platform Committee, obviously, took the report much more seriously than the Democrat members of Congress.

Segregationist Democrats responded with a proposal of their own. They argued in favor of what they called a "States Rights Plank" within the party's platform, which essentially meant that individual states had the authority to deny constitutional rights to anyone they chose.

The States Rights Plank had the support of high-profile convention leaders such as Democrats Texas Governor Dan Moody and Mississippi House Speaker Frank J. Myers, who also claimed that the adoption of Truman's agenda would destroy the Constitution.

The States Rights Plank failed to pass in the committee therefore the proposal did not make it to the floor for debate between the convention delegates. But the committee did support Truman's agenda.

When the committee chairman offered the party platform to the convention delegates, Truman's the civil rights plank ignited a fierce debate between Southern Democrats and Democrats from other regions of the country.

For many of the southern Democrats the issue was not about right versus wrong—it was change versus tradition. Many Southern delegates couldn't bear the thought of changing their tradition. It would be the equivalent to admitting their way of life, their highly esteemed timeless traditions, honored by previous generations, were wrong.

When the debate ended, and the delegates voted, and President Truman and his forces prevailed.[59] Truman and his friends persuaded about 52 percent of the convention delegates to adopt the new civil rights plank in the party's platform by a vote of 651 to 582.

President Truman achieved something many believed to be impossible. He and his supporters successfully persuaded a majority of hard-hearted and racists Democrats to change their ways. For the first time in its history, the Democratic Party officially supported civil rights for blacks.[60]

The States Rights "Dixiecrat" Party

Not all Democrats agreed to change. After the adoption of the new platform, most of the delegates from Alabama, Mississippi, and Georgia stormed out of the convention hall.

Led by South Carolina Democratic Governor Strom Thurmond and Mississippi Democratic Governor Fielding L. Wright, the angry and embittered Democrats broke away from their party to form a new party under a "States' Rights" plank. They called it the States' Rights Democratic Party, which later became known as the "Dixiecrat Party."

The Dixiecrats offered Governor Strom Thurmond as a presidential candidate. And because neither Truman or the Republican candidate Thomas Dewey was acceptable to them, their goal was to deny both of them enough electoral college votes to win the presidency, so that the election of the presidential race could be decided by Congress.

On election day, President Truman defeated Dewey, and the Democrats' "solid South" was significantly divided on civil rights. President Truman won nine Southern states, and Governor

---

[59] Detroit Tribune, July 24, 1948, P. 1

[60] https://www.trumanlibrary.org/whistlestop/study_collections/trumancivil-rights/documents/index.php?documentid=3-2&pagenumber=2

Thurmond won the states of Louisiana, Mississippi, Alabama, and South Carolina.[61]

President Truman was very clear about his position on civil rights to Southern voters. Yet the people of North Carolina, Georgia, Florida, Arkansas, Texas, Missouri, Tennessee, Kentucky, and Virginia all supported him. This was a clear indication that Southerners were beginning to change their long-held views about the South's oppressive social order.

The Domino Effect in the Courts

Judge Julius Waring

The States' Rights "Dixiecrat" Party dissolved about a year after its creation. After they failed to force Congress to make the choice in the 1948 presidential race, the angry and embittered segregationists returned to the Democratic Party, vowing to stand their ground on segregation.

The rest of the country, however, appeared to be following Truman's lead on the issue, making great strides in the right direction. In 1949, for example, the California Supreme Court ruled that California's law banning interracial marriage was unconstitutional: Wisconsin and Indiana both passed state laws ending segregation in their public schools; private schools, nationwide, opened their doors the black students; and South Carolina Federal Judge Julius Waring reversed a long-standing Democrat tradition, ruling that blacks must be allowed to become members of the Democratic Party.[62]

61 https://www.270towin.com/historical-presidential-elections/timeline/
62 https://www.trumanlibrary.org/whistlestop/study_collections/trumancivil-rights/documents/index.php?documentid=11-9&pagenumber=3

According to many, Judge Waring's ruling was the final nail in the coffin of the Dixiecrat Party.

Also, during that period, a great wave of pro-civil rights legislation and court rulings swept through the country.

From one state to another and from one court room to another, America started the processes of cleansing its soul of institutionalized racism.

Unfortunately, there remained several stubborn and steadfast pockets of discrimination, not only in the South but in the federal government. In July of 1948, President Truman issued an executive order to desegregate the armed forces. But in many military bases throughout the country, commanders refused to carry out the order—those bases were still segregated by the end of Truman's last term in office.

These base commanders had the full support of those Democratic senators who stubbornly refused to change their thinking. Also, after the 1948 elections, the Democrats regained control of both houses of Congress. When the dust settled, the Democrats held 263 seats in the House of Representatives and the Republicans 171. In the Senate, the Democrats controlled 54 seats and the Republicans 42 seats.

Perhaps Truman projected his own sensibilities and values upon his fellow Democrats, or perhaps he was simply naïve. But just as the Democratic Party held no regard for the Fourteenth and Fifteenth Amendments to the Constitution, they showed no respect for the new civil rights plank in their own official platform.

The Democrats held the presidency as well as both houses of Congress. They could have easily achieved what their party platform called for. But except for Truman, the party's national leadership fought against all civil rights legislation and desegregation.

All of Truman's efforts to improve civil rights were undermined by his fellow Democrats—especially the Democrats in the Senate. They were determined to continue their outdated social order no matter the cost. And clearly, Truman had been successful in getting the Democrats to accept civil rights on paper, but he had failed to get them to accept it in their hearts.

But as blind and unyielding as they were, the Democrats saw that the nation was changing its views about race relations. They very likely realized that they could not hold their position much longer, no matter how much they believed in it.

So the Democrats did what many politicians would do in such a situation—they appeared to stand on both sides of the issue, but with outcome of all civil rights legislation ending with their true desire: failure.

The Democrat-controlled House of Representatives passed many pro-civil rights bills—including an end to all poll taxes in the South. They supported Truman's civil rights agenda with help from Republicans.

But it was the Senate Democrats who did the dirty work—it was on the floor of the Senate where the truth and what really lived in the hearts of Southern Democrats were on full display.

The Senate Democrats did not have to face the voters as often as the House Democrats. Therefore, they felt free to govern against will of the people and the growing favorability of civil rights. All of Truman's civil rights bills died in the Senate, either in committee or on the Senate floor.

Chapter 8: 1953–1957
Dwight Eisenhower, the Civil Rights President

Sadly, President Truman completed his final term in office with the most important part of his domestic agenda unfulfilled. He had done everything in his power to correct the discriminatory laws and practices of his country and the historic evil of the Democratic Party.

But Republican President Dwight D. Eisenhower, Truman's successor, once said during a speech in Wheeling, West Virginia, "*An ounce of leadership is worth a pound of law.*"

President Dwight Eisenhower

Eisenhower was not referring to Truman when he said this, but it certainly applied. Although Truman's civil rights agenda never made it through Congress, southerners saw him stand courageously against the barbaric Congressional leadership of his own party and they heard what he had to say to other southerners as individuals.

It's impossible to quantify anyone's leadership. But if Truman did provide southerners at least "an ounce of leadership" it was enough to begin moving the hearts of many southerners in the right direction. And even though Truman's agenda was not enshrined in federal law, most southerners began to follow him. Perhaps the people of the South needed to hear one of their own leaders say that they had to treat their black neighbors as they would like to be treated. No one will ever know if that's what it took, but the most important thing is that most southerners began to follow Truman's lead whether Congress liked it or not.

But as Truman's final term ended, it was clear that the primary battlefield for civil rights progress would not be in Congress—and that the greatest challenge to institutionalized racism would not come from the White House. Jim Crow's greatest challenge would come from the courts—more specifically the US Supreme Court.

For about 50 years, the Supreme Court ruling in the 1896 case of *Plessy vs. Ferguson* had provided a legal foundation for the doctrine of "*separate, but equal.*" The case was continuously cited by Democrat lawyers as justification for states that resorted to great extremes to keep black and white school children away from one another.

In *Plessy vs. Ferguson*, the Court ruled that the state of Louisiana could legally separate the races in public transportation systems if the method of transportation for both races was of equal quality. The Court also determined that although the Fourteenth Amendment to the Constitution addressed equality of all people under the law, it was silent on "*the commingling of the two races.*"

Plessy vs. Ferguson Attacked in the Courts

By the fall of 1950, there were five separate cases headed for the Supreme Court from South Carolina, Virginia, the District of Columbia, Delaware, and Kansas. Each case had *Plessy vs. Ferguson* squarely in their sights with the intent to overturn the 54-year-old ruling that had helped keep blacks tethered to the 19th century.

As the Supreme Court showdown drew closer, Republican President Eisenhower first set his sights on Washington, DC, itself. Racial discrimination prevailed just as strongly in the nation's capital as it did in any Southern town thanks to the Democratic President Woodrow Wilson during the early 1900s.

Many of the city's residents were federal employees who had to live by federal Jim Crow policies. As the chief executive of the federal government and its employees, President Eisenhower saw an opportunity to advance his civil rights agenda for the entire city.

Most public places such as restaurants, sandwich and coffee shops, movie theaters, schools, and public housing were completely segregated in Washington, DC. And black people could not stay in the city's downtown hotels overnight.

Any black person who traveled by train or bus from the North into the Southern states had to switch to segregated trains or move to the back of the bus in Washington, DC, before the trains and buses could proceed into the South.

One of the numerous cases on track to challenge Jim Crow in Washington, DC, was *District of Columbia v. John R. Thompson Co.* The arguments were heard in the US Supreme Court on April 30, 1953.

Eisenhower instructed his Attorney General Herbert Brownell Jr. to file an amicus-curiae brief in support of the plaintiffs. Brownell

and the plaintiffs' attorneys argued that, during the late 19th century, the local governments banned racial discrimination in the capital city. And they pointed out that although those laws were ignored, they were never repealed.

On June 8, 1953, the Supreme Court ruled in favor of the plaintiffs and ended "Whites Only" businesses in the city.

**Attorney General
Herbert Brownell Jr.**

Eisenhower then turned his attention to finishing what President Truman started with the armed forces. About 60 military base commanders continued to openly defy President Truman's 1948 order to desegregate their bases. They no doubt believed they'd be free to continue their discriminatory practices after President Truman left office.

But President Eisenhower ordered Secretary of the Navy Robert Anderson to completely eradicate all signs of racial segregation on all naval bases and to do it quickly. High-ranking naval officials first responded to bases in Norfolk, Virginia, and Charleston, South Carolina, and found segregated washrooms, cafeterias, and drinking fountains. The naval officers ordered the base commanders to take down the signs, and the signs were removed before the navy officials returned to Washington.

In August of 1953, President Eisenhower also ordered the removal of all "Colored" and "White" signs over water fountains, bathrooms, and several other areas intended for use by sailors. By November 1, 1953, President Eisenhower had eliminated all signs of racial segregation in the US military.[63]

NAACP Chief Legal Counsel Thurgood Marshall

Furthermore, in August of 1953, President Eisenhower declared the creation of the Committee on Government Contracts. The committee was charged with the duty of ensuring that racial discrimination did not exist in any private company that received federal contracts.

Eisenhower made great progress in the advancement of civil rights during his first eight months in office. He and Attorney General Brownell received great praise from NAACP leaders, particularly NAACP chief legal counsel Thurgood Marshall.

The entire NAACP leadership saw the desegregation of Washington, DC, as a major victory.

Thurgood Marshall also played a vital role in the next major step in the march for equality. Marshall and the NAACP Legal Defense Team made the strategic decision to combine all cases that targeted

---

[63] William Hitchcock, The Age of Eisenhower: America and the World in the 1950's. New York, London, Toronto, Sydney, New Delhi. Simon and Schuster, P. 219

Plessy v. Ferguson. The cases were joined when the Supreme Court heard the case of *Oliver Brown v. the Board of Education of Topeka.*

Brown vs. the Board of Education
Creates National Anxiety

Brown v. the Board of Education drew considerable public attention because everyone knew what was at stake—the desegregation of public schools in the South. The Court, likely, had not received so much attention since 1883 when it ruled the Civil Rights Act of 1875 as unconstitutional.

All Americans knew their Southern neighbors well enough to know that if the Supreme Court ruled against racial segregation, the South would erupt into violence. The only question to be answered was how intense and bloody the violence would become.

Political leaders throughout the country were fearful of the outcome. Anger and anxiety also gripped blacks and whites throughout the South. Many of them knew the right thing had to be done regardless of the consequences. But they trembled at the thought of facing the unrestrained wrath of the Southern people and the Southern Democrats.

Left to Right: Attorney General Brownell, President Eisenhower, and FBI Director J. Edgar Hoover discuss the civil rights issue.

The Supreme Court justices wrestled with their own anxieties as well. When the entire country expected to hear a ruling during June of 1953, but the Supreme Court announced it was delaying final ruling until more arguments had been heard.

And there was a lot happening behind the scenes. During the postponement, most Americans did not realize that Chief Justice

Fred Vinson asked Eisenhower's Attorney General to file a brief as "a friend of the Court."[64]

Justice Vinson was a Democrat from Kentucky appointed by President Truman. Eisenhower described him easygoing and decent. He was a moderate on civil rights issues and would likely be described in today's political terminology as a moderate swing vote.

But President Eisenhower was very reluctant to respond. He wanted the matter to be decided exclusively by the Supreme Court without appearing to be an influence on the Court one way or the other.

Everyone in Washington knew Attorney General Brownell's position on civil rights. Brownell, who was also a former chair of the Republican National Committee, was a strong and very outspoken advocate in favor of desegregation. His participation in the desegregation of Washington, DC, was highly publicized. No one will ever know if the NAACP's legal team would have been successful without him, but they were very grateful for his help.

So, it appears as if the chief justice delayed the Court's ruling to search for a stronger legal position in favor of desegregation. After extensive consultation with the president, Brownell told Eisenhower that the administration had to respond. Because the chief justice of the Supreme Court had made an official request, the administration would be neglecting its duty if the brief was not filed.

Democrats Urge the Courts to Uphold Segregation

Eisenhower agreed and Brownell and his legal team proceeded. But before Brownell could submit his brief to the Court, Eisenhower began to feel pressure from the Southern Democrats to refuse the request from Chief Justice Vinson.

In a letter to the president dated July 16, 1953, Texas Democratic Governor Allan Shivers wrote: *"There is nothing more local then the*

---

[64] William Hitchcock, The Age of Eisenhower: America and the World in the 1950's. New York, London, Toronto, Sydney, New Delhi. Simon and Schuster, P. 348

public-school system. The decision in these cases will have a wide influence in the future economic and political life of our nation, particularly in the 17 southern and southwestern states where this problem is being solved on the local level as it must and should be."[65]

Texas Gov. Allen Shivers opposed desegregation of public schools.

Louisiana Democratic Governor Robert Kennon wrote, "*The controlling consideration is preserving our dual system of federal and state government. I trust that the guiding principle of states' rights, local self-government and community responsibility will be given the prime consideration it deserves, and that the position of the Department of Justice will be towards sustaining the fundamental American concept of state sovereignty.*"[66]

Eisenhower received a multitude of letters asking, and demanding, the preservation of school segregation in the South and he did not like being placed in this position. Eisenhower knew that however the Court ruled, the outcome would be felt for generations to come and he did not want his fingerprints on it.

As the American people waited for the Court's decision, an unexpected event added to the drama—Chief Justice Fred Vinson died. He died of a heart attack on September 8, 1953, at the age of 63.

President Eisenhower had to select a replacement. During October of 1953, Eisenhower made a recess appointment of Earl Warren, a moderate who was a former Republican governor and attorney general of California. The Senate confirmed Warren in March of 1954.

---

[65] https://eisenhower.archives.gov/research/online_documents/civil_rights_brown_v_boe/1953_07_16_Shivers_to_DDE.pdf

[66] https://www.eisenhowerlibrary.gov/sites/default/files/research/online-documents/civil-rights-brown-v-boe/1953-11-20-kennon-to-dde.pdf

Brownell Tips the Scales of Justice in Favor of Civil Rights

Attorney General Brownell, along with his legal team, conducted extensive research on the language and original intent of the Fourteenth Amendment. In Brownell's brief, he said that the amendment was clearly intended to *"strike down distinctions based on race or color and establish equality of all persons under the law."*

Chief Supreme Court Justice Earl Warren

The big question was whether the Fourteenth Amendment applied to public schools. Brownell wrote that when the amendment was drafted, Congress did not list in detail all the specific applications of the amendment, but that the *"great and pervading purpose"* of the amendment was to establish equality and the enjoyment of basic human rights for blacks.

On November 27, 1953, Attorney General Brownell filed his brief with the Supreme Court. Not long afterward, the national media published that the GOP and the Eisenhower administration were urging the Supreme Court to eliminate the Jim Crow laws.

The backlash against the Eisenhower administration was tremendous. Angry and hate-filled letters poured into the White House, and Democratic congressmen throughout the South condemned the White House's position.

They also deeply criticized Brownell because he tipped the scales against them. Georgia Democratic Governor Herman Talmadge said that both the Court and the White House wanted to destroy the South.

Finally, on May 17, 1954, the US Supreme Court unanimously ruled that segregation of school children by race denied minorities of equality of education. The Court wrote, *"We conclude that in the field of public education the doctrine of separate but equal has no place. Separate educational facilities are inherently unequal."*

Plessy vs. Ferguson was overturned. And shock and anger filled the hearts of many Southern Democrats.

Segregationist Democrats React Vehemently

The South's reaction to the Court decision was additional proof that Democratic Congressman Alexander Hamilton Stephens's statement, years earlier, was very true. On March 21, 1861, Stephens, who was the vice president of the Confederate States, said *"the cornerstone of the South's new government rests upon the great truth that the Negro is not equal to the white man; and subordination...is his natural and moral condition."*

The cornerstone of Southern tradition was destroyed, and its foundation began to crumble in front of their eyes. Irrational, seething rage took hold of the minds Southern Democrats. Governor Talmadge vowed to ignore the ruling and continue segregation in Georgia. Other Southern Democrat lawmakers made the same promise.

Many feared that the South would immediately erupt into violence. Instead, at first, Southern political leaders at every level tried to delay implementation of desegregation indefinitely. And the untimely death of Associate Justice Robert Jackson helped them achieve this. Justice Jackson died of a massive heart attack on October 9, 1954.

Justice John Marshall Harlan II

After losing two Supreme Court justices to heart attacks within a year and a half, it was clear that the stress of the entire situation was taking its toll on them.

Chief Justice Warren decided to suspend discussions about implementation of desegregation of public schools until Jackson was replaced. And in a move that can easily be interpreted as mockery of the Democrats, President Eisenhower nominated John Marshall Harlan II to replace Justice Jackson.

John Marshall Harlan II was the grandson of Associate Justice John Marshall Harlan, who served on the US Supreme Court in 1896 and was the lone dissenter in *Plessy vs. Ferguson*. In his dissent, Justice Harlan harshly criticized his colleagues for their final ruling. In his decision he wrote, "*In view of the Constitution, in the eye of the law, there is in this country no superior, dominant, ruling class of citizens. There is no caste here. Our Constitution is color-blind, and neither knows nor tolerates classes among citizens. In respect of civil rights, all citizens are equal before the law. The humblest is the peer of the most powerful. The law regards man as man and takes no account of his surroundings or of his color when his civil rights as guaranteed by the supreme law of the land are involved.*"[67]

Justice Harlan was also the lone voice of dissent, in 1883, when the Supreme Court ruled that the Civil Rights Act of 1875 was unconstitutional. In that dissent Justice Harlan wrote: "*There cannot be, in this republic, any class of human beings in practical subjection to another class with power in the latter to dole out to the former just such privileges as they may choose to grant.*"

Eisenhower's nominee had a family history of fighting for civil rights from the bench, which clearly showed which way the president was leaning. It seems very appropriate that the grandson of the only Supreme Court justice who tried to stop institutionalized segregation in *Plessy vs. Ferguson* was seated as a member of the Court when desegregation was implemented. No doubt that Harlan's grandfather would have been very pleased.

There is no evidence to indicate that Eisenhower intended Harlan's presence on the Supreme Court to be a "slap in the face" of Democrats. Regardless, the Democrat-controlled Senate confirmed Harlan to the Supreme Court on March 17, 1955, after delaying the process for as long as possible.

---

[67] https://supreme.justia.com/cases/federal/us/163/537/

With All Deliberate Speed

In April of 1955, the Supreme Court resumed discussion of implementation of the desegregation of schools. Thurgood Marshall and the NAACP's legal team argued for quick and immediate action with full implementation in place by the fall of 1956.

Lawyers for the defendant, however, argued for an indefinite period of time. They said that quick action would certainly ignite unparalleled racial violence not been seen since the Reconstruction Era.

The opposition's strategy was clear. Its plan was to create fear in the minds of Thurgood Marshall, the NAACP, and all supporters of

Eisenhower's Attorney General Herbert Brownell Jr. greatly influenced the Court's decision and implementation of Brown vs. the Board of Education.

desegregation. The defense lawyers conjured images of Klansmen riding through the night, inflicting violence and even death on anyone in favor of school desegregation. The defense attorneys said that it was the duty of the Court to ensure that desegregation could be implemented safely—any quick action would be irresponsible, which meant waiting for tempers to cool.

The NAACP knew that its opponents were right. Even as the lawyers argued before the Court, white community leaders were gathering support throughout the South and planning economic and violent retaliation against blacks. The NAACP knew that the unfettered anger of Southerners would eventually drive them to violence. And they knew that state and local law enforcement officials would be of little help.

But the NAACP could not back down—it could not agree to wait for "tempers to cool." That would place the future of Southern blacks right back in the hands of their oppressors. And it would be entirely inappropriate for the Court to yield to the temperament of angry Southerners.

Marshall and the NAACP pressed forward despite the threat of violence in the South. During the proceeding, Marshall declared that *"there can be no moratorium on the 14th Amendment."* The Court, however, asked the Eisenhower administration to submit another "friend of the court" brief on the implementation of desegregation.

Mindful of the threats toward Southern blacks, President Eisenhower initially wanted the school districts to submit plans for full implementation within a certain time frame, with no hard date set for implementation. But in the brief submitted to the Court, Brownell wrote: *"Relief, short of immediate admission to non-segregated schools, necessary implies the continued deprivation of the rights of blacks."*

Eisenhower's administration stood shoulder to shoulder with the NAACP in full agreement on the issue. And on May 31, 1955, the US Supreme Court ruled that the burden rested on the defendants to show why any delay was needed and that simple disagreement with the Court was not a valid reason. Desegregation had to proceed under court supervision with *"all deliberate speed."*[68]

Democrats Call on Southerners to Resist the Court Decision

The events that followed can be characterized as nothing less than a temper tantrum led by Democrats in Congress.

Prior to the Court's implementation ruling, Democrats in the House of Representatives had the luxury of hiding behind Senate Democrats.

But not anymore.

---

[68] William Hitchcock, The Age of Eisenhower: America and the World in the 1950's. New York, London, Toronto, Sydney, New Delhi. Simon and Schuster, P. 232

Democrats in Congress believed that Southern voters would no longer tolerate them playing games on this issue.

Virginia Democratic Congressman Howard Smith and Georgia

US Senator Walter George went to the floor of their respective chambers and read a document that became known as the *"Southern Manifesto."*

The document declared the Supreme Court decision in *Brown vs. the Board of Education* as a tyrannical use of judicial power. It also declared that the signers of the document would do everything in their power to stop the implementation of desegregation and encouraged Southern state and local officials to fall in line.

Senator Walter George

The document also stated, *"This unwarranted exercise of power by the court, contrary to the Constitution, is creating chaos and confusion in the states principally affected. It is destroying the amicable relations between the white and Negro races that have been created through 90 years of patient effort by the good people of both races. It has planted hatred and suspicion where there has been heretofore friendship and understanding. Without regard to the consent of the governed, outside agitators are threatening immediate and revolutionary changes in our public-school systems. If done, this is certain to destroy the system of public education in some of the states".*[69]

The *Southern Manifesto* was signed by 82 members of the House and 19 members of the Senate. All of them were Democrats, except for two Republicans from Virginia. Not only did the document advocate noncompliance and massive resistance, but its authors used

---

[69] The Arkansas Historical Quarterly Vol. 55, No. 2, Article by Brent J. Aucoin, The Southern Manifesto and Southern Opposition to Desegregation. Arkansas, Arkansas Historical Association, 1996, P. 173

the same condescending language slave owners had used when they claimed that slaves were grateful and content in their situation.

Many historians agree that *the Southern Manifesto* was the equivalent to the Confederate attack on Fort Sumter that started the Civil War. The South followed its congressional leaders and rebelled against the ruling throughout state and local governments.

Local officials in Prince Edward County, Virginia, refused to pass a budget and planned

Left to right: Roy Wilkins, Autherine Lucy, and Thurgood Marshall during a press conference in 1956.

to close all public schools; state government officials in Georgia, including the governor and the attorney general, agreed to stop all state funding of schools; and state officials in Alabama passed legislation to ensure the continuation of segregation and passed a resolution calling for the impeachment of the entire Supreme Court. Additionally, the states of Virginia, Alabama, Georgia, Mississippi, South Carolina, and Tennessee each passed laws designed to nullify the *Brown vs. Board of Education* decision.

After the University of Alabama denied admission to Autherine Lucy, a black woman, she took her case to the Supreme Court, with help from the NAACP. The Court ruled unanimously in her favor. But when she tried to go to classes, on February 3, 1953, she was stopped by a mob of about 3,000 people and assaulted.

The NAACP filed a complaint against the school and University of Alabama officials expelled Lucy, blaming her for the problem.

Racial tension and violence did not discourage Attorney General Brownell, however, who aggressively pursued the establishment of the strongest civil rights laws possible. Shortly after Democrats in Congress published the *Southern Manifesto*, Brownell proposed the passage of civil rights legislation allowing the attorney general's office to investigate and enforce civil rights violations.

Eisenhower's entire cabinet was opposed to the idea, especially FBI director J. Edgar Hoover. Because many blacks had supported the Communist Party, Hoover believed Russian Communists were still active within the civil rights movement. So, Hoover insisted that the Eisenhower administration should have nothing to do with civil rights organizations. Other cabinet members thought the bill gave too much power to the attorney general's office.

Eisenhower supported the proposal if the power of the attorney general's office was slightly reduced, and Brownell agreed. Brownell revised the bill, and the Civil Rights Act was sent to the House of Representatives.

New York Republican Congressman Kenneth Keating, however, restored the provisions Brownell had removed in support of a much stronger bill. The bill passed the House 276–126, but, predictably, it died in the hands of Senate Democrats.

Eisenhower was determined and renewed his promise to pass a strong civil rights bill during the State of the Union address in January of 1957. The bill was reintroduced in the House that summer and passed 286–126, with nearly the same support as it had before.

The Democrat-controlled Senate, however, had become known as the burial ground for all civil rights legislation. Everyone expected Eisenhower's bill to languish in the Senate indefinitely just as it had the year before alongside other civil rights proposals.

Chapter 9: 1957–1960

Senator Lyndon Johnson, the Fake Civil Rights Leader

No one had considered the unquenchable and completely ravenous ambitions of Texas Democratic Senate Majority Leader Lyndon Johnson.

Senator Johnson would be the next Democrat to play a long-lasting role in black political history. But unlike President Truman, Lyndon Johnson was not motivated by a desire to see the rights of blacks protected.

Senator Lyndon Johnson

Senator Johnson was a traditional Southern Democrat. He supported segregation himself and fought against Harry Truman's genuine efforts to protect the rights of blacks in the South. Throughout his 20 years in public office, Senator Johnson opposed all legislation that strengthen the civil rights protections and often referred to Eisenhower's Civil Rights Bill as *"the nigger bill."*

Like all prominent Democrats, Johnson believed that the social place of blacks throughout America should be determined by whites—and preferably by Southern whites because they had the most experience with blacks.

Johnson believed that Southern whites knew everything there was to know about blacks. He believed Southerners knew what blacks could do and could not do even better than the black people themselves. And Johnson believed that American society would function better if blacks would accept this and not strive for more than what whites believed they should have. Johnson subscribed to the 19th-century belief that blacks would only succeed when the Democrats said they were ready—and not before.

Lyndon Johnson was motivated by an insatiable lust for power and prestige. And the opportunity to lay hold of it was right in front of him.

After Eisenhower defeated Adlai Stevenson for the presidency, for the second time, Johnson knew that Democratic Party officials and supporters were looking for a new leader. His only competition was Senator John F. Kennedy from Massachusetts. Johnson wanted to step into the role.

Johnson's desire for more power outweighed his shameless commitment to segregation—so even the Southern traditions that were dear to his heart yielded to anything that would help him achieve his personal agenda.

That meant Johnson had to perform a very delicate balancing act to get the Civil Rights Bill through the Senate while appeasing his Democrat colleagues, so he would appear to be a national leader. But most of Johnson's fellow Democrats preferred to see the bill die a quick death. So, getting their cooperation would not be easy.

Democrats Destroy the Civil Rights Act of 1957

Senator Johnson decided to try to strip the bill of two of its enforcement provisions, Section 3 and Section 4, to placate his fellow segregationists. He wasn't sure how the White House would react, but that did not matter at this point because if he couldn't get the bill through the Senate the president would never see it anyway.

Sen. Lyndon Johnson (left) and Sen. Richard Russell (right) work to neutralize the Civil Rights Bill.

Johnson persuaded other Democratic Senate leaders to have the bill bypass the Senate Judicial Committee and move straight to the Senate floor. This was necessary to avoid Mississippi Democratic Senator James Eastland, the committee chairman. Eastland would certainly let the bill die in his committee rather than support Johnson's plan.

Johnson managed to avoid the committee, which was an important step in his scheme. Johnson then contacted Eisenhower and spoke to him in regretful, sorrowful tones that the entire bill would probably fail because of Section 3.

Section 3 allowed the attorney general's office to enforce court orders and other orders issued by federal judges. Johnson appeared to be disappointed that the entire bill would likely fail because of Section 3, talking as if he supported the provision. In truth, Johnson wanted Section 3 and Section 4 removed. But he focused upon one provision at a time.

After Johnson expressed his deepest, but false, regrets to the president about the difficulty he was encountering as he navigated the bill through the Senate, Georgia Senator Richard Russell went to the Senate floor and delivered a very angry speech about Section 3 of the bill.

Senator Russell hurled the most outrageous accusations conceivable at the Eisenhower administration. Russell accused Eisenhower of orchestrating the destruction of Southern local law enforcement, state courts, and social customs through Section 3 of the bill. Russell also said that Section 3 would force the races to commingle and produce unwanted interracial children.

In fact, government coercion of interracial marriage for the production of mixed-race children was one of the arguments used by 19th-century Democrats to defeat the Civil Rights Bill of 1875. On December 19, 1873, Kentucky Democratic Congressman James B. Beck insisted that the passage of the bill required blacks and whites to have children with each other.[70] This clearly shows that, by the

---

[70] The Congressional Record, House of Representatives, 43rd Congress, 1st Session, P. 343.

1950s, Democrats' demonization of peace between the races had not changed in over 80 years.

During his speech on July 2, 1957, Senator Russell spewed the most sickening type of racist bile. He led the entire nation to believe that Section 3 marked the coming of an apocalyptic age if it were not dealt with.

Russell's speech inspired fear and suspicion of the Civil Rights Bill not only among Southerners but across the entire country.

Dr. King and Vice President Nixon discuss the Civil Rights Act of 1957.

Section 3 did not advocate the destruction of Southern law enforcement agencies and courts, and it certainly did not force blacks and whites to intermarry. The wild accusations were likely a big part of Lyndon Johnson's plan to gut the bill. In fact, Senator Russell clearly mischaracterized a portion of the bill publicly to force the Eisenhower Administration to abandon it.

In an attempt to clarify the language of Section 3, Attorney General Brownell explained that it gave power to the attorney general to appeal to federal courts for injunctions against any individual who obstructed, or was planning to obstruct, a person's right to equal protection. If the injunction was violated or the court order ignored, a judge could assess penalties, fines, or imprisonment without reference to a jury trial.

Section 3 did not destroy Southern law enforcement agencies or its courts. But it did allow the Justice Department to use the federal courts to circumvent state and local authorities when a person's civil rights were being threatened.

As always, Attorney General Brownell was very intelligent and cerebral in his clarification of Section 3. But Russell and the Democrats were very emotional. They built their entire case against the provision on the emotions stirred up by Russell's mischaracterization of the law.

Republican lawmakers wavered, as did President Eisenhower. In the end, Eisenhower agreed to remove Section 3 from the bill.

The administration thought the bill would certainly pass now. Concerns were addressed, and compromises made. What more could the Democrats want?

After the successful removal of Section 3 from the Civil Rights Bill, Senator Johnson and the Senate Democrats turned their attention to Section 4.

Section 4 of the Civil Rights Bill allowed the attorney general to go to a federal court to get an injunction against any state or local official who tried to deny black people the right to vote.

It's unclear whether Eisenhower underestimated the desire of the Democrats to keep blacks under their subjugation, or if he was simply naïve. Either way, Eisenhower truly believed that the Democrats would be willing to accept Section 4 if he conceded to their wishes on Section 3.

But they did not. However, the Democrats did not want to appear to oppose voting rights and unwilling to enforce civil rights. So rather than have Section 4 removed, they proposed an amendment to the bill that declared if state or local officials tried to deny blacks their right to vote, the case would be decided by a jury and not a judge. So, if the amendment passed, Section 4 would be useless because it would take civil rights cases out of the hands of federal judges and into the hands of southern juries. And the Democrats presumed that southern juries would always decide in favor of segregation.

Once again, the Democrats went before all available media outlets to make the most outlandish claims to demonize the Civil Rights Bill. They said that if their amendment was not adopted, federal judges would have the right to randomly throw Southerners into jails throughout the South without a trial.

It was common, and legal, for judges to issue penalties for contempt of court without a jury. The people of the South knew that. But once again the Democrats inspired and fed the fears and suspicions of the people and America, all in the context of the Civil Rights Bill.

Eisenhower strongly denied that the bill would allow judges to randomly throw Southerners in jail. And Attorney General Brownell tried to explain the truth about Section 4.

The Democrats, however, were very skilled at emotionally manipulating the public, which is a long-standing truth about the Democratic Party. Throughout the first part of the 20th century, the Democrats created and inspired fear and hatred for blacks throughout the country. Because of Democrat propaganda, most people truly believed that black men were animals lurking behind every bush waiting to attack white women. Many southerners believed that black men were dangerous, which is why so many agreed that their freedom had to be suppressed.

Because Democrats were experts on emotional manipulation, it did not matter how factual the Eisenhower administration was or how eloquently the bill was explained.

Johnson twisted a lot of arms, made a lot of promises, and offered a lot of incentives to achieve his aim. And on August 1, 1957, Lyndon Johnson successfully navigated the bill through the Senate with the addition of the jury trial amendment and it passed 51–42.

President Eisenhower was stunned. The jury trial amendment completely handicapped federal judges from enforcing federal law. It provided power to the attorney general to enforce voting rights, but then placed local juries in the way. The entire Justice Department was disgusted with the bill.

Lyndon Johnson, in contrast, was very pleased. The situation could not have turned out any better for him. He had successfully helped pass an ineffective Civil Rights Bill. He also helped to preserve the Southern tradition that allowed state and local officials to continue disenfranchising black voters. The bill protected state and local officials from federal judges. And, at the same time, it made Johnson appear to be a national leader who was in favor of civil rights.

Eisenhower was clearly outmaneuvered and forced to consider whether to veto the bill. He agonized over it for a long time. Lyndon Johnson had trapped him into the choice of signing a completely toothless Civil Rights Bill or appearing to be against civil rights for blacks.

Congressional Republicans urged the president to sign the bill. They knew that any attempt to explain the bill's flaws would fall on deaf ears for the most part. And they reminded the president that there was hope the bill could be improved in the future.

For now, the general public, especially the black community, was so emotionally wrapped up in the passage of a Civil Rights Bill, it did not matter if the law had any real substance.

The Eisenhower administration had failed in its attempts to enlighten the public about the merits of Sections 3 and 4, so it was very unlikely it would succeed in showing everyone why the Civil Rights Bill was now powerless. So, with great reluctance and a very bad taste in his mouth, President Eisenhower signed the Civil Rights Act of 1957 into law on September 9, 1957.

Dr. Martin Luther King Jr. and the Montgomery Bus Boycott

Even though the bill was useless in enforcing civil rights, Southern Democrats still railed against it! Senator Russell, again, went to the floor of the Senate and falsely prophesied that the passage of the bill heralded the destruction of the South and that all good Southerners must prepare themselves. Other Democrats, some who supported Johnson and some who preferred to see the bill fail, also strongly denounced the new law.

Civil Rights leaders, however, saw the bill somewhat differently. For example, Martin Luther King Jr. was fully aware of the bill's flaws, but he wrote to the president and thanked him for signing the bill.

In his letter, Dr. King pointed out that the passage of the bill proved that Congress would now address an important domestic issue that had been ignored for decades. The bill also helped keep a spark of hope flickering in the hearts of the black community, which was important to Dr. King. Dr. King believed that the civil rights struggle was just as much a spiritual battle as it was a political battle. And failure to sign the bill would have weakened their spirits.

President Eisenhower believed that racial equality would be achieved by action from the federal government, but Dr. King believed that racial equality would be won primarily through the

strength, courage, and sheer determination produced in the hearts of blacks. Eisenhower was discouraged, but Dr. King tried to show the situation from a spiritual perspective.

Senator Johnson did not share Dr. King's perspective either. In his mind, he and his fellow segregationists had

Dr. Martin Luther King Jr. and President Eisenhower

achieved a great victory. Johnson was completely unaware that seeing the president of the United States sign a Civil Rights Bill had completely emboldened and encouraged Southern blacks to continue fighting for civil rights.

They were now ready to continue the struggle armed with nothing more than their own courage and sheer determination. And that was something Senator Johnson and his friends in the Senate did not want.

Dr. King's highest priority was to keep the black community's collective spirit aroused because he saw firsthand what they could achieve when they were constantly encouraged and motivated.

About a year after Dr. King accepted the full-time position of pastor of Dexter Avenue Baptist Church in Montgomery, Alabama, the city's black community was in an uproar when Rosa Parks was famously arrested on December 1, 1955 for violating the state's segregation laws. Mrs. Parks refused to give a seat to a white male passenger who had just boarded the bus.

To add insult to injury, Mrs. Parks was already seated in the "Colored Section." But when the bus became full, blacks were required to relinquish the Colored Section to whites and forced to stand.

Some of the city's blacks were apathetic to the issue and some were very sensitive. Not only did they have to give the seats in the Colored Section when they White Section became full, but they often were forced to get off the bus after they had paid their fare and get onboard through the back door.

Dr. King speaks at Dexter Avenue Baptist Church.

They all endured the same humiliation throughout their lives and related very easily to Mrs. Parks. They suffered embarrassment, suppressed their anger, submitted to their fears, and remained silent for decades.

But each time they held their peace, more pressure was building in their hearts and minds until it finally erupted. To Montgomery's black community, Rosa Parks spoke for everyone when she openly defied the bus driver and the police.

Dr. King was contacted by Edgar Dixon, the president of the local chapter of the NAACP. Dixon paid the bond for Mrs. Parks and called leaders of black churches about the incident. Dixon also contacted Reverend Ralph Abernathy, a minister from Montgomery's First Baptist Church.

Dr. King agreed to host the meeting of ministers and civic leaders at Dexter Avenue Baptist Church.[71] But prior to the meeting,

---

[71] Edited by Clayborne Carson, The Autobiography of Martin Luther King, Jr., New York, Boston, Intellectual Properties Management, Inc. in association with Grand Central Publishing, 1998, P. 52

Dixon suggested that only a major act of civil disobedience could bring the change they wanted. So, Dixon asked the community leaders to consider a boycott of the city buses. Dr. King and Reverend Abernathy agreed that it seemed like a good plan and pledged their support for it during the meeting.

Pastors and civic leaders called on friends and neighbors and circulated information about the meeting at Dexter Avenue Baptist Church. Dr. King was unsure about how many would attend. But he was pleased to see the response and his church filled with church leaders, pastors, preachers, and civil rights leaders who wanted to fight segregation on public transportation.

At the meeting, Reverend L. Roy Bennett, a minister from Mount Zion AME Church offered the plan of a bus boycott in protest of the arrest of Rosa Parks and the state's segregation laws. The attendees agreed that it was a proper course of action. They decided to begin on the morning of Monday, December 5. They sent word and asked all blacks to support the boycott by not using public bus transportation.

They asked the community to share rides with others, share cabs, or make other arrangements to get to work, to school, or anywhere else. As the leadership fielded questions from the community, they explained that the only reason segregation had continued for so long was because the black community cooperated with it. And it was time to end their cooperation with an evil system.

Dr. King and his wife Coretta arose early on December 5 not sure what they would see. They went to a bus stop near their home to get an idea of the black community's support for the boycott. They stepped outside and looked in the direction of the bus stop. They were glad to see no one waiting at the stop, but they wanted to see how many black passengers were riding city buses in their neighborhood.

Coretta saw a bus slowly approaching the corner first. She looked through the windows and shouted to her husband, "*The bus is empty!*"

When Dr. King saw it for himself, he could hardly believe it. The buses that went past their home were always filled with black passengers on Monday mornings on their way to their jobs. But that morning, the bus was empty.

They waited for the next bus and were very happy to see that it and the following two buses were completely empty.[72]

Dr. King wanted to see the extent to which blacks were participating in the boycott. He would have been happy to get 60 percent support. So, he got into his car and drove along the bus route himself. As he drove, he saw empty buses and no one waiting at bus stops. Dr. King also drove along the bus routes during peak hours to find the same thing.

Although the organizers of the boycott did not plan for the event to create a stronger bond between the people, that is exactly what happened. Dr. King saw crowded sidewalks with many blacks walking, talking, and in fellowship with one another throughout that day. Students from Alabama State College were also walking and cheerfully hitchhiking.

Dr. King speaks as president
of the Montgomery
Improvement Association.

Dr. King even saw people riding mules and several horse-drawn buggies that day.

It appeared that the Montgomery Bus Boycott received 100 percent support from the black community, which was much more than what Dr. King hoped for.

Reverend Abernathy, Edgar Dixon, Dr. King, and other civic leaders called for another meeting to celebrate their early success and discuss how to proceed and keep the boycott operating. They

---

[72] Edited by Clayborne Carson, The Autobiography of Martin Luther King, Jr., New York, Boston, Intellectual Properties Management, Inc. in association with Grand Central Publishing, 1998, P. 54

decided to form a new civic organization whose president and chairman would be the official voice of the Montgomery Bus Boycott. They agreed to call the organization the Montgomery Improvement Association and unanimously elected Dr. Martin Luther King Jr. as its president.

After the election of King and other officers, the group discussed how to proceed, how to deal with the media, and how to organize more alternative methods of transportation for the black community.

Some wanted to hide the names of the group's leadership because of concern about violent retaliation from whites. Dixon and King, however, denounced the act of the group's leaders cowering in fear while asking blacks to openly and publicly support them.

They agreed that the boycott would continue until their demands were met. They also agreed to map out neighborhoods and organize carpooling systems to help everyone get to work, school, and run routine errands.

On Sunday morning, December 11, 1955, Dr. King spoke as the president of the Montgomery Improvement Association (MIA) with his church filled with supporters, members of the media, and curious onlookers. He was about to give the first official statement of the MIA, and he was virtually speaking for 100 percent of Montgomery's black community.

Dr. King had to deliver a very powerful speech and simultaneously perform a very delicate balancing act. His speech had to inspire hope and a willingness to endure the great persecution that would certainly come.

The speech also had to be free of bitterness and anger, while communicating strength and determination to whites as well as honor and respect for the local and state governments.

Dr. King struggled with feelings of anxiety and inadequacy about how to deliver such a message. And justifiably so. The stakes were high and many people were relying upon his effectiveness.

Dr. King rose to the pulpit: *"My friends, there comes a time when people get tired of being trampled over by the iron feet of oppression and plunged into the abyss of humiliation where they experience the bleakness of nagging despair.*

"We are not wrong in what we're doing. If we are wrong, the Supreme Court of this nation is wrong. If we are wrong, the Constitution of the United States is wrong. If we are wrong, Jesus of Nazareth was merely a utopian dreamer that never came down to earth. And we are determined here in Montgomery to work and fight until justice runs down like water and righteousness like a mighty stream. We, the disinherited of this land, we who have been oppressed so long, are tired of going through the long night of captivity. And now we are reaching out for the daybreak of freedom and justice and equality.

"As we stand and sit here this evening and prepare ourselves for what lies ahead, let us go out with a grim and bold determination that we're are going to stick together. We are going to work together. Right here in Montgomery."

Rev. Ralph Abernathy

A sustained, enthusiastic applause filled the church as Dr. King took his seat. The crowd responded favorably, and members of the media noted every word and recorded the reaction of the crowd.

Reverend Abernathy, then, stood before the crowd to talk about the adoption of the Montgomery Bus Boycott Resolution. The resolution called upon blacks to not ride public transportation until they received courteous treatment from bus drivers; that passengers be seated on a first-come, first-serve basis; and that black bus drivers be employed through predominately black neighborhoods.

Reverend Abernathy asked all those in favor of the motion to stand, and everyone present, except for members of the media, stood and cheered.

The Strategy

Not only did the meeting stir the hearts of Montgomery's black community, but it created national interest. The eyes of the nation were suddenly focused on Montgomery, Alabama. And all events related to the Montgomery Bus Boycott would echo across the country and face various forms of criticism.

Montgomery city buses were empty as they drove through the city's black neighborhoods.

That was all part of Dr. King's plan. King hoped to use the combined outrage of the entire nation as leverage to achieve his objectives in Alabama, a tactic that had been used by 19th-century Abolitionists with little success.

During the slavery era, many Americans were ignorant of the great horrors inflicted upon blacks to maintain slavery. Abolitionists tried desperately to inform the public as much as possible. They believed that if the American people knew the atrocities committed in the name of slavery, they'd be shocked and appalled and demand an end to it. The Abolitionists circulated pamphlets, published newspapers, and circulated other printed materials throughout the North. They also communicated the displeasure of the rest of the nation with the institution of slavery throughout the South as much as possible.

Abolitionists also hoped most Southerners would feel ashamed about slavery if it were exposed and a bright light was shined upon it. Likewise, Dr. King hoped to produce a desire for correction within the white people of Alabama, which would only come as a result of a profound sense of shame, embarrassment, guilt, and public scrutiny.

Dr. King believed he would have more success with this method than his 19th-century counterparts because he and his supporters did not suffer the technological limitations of the Abolitionists. He was certain that as the national media reported on the progress of the boycott itself, Alabama's response to the boycott would bring the full weight of American outrage upon them.

Furthermore, Dr. King and his supporters easily captured the moral high ground. He made it clear that their efforts would be kept within the bounds of Christian conduct. By taking a moral position early, the American public would draw a clear distinction between himself, his supporters, and everyone who opposed them.

During the next few days, the boycott itself became better organized. The MIA worked out arrangements with black taxi drivers and organized carpools to take care of the transportation needs of the community. At first, they relied heavily upon taxi services until they could get more volunteers to help with carpools.

Public opposition to the boycott first struck at black taxi drivers. The drivers had some discretion when they charged a fare during that time. And the supporters of the boycott charged as little as possible whenever they transported blacks.

City Officials Attempt to End the Boycott

At this moment, Police Commissioner Clyde Sellers instructed Montgomery's police officers to enforce an obscure law requiring cab drivers to charge a fare that made the use of the taxi service costly to boycott supporters.[73]

Instead of weakening the boycott, the police commissioner's attack only produced more volunteers for carpools. During the next meeting of the MIA, Dr. King explained that the police commissioner targeted black taxi drivers by forcing them to charge more for their service.

Afterward, Dr. King asked for more volunteers for carpools and received a much better response that he could have hoped for. Within

---

[73] Edited by Clayborne Carson, The Autobiography of Martin Luther King, Jr., New York, Boston, Intellectual Properties Management, Inc. in association with Grand Central Publishing, 1998, P. 65

a few days of the meeting, they had a list of 48 more dispatchers and organized 42 new pickup locations for carpools.

Since Dr. King's speech, Montgomery's public officials were suddenly dealing with a lot of unwanted national attention over a very uncomfortable issue. Most of them believed that the anger of the black community would fizzle out and they would eventually return to public transportation. And some believed that the clampdown on black taxi drivers would be enough to discourage them.

But when they saw that blacks were determined to continue the boycott, which only kept unwanted attention upon on them, Montgomery's city officials sent a messenger to Dr. King to inform him that they were willing to negotiate.

At first, Dr. King was hopeful about the outcome. Alabama's public officials had always ignored grievances of the black community. This time, they at least acknowledged them and initiated the conversation.

Montgomery's black citizens carpool as the city bus passes by across the street empty.

Dr. King arrived at city hall with 11 other representatives of the MIA and met in the commissioner's chamber on December 17, 1955. Members of the media were present, and Dr. King and the others walked in confidently, willing to hear what the local officials had to say.

They were greeted by the Democratic Mayor William Gayle, city attorney Jack Crenshaw, and several commissioners. Dr. King spoke first and told the officials the boycott would continue until they had everything outlined in the Montgomery Boycott Resolution.

Crenshaw, who spoke for the other officials, challenged the legality of the resolution. He told Dr. King that everything in the resolution violated state law. He also said that as long as segregation laws were in place, Montgomery's city officials were obligated to enforce them.

Dr. King responded with several attempts to make them see the basic injustice and unfairness of the law. But Crenshaw and Mayor Gayle told him that they were not judges and therefore could not condemn the law.

The meeting did not last long. Dr. King saw that Montgomery's local officials were not interested in the morality of the law. In fact, they tried to appear as if they would have supported Dr. King's position if only his position were supported by state law.

Dr. King and his associates left city hall disappointed but determined to press on.

As the boycott continued, more volunteers signed up to support the carpools. At first, the drivers were local ministers. Later they were joined by housewives, teachers, businessmen, and various types of workers. As the numbers continued to grow, they were even supported by a handful of courageous white people who were willing to suffer the contempt of their family members for their support of Dr. King.

Despite the efforts of the police department and the stubbornness of the local officials, the boycott showed no signs of weakening. Subsequently, Mayor Gayle made another attempt to end the boycott by releasing a statement to the press that declared that he reached a settlement with the MIA less than a month after his meeting with Dr. King.

Dr. King and other leaders of the MIA were shocked to hear this and immediately began making phone calls to discover who among them could have possibly spoken on their behalf. They discovered that the mayor had met with black preachers claiming to be from the MIA who were not associated with the organization at all.

The mayor tried to create enough confusion within the black community so that a significant number of people would return to public transportation. But Dr. King, Reverend Abernathy, and other members of the MIA contacted the media and their supporters quickly enough to make sure people knew that the boycott was still in effect and that no one should resume the use of public transportation.

Not only did the mayor fail to end the boycott once again, but he was publicly humiliated by Dr. King and Montgomery's "uppity" black community. And day after day, the city buses remained empty as they traveled throughout much of Montgomery.

City Officials "Get Tough"

In the wake his most recent embarrassment, they mayor decided to get tougher on the protesters. Mayor Gayle established a local policy that led to a series of arrests for minor traffic violations for many of the boycott volunteers. Police officers arrested volunteer drivers from the carpools for insignificant, and sometimes nonexistent, traffic violations.

The harassment of drivers was a very effective weapon against the protesters. After multiple arrests and intimidating encounters with police officers, many volunteer drivers ended their support for the boycott. And because of this, Montgomery's black community was faced with the difficulty of getting to their jobs on time and began to express their frustration toward Dr. King.

Perhaps the most disturbing and frightening incident for all the boycott supporters at this point was when Dr. King himself was arrested for a trumped-up traffic violation and taken to jail. When the news of King's arrest spread across the city, a multitude of supporters gathered at the front of the jail and demanded his release.

Reverend Abernathy paid the bond and Dr. King addressed the crowd outside the jail. He thanked them for gathering so quickly and for their support. He also encouraged the crowd to continue their support for the struggle.

Dr. King warned them that the police's harassment was an indication that the enemies of black freedom were very determined to keep them in bondage. And he warned that even though the opposition turned to the use of harsh and unjust tactics, they may use even more extreme methods. The community had to be willing to endure hardness as good soldiers and prepare themselves for even greater harassment to come.

It was not very long before Dr. King's prophecy came true. As the boycott continued, many of the white people of Montgomery could no longer bear the open defiance of blacks, whom they had always deemed weak and servile and now refused to accept their place in the South's social order. They also could not bear the thought of their city and neighbors being so harshly judged by the entire nation.

Dr. King arrested.

So, some of Montgomery's white people took matters into their own hands and tried break the will of the protesters. On January 30, 1956, while Dr. King was attending a church service at First Baptist Church, a bomb exploded on the front porch of his home while his wife, Coretta, and his daughter Yoki were inside.

Dr. King returned home and was relieved that his family was not injured. But he also returned to see hundreds of people had surrounded his home shouting and arguing along with several police officers. Mayor Gayle was also there along with the police commissioner and members of the media.

The mayor expressed his regrets about the incident, but Dr. King laid the responsibility at his feet. Dr. King, visibly angry and very animated, told the mayor and the police commissioner that this attack was a direct result of their "get tough" policy. And that now the white people of Montgomery felt free to terrorize, or even kill, blacks who supported the boycott.

Dr. King's supporters were enraged! They shouted and argued with the police, the mayor, and others, who cast the blame for the bombing on the protesters themselves. Some of the protesters called for all blacks to arm themselves and openly retaliate against white people and Montgomery's public officials.

Dr. King then stood upon the steaming wreckage of his front porch and addressed the crowd and said, *"Don't get your weapons. He who lives by the sword will perish by the sword. Remember that is what God said. We are not advocating violence. We want to love our enemies. I want you to love your enemies. Be good to them. Love them and let them know you love them. I did not start this boycott. I was asked by you to serve as your spokesman. I want it known throughout the length and breadth of this land that if I am stopped this movement will not stop. If I am stopped our work will not stop. For what we are doing is right. What we are doing is just. And God is with us!"*[74]

King's supporters responded to his impromptu sermon with shots of *"amen."* And those who called for armed conflict and a violent response suppressed their anger that night. At least for the moment, their desire for vengeance was subdued by King's message of love.

Once again, the attack against the movement produced the opposite of what the attackers expected. Rather than seeing the boycotters run away frightened and scattered, they rallied and became stronger in their support and more determined than ever.

But their restraint and faith in nonviolent resistance would be tested again and again. Several days later, a bomb was detonated on the front lawn of E.D. Dixon's home. No one was injured, but the message of terror and intimidation was clear. Hundreds of people gathered, including law enforcement and media, just as before. But this time, there were no calls for a violent response by the protesters.

King's close friends, family members, and associates urged him to hire armed security guards to watch his home, his family, and the church. They said he should, at least, have security guards watching his home.

---

[74] Edited by Clayborne Carson, The Autobiography of Martin Luther King, Jr., New York, Boston, Intellectual Properties Management, Inc. in association with Grand Central Publishing, 1998, P. 80

Dr. King struggled with the question for a long time. He publicly called for nonviolent resistance, and he certainly wanted to protect his family. But how could the leader of a nonviolent movement walk around with armed guards? Those guards would certainly use their guns if it became necessary. How could he continue to encourage the supporters of the boycott to restrain themselves if he had armed guards who did not?

Dr. King decided to mount floodlights around his home and the church. He also hired unarmed watchmen to guard them. The compromise satisfied his supporters and allowed him to hold onto his message of nonviolent resistance.

Meanwhile, a group of civil rights leaders met with NAACP officials and attorneys to determine a stronger course of action—a course of action much stronger than the boycott.

Civil Rights Leaders "Get Tough" with Mayor Gayle

The MIA was fed up with Mayor Gayle and his "get tough" policy. They had enough of the police harassment and listening to white public officials blaming blacks for not being content with their social status. And they wanted to find a way to defeat the segregationists and once and for all end the suffering of blacks in Montgomery.

Attorneys from the NAACP, including NAACP Chief Counsel Thurgood Marshall, considered filing a federal lawsuit against the Mayor Gayle and the city of Montgomery.

The attorneys wanted to consolidate every incident in which black passengers were arrested for not giving their seats to a white person. And they wanted to file a suit in federal court arguing that segregation enforcement was a violation of their rights under the Fourteenth Amendment.

After considerable research, the attorneys discovered a path in which they could file the case in federal court. Rosa Parks agreed to be a plaintiff in the lawsuit. The NAACP then contacted the family of Claudette Colvin. Colvin was a 15-year-old black girl who was arrested for refusing to give her seat to a white person nine months before Rosa Parks. They also contacted Aurelia Browder, Susie McDonald, Mary Louise Smith, and Jeanetta Reese.

All of them were arrested for refusing to give up their seats on public buses and all agreed to be plaintiffs in the lawsuit.

One of the lawyers, Virginia Durr, was very concerned about some of the details in the Rosa Parks case. Durr did not believe that Mrs. Park's case should be used because of a criminal charge, possibly resting arrest, that distinguished Parks case from the others. And because of the criminal charge, Durr believed that their case may be dismissed or the federal courts might refuse to hear it.

Claudette Colvin

The other attorneys reluctantly agreed. So, Rosa Parks was removed as a plaintiff and the suit was filed in US District Court on February 1, 1956 as *Browder vs. Gayle*. Shortly after the filing, Jeanetta Reese asked to be removed as a plaintiff and the NAACP attorneys removed her from the lawsuit as well. The reason for her request was not made clear, but many believed that she had become the target of white segregationists and was intimidated.

Montgomery's segregationists were infuriated by the lawsuit. They were also frustrated when they saw the boycotters continue to persevere even after cruel and potentially deadly acts of violence. As the news of the bombings spread across the country, the entire state of Alabama was viewed harshly by the American public, and shouts of condemnation were heard from every corner of the country. For that reason, the city's segregationist decided to return to a less lethal method and raise the stakes at the same time. Mayor Gayle turned to mass arrests to achieve his goal of ending the boycott.

On February 13, 1956, a Montgomery County Grand Jury was convened to determine if Dr. King and his supporters were in violation of another obscure, unused, and very old state law against boycotts. An indictment could lead to arrests of hundreds of people and heavy fines that were well out of the economic range of the protesters.

Aurelia Browder

The grand jury was composed of 17 whites and one black person. And after about a week of deliberations, they indicted Dr. King and about 100 protesters of operating an illegal boycott. Dr. King was told of the indictments while participating in a lecture series at Fisk University in Nashville, Tennessee. He went back to Montgomery to submit himself to be arrested.

Protestors Not Afraid of the Police or Time in Jail

During his return to Montgomery, King prayed that this latest development would not discourage the protesters. The boycott itself had virtually turned the lives of his supporters upside down. They walked everywhere and had dramatically adjusted their personal lives to support it.

And they endured too much persecution and too much hardship to stop short of their goal.

The police had already rounded up everyone whose name appeared on the indictment and Dr. King was the last of them to arrive at the jail. He was unsure about the state of mind and the morale of his supporters.

When he arrived at the Montgomery County Jail, he was surprised to see that his supporters embraced a very cheerful attitude and expressions of happiness were on their faces. They shouted and cheered for him as he was processed. The entire building was filled with a very joyous and festive spirit—much to the dismay and confusion of the police.

Some sang songs and hymns, others told jokes, and some talked about their daily lives as if the police were not there.[75]

Dr. King's heart was lifted to new heights when he saw his people rejoicing in persecution. And he joined them in laughter as they watched the confused faces of the jailers and the police. Dr. King realized that his supporters had overcome the greatest obstacle to their movement—fear.

Throughout the boycott, they were afraid of being arrested, afraid of the police, and afraid of the violence. But when he saw his people turn a massive police arrest into a festive occasion, he knew that they had broken through the greatest spiritual barrier that stood between them and their goals.

The movement's supporters were no longer afraid to be arrested. Perhaps it was because they had been arrested so much, they became used to it. Or perhaps it was due to the prayers of Dr. King for spiritual strength. Or perhaps both.

Regardless of which, the segregationists' greatest weapon was taken from them. And Dr. King knew that now that his supporters were not afraid to be arrested, nothing could stop them.

And Mayor Gayle had greatly miscalculated once again. The bombings certainly left the America public with a horrible perception of Montgomery. And for some reason, the mayor believed that the mass arrest of about 100 blacks would be more acceptable—but it was not.

The bench trial began on March 19 with Judge Eugene Carter presiding. The trial drew a massive amount of media and public attention. Judge Carter certainly had more media attention than he was used to.

The trial lasted for four days, and Dr. King faced the possibility of 14 months of hard labor, in the Montgomery County Jail, or a $500 fine and court costs. After both sides made their cases, Judge Carter ruled that King was guilty of violating Alabama's anti-boy-

---

[75] Edited by Clayborne Carson, The Autobiography of Martin Luther King, Jr., New York, Boston, Intellectual Properties Management, Inc. in association with Grand Central Publishing, 1998, P. 87

cotting law. Judge Carter then pronounced the minimum penalty allowed by law, which was the $500 fine.

The judge said the reason Dr. King received the minimum penalty was because of his efforts to prevent violence during the boycott. And although he was pronounced guilty Dr. King was relieved to hear the ruling and happy that he would not spend any time in jail. He considered that a victory in itself.

His lawyers announced they would appeal the decision. It is not clear whether Judge Carter was sympathetic to the protesters or if he submitted to the media pressure, but after King's lawyers said they would appeal the decision, Judge Carter issued continuances for all of King's supporters who were arrested for the same violation.

The judge said he would hear the cases after King's appeal was heard in the appellate court.

Dr. King and his allies experienced a very significant victory in the months to follow. On June 5, 1956, a federal three-judge panel ruled 2–1 in the case of *Browder v. Gayle*. The court ruled that *"the enforced segregation of black and white passengers on motor buses operating in the City of Montgomery violates the Constitution and laws of the United States because the conditions deprive people of equal protection under the Fourteenth Amendment. The court further enjoins Alabama and Montgomery from the continued operation of segregated buses."*

Judge Frank Johnson

The panel consisted of Judge Frank Johnson, Judge Seybourn Harris Lynn, and Judge Richard Rives.

Judge Lynn was the dissenting jurist.

This was a major victory. The federal court ruled in favor of the protesters and at long last a dim but visible light appeared at the end of the long, difficult tunnel for the protestors.

The attorneys for Gayle appealed the ruling to the US Supreme Court. King and the NAACP were cautiously optimistic about their chances.

The recent court victory, however, was followed by another setback. Mayor Gayle was determined to find a quiet and nonviolent way to end the boycott. And somehow the mayor, and other pro-segregation forces, discovered which insurance companies were working with the carpool. Each company canceled the insurance policies of the carpool volunteers almost simultaneously.

The reason given by insurance agents was that the risk was too high for any vehicle that participated in the carpool. In response, Dr. King was able to find alternative coverage for the vehicles through friends in Atlanta who were supportive the boycott.

The determined Mayor of Montgomery attacked the boycott once again in the courts. The City of Montgomery filed a petition asking the court to order the Montgomery Improvement Association to end to the boycott and compensate the city for the damages it caused. The hearing was scheduled for November 13.

The hearing was convened that morning, with Judge Eugene Carter presiding once again. The courtroom was filled with reporters, casual observers, and interested parties from both sides. The hearing went into recess around noon.

Victory at Last!

The day took a very dramatic and unexpected turn for both sides. During the recess, Dr. King could see someone delivering important news to the attorneys representing the city of Montgomery. The news caused an uproar among them.

Shortly afterward, several reporters were talking loudly and impatiently on telephones. Shock and surprised expressions appeared on all their faces.

Then a reporter from the Associated Press delivered the news release to Dr. King and his attorneys. Earlier that day, the United States Supreme Court affirmed the ruling of the three-judge panel declaring Alabama's state and local laws requiring segregation on buses as unconstitutional in *Browder vs. Gayle*!

The excitement among King's supporters could barely be contained. Shouts and joy mixed with expressions of contempt and anger from the courtroom were heard throughout the building.

Dr. King's hard-fought battle against the forces of segregation, alongside the black people of Montgomery, Alabama, was finally won!

After everyone collected themselves, the hearing resumed and Judge Carter, who was aware of the news, continued to hear arguments from both sides.

Judge Carter ruled in favor of the City of Montgomery and issued a temporary restraining order

Dr. King and his supporters celebrate their victory on Browder vs. Gayle.

against the carpool. But the order was moot. In the minds of the people who fought on the front lines of this battle, November 13, 1956, was a day of tremendous irony. It was the day that Mayor Gayle achieved his greatest victory against them but also suffered his greatest defeat. As for Dr. King and his supporters, it was a day that started with anxiety and sorrow and ended with shouts of joy.

Dr. King went home and contacted friends, family, and other members of the press and told them of the day's events. Montgomery's black community dropped whatever they were doing and celebrated their victory in the streets, in their homes, and at their jobs all night long.

Dr. King called a meeting of the MIA that week to discuss the status of the boycott and how to proceed considering the affirmation of the Supreme Court. Meetings were held in several churches simultaneously because of the overwhelming response from the black community.

After consulting with their attorneys, they decided to officially end the boycott. But they would not return to the buses until the Order from the Supreme Court was received by Alabama's state and local officials.

Typically, it only took a few days for documents to reach Montgomery from Washington, DC. But for some reason, the Order was not received until December 20, 1956. Montgomery's black citizens returned to the buses 384 days after the boycott began.

Of course, the segregationist forces that wanted to hold onto their way of life howled with rage! Dr. King received vulgar, threatening phone calls from Montgomery's white population that simply refused to accept the Court's decision.

Other leaders of the boycott were told that if blacks tried to sit in white sections or refused to get up for a white person, they would be lynched. The Ku Klux Klan also marched through downtown and demanded that whites openly defy the Supreme Court.

Before the boycott, Montgomery's blacks would typically retreat into their homes and lock the doors whenever the Klan marched through town and threatened them. But this time, as Klan members marched and drove slowly through the downtown area, they were also greeted by a multitude of blacks watching them go by with no expression of fear on their faces.[76]

Some blacks acted as if they were watching a parade go by.

Dr. King's experience during the Montgomery Bus Boycott demonstrated that the fight for civil rights was a spiritual battle just as much as it was a political battle. The boycotters stepped out in faith knowing full well the opposition was much more powerful. When they encountered resistance, they persisted. And when they encountered violence, they held on to their Christian principles.

When they stopped being afraid of their enemies—when they no longer trembled at the thought of being arrested or stopped by

---

[76] Edited by Clayborne Carson, The Autobiography of Martin Luther King, Jr., New York, Boston, Intellectual Properties Management, Inc. in association with Grand Central Publishing, 1998, P. 95

the police, thrown in jail, or ordered to appear in court—everything moved much more quickly for them.

But the battle certainly was not over. Dr. King would try to teach this lesson to other blacks throughout the South as it continued.

But at the time, he tried to explain it to President Eisenhower, who was dealing with radical segregationists on the state level across the South, as well as in Washington, DC.

Democrat Extremists Sacrifice Schools

During that time, President Eisenhower was contending with segregationist Democratic governors who would rather see chaos in their streets than comply with the Supreme Court decision.

They resorted to great extremes—including military force—in defiance of the Supreme Court. Texas Democratic Governor Allan Shivers sent the Texas Rangers to keep blacks out of public schools in Mansfield. Other governors threatened to do the same thing.

But one of the most extremist segregationists was Arkansas Democratic Governor Orval Faubus, who initiated a crisis in Little Rock.

In 1955, Little Rock's school board adopted a plan to desegregate Little Rock Central High School beginning in the fall of 1957.

Segregationist groups, such as the Capital Citizens' Council and the Mothers' League of Central High School, demanded the governor to block the school board from implementing the plan. The governor was able to get an injunction against the school board and their integration plan was stopped.

Federal Court Judge Ronald Davies, from the Arkansas Eastern

Arkansas Gov. Orval Faubus

District, overruled the local court. When the governor's lawyers appeared before the judge, they argued that the injunction was necessary because various weapons were found among the students. Therefore, the school could not be integrated safely.

The school's superintendent, Virgil Blossom, vehemently denied the allegation. Blossom made it clear to the public, especially the parents, that there were no weapons found in the school.

Judge Davies ordered the continuation of the school board's desegregation plan with appropriate safeguards, and the school board resumed the process.

Governor Faubus railed against Judge Davies through the media, vowing that he would not allow the school to desegregate. On September 2, 1957, the governor dispatched 200 members of the National Guard to surround the school.

Of course, the deployment of the state's militia drew considerable media attention. Faubus said he only sent the military to keep peace and order because desegregation was a threat to peace. He also said that the presence of the armed militia was not intended to intimidate blacks from coming to the school.

The Little Rock Nine

Hundreds of people gathered around the school to see what would happen. The menacing crowd chanted threats and violence, and no blacks dared go near the school.

Judge Davies once again ordered the school board to proceed with the desegregation process, noting that the governor claimed the guardsmen were only there to keep order.

Judge Ronald Davies

The school board arranged for nine black students to go to the school under the care of NAACP official Daisy Bates. They were joined by black journalists, local ministers, and several other civil rights leaders.

They got as far as the school's entrance when they were turned away by the National Guard. As they walked back to their vehicles, the angry mob shouted and harassed them all the way to their vehicles. The crowd shouted, "Lynch, them…lynch the niggers now!"

The ministers and civil rights leaders encircled the children to keep them safe. But the black journalists were taken by the mob and badly beaten.[77]

The event not only drew national attention, but the shameful display traveled quickly around the world and drew harsh criticism from other countries.

Governor Faubus had lied to Judge Davies, and Davies was furious! Faubus said that the National Guard was there to keep the peace—not to deny black students' entry into the school or intimidate them. Not only did the guardsmen block the students from entering the school, but they failed to keep the peace and allowed blacks to be assaulted.

Black student harassed by white protesters.

Judge Davies issued a summons to Governor Faubus compelling him to appear in court to explain his actions. Davies also contacted the Justice Department and asked them for an injunction against the governor.

Shortly afterward, President Eisenhower sent a telegram to Governor Faubus that can be easily interpreted as a threat if you read between the lines.

---

[77] William Hitchcock, The Age of Eisenhower: America and the World in the 1950's. New York, London, Toronto, Sydney, New Delhi. Simon and Schuster.

In the telegram, Eisenhower wrote the following: "*At the request of Judge Davies, the Department of Justice is presently collecting facts as to the interference or failure to comply with the District Court's order.*

"*The Arkansas National Guard is partially sustained by the federal government. When I became President, I took an oath to support and defend the Constitution of the United States. And I will uphold the Federal Constitution by every legal means at my command.*"[78]

At this point, several Arkansas congressmen interceded and asked the president if he would sit down and talk with the governor before the situation became worse. Eisenhower agreed, but Attorney General Brownell was completely against it. Brownell reminded Eisenhower that Governor Faubus lied to Judge Davies about the mission of the guardsmen. Brownell did not believe that Faubus could be trusted.

Nonetheless, Eisenhower proceeded with the meeting. On September 14, 1957, Governor Faubus met with President Eisenhower at the US Naval base at Newport, Rhode Island, for about two hours. During the first 20 minutes, Faubus protested and assailed the Supreme Court.

Eisenhower offered a compromise. Eisenhower said that if Faubus ordered the National Guard to keep the peace and allow the black children into the school, he would ask the Justice Department to talk to Judge Davies about revoking the order for Faubus to appear in court.

Governor Faubus Defies the President and the Courts

Faubus had no desire to see the school integrated, but Eisenhower wanted the governor to comply with the Court's ruling and, to Eisenhower, it was a good deal because the arrangement also allowed Faubus to save face. Faubus waffled and equivocated as they talked about the offer. But in the end, Governor Faubus did not firmly agree to the deal.

---

[78] https://eisenhower.archives.gov/research/online_documents/civil_rights_little_rock/Press_release_DDE_telegram_to_Faubus.pdf

When Faubus returned to Arkansas, he did not withdraw the National Guard and he did not change their orders. So, the stalemate continued.

Given the circumstances, Eisenhower was under no obligation to intercede for Faubus with Judge Davies. When the day came for Governor Faubus to appear before the judge, the governor did not appear. The governor's lawyers were there, however, and they asked the judge to dismiss the case against Faubus. The attorneys argued that federal courts had no authority over the governor of Arkansas.[79]

Needless to say, Judge Davies denied the motion and Faubus's lawyers quickly left the courtroom.

Gov. Faubus holds a press conference about Little Rock High School.

After hearing from other witness, Judge Davies issued an injunction that ordered Governor Faubus to stop using the National Guard to obstruct black students from entering the school.

Several hours later during a press conference, Faubus denounced, complained, and condemned the actions of the federal courts. But he announced that he would comply with the order.

And during an outrageous display of religious hypocrisy, Faubus ended the press conference with a prayer in which he prayed for peace at the school.

The following Monday, Daisy Bates, the nine black students, as well as several community leaders met at Bates's home before going to the school. When they arrived at the school, they were met by a

---

[79] William Hitchcock, The Age of Eisenhower: America and the World in the 1950's. New York, London, Toronto, Sydney, New Delhi. Simon and Schuster. P. 367

handful of local police officers, state police, and about 1,000 angry white protesters screaming and shouting threats of violence.

Daisy Bates (second row, second from the left) and the nine Black Little Rock High School students.

The black students made it into the building, but they could not stay because of the raucous and angry mob disrupting the classes. The white students themselves quickly became inflamed and began repeating the chants they heard coming from the mob outside.

The nine black students, again, left the area encircled by their guardians as well as a few police officers. And several black journalists and photographers were assaulted again.

After this latest incident, Little Rock Mayor Woodrow Wilson Mann sent a telegram to President Eisenhower on September 23, 1957. In the telegram, Mayor Mann informed the president that Governor Faubus arranged for the mob to gather outside the high school and was directing their actions through representatives in the crowd.

The mayor said that he had evidence to support his claim and wanted to share it with the Justice Department. In his telegram Mayor Mann wrote: "*The mob that gathered was no spontaneous assembly. It was assembled, agitated, and aroused by a concerted plan of action. One of the principle agitators in the crowd was Jimmy Karam, who is a political and socially close ally to Governor Faubus. Karam has a long history and experienced at strike-breaking, and other activities such as what he engaged in at the high school. The way the mob formed, and the presence of Jimmy Karam leads to the inevitable conclusion that Governor Faubus was aware of what was going to take place. If the Justice Department desires to enforce the orders of the federal court regarding integration, the city police will be available to lend such support as you may require.*[80]

Eisenhower was very angry. Governor Faubus lied to Judge Davies, to him, and to the people of Arkansas. Governor Faubus stood before the entire nation and prayed for peace out of one side of his mouth and organized mob violence out of the other side.

But the mayor's telegram also provided Eisenhower with exactly what he needed. In the telegram, the mayor also asked for help. The mayor said, *"In the interest of humanity, law and order, please send federal troops to restore order to our city."*

Eisenhower Deploys the 101st Airborne to Little Rock Central High School

Before the president or the attorney general could legally respond to any city, they needed a local official to ask for help. And that's exactly what the mayor did. On September 24, 1957, President Eisenhower ordered the army chief of staff to send 1,000 soldiers from the 101 Airborne to Little Rock Central

President Eisenhower addresses the nation about the situation in Little Rock.

High School to control the mob as the black students entered the school. Eisenhower also issued an executive order and federalized the Arkansas National Guard.

The troops converged around the school that night and took position on every side. Their orders were to control any mob that gathered the next morning and to protect all black students as they entered the school. Afterward, President Eisenhower addressed

---

[80] Archives.gov. National Archives Identifier: 12237734

the nation through radio and television about the dramatic events unfolding in Little Rock.

"In that city, under the leadership of demagogic extremists, disorderly mobs have deliberately prevented the carrying out of proper orders from a federal court. Local authorities have not eliminated the mob threat, and, under law, I yesterday issued a proclamation calling upon the mob to disperse. But the mob, again, gathered in front of Central High School of Little Rock for the purpose of again preventing the carrying out of the Court's order relating to the admission of Negro children.

"Our personal opinions about the decision have no bearing on the matter of enforcement; the responsibility and authority of the Supreme Court to interpret the Constitution are clear. Local federal courts were instructed by the Supreme Court to issue such orders and decrees as might be necessary to achieve admission to public schools without regard to race—and with all deliberate speed.

"Mob rule cannot be allowed to override the decisions of the courts. Let me make this clear. The federal troops are not being used to relieve the local and state authorities of their primary duty to preserve the peace and order of the community. Nor are the troops there for the purpose of taking over the responsibility of the school board and other local officials. The troops are there, pursuant to law, solely for the purpose of preventing the interference with the orders of the Court."[81]

Governor Faubus and Democrats Accuse Soldiers of Harassing High School Girls

Not to be outdone, Governor Faubus also addressed the nation and characterized the event as an act of war. He tried to inflame the entire South against the White House and the courts by rekindling historic hatred against the North.

"We are now occupied territory," Faubus told the nation. *"And we're occupied by Yankee soldiers."*[82]

---

[81] https://eisenhower.archives.gov/research/online_documents/civil_rights_little_rock/1957_09_24_Press_Release.pdf

[82] https://www.upi.com/Archives/1981/06/07/Orval-Faubus-Recalls-crisis-of-57-A-world-rep-as-a-racist-endearment-to-Arkansas/7395360734400/

Predictably, Southern Democratic congressmen were also outraged. They saw the deployment of troops as a serious abuse of presidential power and nothing less than an assault upon the South.

Governor Faubus also accused the troops of "*invading the girls' dressing room*" at Little Rock Central High School and sent a letter to Major General E.A. Walker. Faubus addressed the general as "*the Commander of the Occupation Troops*" and asked him to send the Women's Army Corps to Little Rock so that the soldiers would stop harassing high school girls.[83]

Black students escorted into Little Rock High School by the US Military.

The White House responded with a press release that said that the governor's charges were untrue and completely vulgar. School Superintendent Virgil T. Blossom said that "*federal troops are not following the girls into the dressing rooms and that the accusations are absolutely ridiculous.*"

Arkansas Congressman Oren Harris and Georgia Senator Richard Russell joined Governor Faubus in hurling unthinkable

Senator John Stennis

accusations against the military. Harris demanded that the president withdraw the federal troops and leave the matter to the local authorities. And Senator Russell wrote the following: "*I must vigorously protest the highhanded and illegal methods being employed by the Armed Forces of the United States, under your command, who are carrying out your orders to mix the races in*

---

[83] The Detroit Tribune. Oct. 12, 1957, P. 1

our public schools. And if reports of reputable press associations and news writers are to be believed, these soldiers are disregarding and overriding the elementary rights of the American citizens by applying tactics which must have been copied from the manual issued by the officers of Hitler's Storm Troopers. These reports agree that an unarmed citizen was cracked in the head by a rifle butt while standing peacefully on private property. Another account relates that three or more citizens were pushed down a street with bayonets at their throats."[84]

Although others expressed their objections in a more moderate tone, their positions were no less extreme. Mississippi Senator John Stennis, for example, was one of many that held an apocalyptic view of desegregation of schools.

In a letter to President Eisenhower, Senator Stennis wrote: "*The real issue at stake is the survival of our public schools. The schools are sustained through the combined support of parents and teachers. Opposition to integration is the overwhelming voice of mothers and fathers of these children. Their objections contain no spirit of defiance or lawlessness. They are sincere, patriotic, and law-abiding citizens. Their support will end if schools are integrated by force. And the continued use of the military and the threat of soldiers marching from school to school will totally destroy the public-school system in great areas of the South.*"[85]

But the parents of the nine black students held an entirely different point of view. In a joint letter to the president, on September 30, they wrote: "*We, the parents of the nine Negro children enrolled at Little Rock Central High School, want you to know that your action in safeguarding their rights has strengthened our faith in democracy. We believe that freedom and equality can be maintained only through freedom and equality of opportunity for self-development, growth, and purposeful citizenship. You have demonstrated to us, profoundly, that you believe in this concept. For this we are deeply grateful and respectfully*

---

[84]   https://eisenhower.archives.gov/research/online_documents/civil_rights_little_rock/1957_09_27_Russell_to_DDE.pdf

[85]   https://eisenhower.archives.gov/research/online_documents/civil_rights_little_rock/1957_10_01_Stennis_to_DDE.pdf

extend to you our heartfelt and lasting thanks. May the Almighty and All wise Father of us all bless you and guide you always."[86]

The 101st Airborne remained in place for about a month and a half. And although no evidence was every provided to substantiate Senator Russell's ridiculous and extremely offensive accusations about the soldiers' conduct, Eisenhower thought it was wise to replace the federal troops with the Arkansas National Guard while under the command of the federal government.

This time, the National Guard's orders were to truly keep the peace and protect the black children from any mob that Governor Faubus, or his white supremacist associates, attempted to organize. The National Guard remained at the school throughout that school year to protect the black students and escort them safely onto school grounds.

For those, such as Senator Stennis, who believed that black and white students seated next to each other in classrooms would cause the apocalypse, well…an apocalypse did come.

The destruction of the schools, however, was not the result of integration, but due to the extremist that occupied the governor's mansion. On September 18, 1958, Governor Faubus called for a public vote to close all Little Rock public schools in defiance to Eisenhower and the Supreme Court.

Segregationist Democrats Close Little Rock Schools

As the day approached for the people of Arkansas to vote, Faubus tried to persuade businesses to support private, white-only schools, but they refused. And on the eve of the vote, Governor Faubus addressed the people of Arkansas:

"*It was with a heavy heart that I found it necessary to sign the bills of the Extraordinary Session of the General Assembly and to close the High Schools in the City of Little Rock. I took this action only after the last hope of relief from an intolerable situation had been exhausted. The*

---

[86] https://eisenhower.archives.gov/research/online_documents/civil_rights_little_rock/Little_Rock_Telegram.pdf

Supreme Court shut its eyes to all the facts, and in essence said—integration at any price, even if it means the destruction of our school system, our educational processes, and the risk of disorder and violence that could result in the loss of life—perhaps yours."[87]

On September 27, 1958, the people of the Little Rock School District voted 129,470 to 7,561 to close all four public schools in the city of Little Rock. And a total of 3,665 students, black and white, were unable to acquire a free public education during the 1958–59 school year.[88]

Gov. Faubus calls for public schools to close to fight racial integration.

Most of the city's 177 teachers worked in empty classrooms and some worked as substitutes at other schools.

Apparently, Gov. Faubus and the people of Little Rock were so engulfed by rage, they did not think through this decision. They closed their public schools without developing a viable alternative and the people of Little Rock suffered greatly because of it. Hundreds of students were displaced from families to attend other schools, about 45 teachers were fired without due process, and many black and white students joined the military.

After trying to live without their schools, the people of Little Rock surrendered and agreed to limited desegregation. On June 18, 1959, a three-judge federal panel declared that the closing of Arkansas public schools was unconstitutional. The four schools reopened on August 12, 1959.

Although Southern schools eventually submitted to desegregation, they didn't comply *"with all deliberate speed"* as ordered by the Supreme Court. Resistance continued throughout the South as each

---

[87] https://blackpast.org/1958-governor-orval-e-faubus-speech-school-integration

[88] http://www.encyclopediaofarkansas.net/encyclopedia/entry-detail. aspx?entryID=737

school district desegregated at their own pace. Five years after the *Brown vs. Board of Education* decision, less than 10 percent of black students attended desegregated schools.

But each school district enrolled just enough blacks into white schools to argue successfully that its school district was integrated.

Chapter 10: 1960–1963
Kennedy Tries to Please Everyone

As the 1960 presidential election approached, America was still staggering from the seismic shift of social changes of the 1950s. Long-held traditions were crumbling before the eyes of many who greatly valued them. America took a giant step toward the society envisioned by its founders when they wrote the words, *"We hold these truths to be self-evident, that all men are created equal."*

About 90 had years passed since the ratification of the Fourteenth Amendment. During that time, many people believed that blacks would never truly experience equal treatment under the law. But now, it appeared as if America was experiencing a new birth—complete with birth pains!

The Sit-In Movement

For example, the 1960 Sit-In Movement, which seemed to have ignited spontaneously, changed the way blacks were treated at diners in many communities throughout the South. Planned and executed by students who attended black colleges, owners and managers of diners and restaurant saw young blacks

"One of the most significant developments in the whole civil rights struggle."—Dr. King

walk through the front doors of their businesses, take a seat at lunch counters and tables designated for whites only, and demand to be served as equals to whites.

Each of these businesses required blacks to enter and exit through the side or the back door and sit in designated sections for blacks. But the college students involved in the movement refused to comply with those requirements and they refused to leave the businesses until they were served.

The movement began when four black college students from North Carolina A&T walked up to a lunch counter at Woolworth's Department Store in Greensboro, North Carolina. They asked for coffee and were refused service because of their race. Despite the taunts and threats from some of the white customers, the students sat there peacefully and refused to leave.

News of the incident spread nationwide quickly. And throughout that year, black college students throughout the South repeated the actions of the Greensboro students. Suddenly, owners and managers of diners and restaurants throughout the South had to contend with young black people demanding equality.

The movement embraced the same methods used by Dr. King during the Montgomery Bus Boycott. The students were peaceful and very respectful. When confronted by the police or white thugs in the area, the students remained nonviolent throughout the course of their protests. Many were taken to jail and many were expelled from their schools. But they returned to the businesses and sat in until they were served or arrested.

Dr. King referred to the student movement as *"one of the most significant developments in the whole civil rights struggle."*

Senator Kennedy stands with segregationist Senator Richard Russell.

As the 1960 presidential election year unfolded, the nation braced itself for more birth pains, guaranteeing that the civil rights issue would be front and center during the election.

The Montgomery Bus Boycott, *Brown vs. the Board of Education*, *Browder vs. Gayle*, the Civil Rights Act of 1957, and the dramatic standoff between President Eisenhower with Arkansas Democratic Governor Orval Faubus at Little Rock Central High School were events born from an issue that had to be acknowledged by the candidates.

Prior to 1948, presidential candidates never addressed, or even seriously considered, civil rights, mainly because they were afraid to alienate white voters or because they wanted to keep blacks under subjection indefinitely without saying it publicly.

But the events of the previous 10 years, however, had been so significant, so consequential, that there was no escape for either side. Both presidential candidates, Senator John F. Kennedy and Vice President Richard Nixon, had to take a public stand.

Senator Kennedy emerged as the Democratic nominee for president out of a field of seven candidates, including Senator Lyndon Johnson. For the Republicans, Vice President Richard Nixon was the only serious contender and won his party's nomination easily.

Senator Kennedy was nothing like Harry Truman. President Truman was the exception among the Democrats, a leader who truly wanted to see black Americans enjoy equal rights and for the federal government to protect those rights.

That certainly was not the case for Senator Kennedy. Throughout his career in the US Senate, Senator Kennedy had supported the position of segregationists Democrats. And Kennedy was just as ambitious as Lyndon Johnson, who planned to run for the presidential nomination himself.

When they had been in the Senate together, Kennedy cared more about appeasing the segregationists, whereas Johnson worked to appear in favor of civil rights while privately opposing them.

To help secure Southern support, Kennedy helped segregationist Democrats to remove Section 3 of the Civil Rights Act of

1957 and he supported the amendment to Section 4 which made the entire law useless.

In his book *Profiles in Courage: Decisive Moments in The Lives of Celebrated Americans*, Kennedy expressed strong belief in the 19th-century myths and propaganda about black men.[89-90] Alabama Democratic Governor John Patterson was comfortable enough with Kennedy to endorse him for president as early as 1957.

On the other hand, Nixon sought the endorsement of Dr. Martin Luther King Jr., but Dr. King refused to publicly endorse any presidential candidate. The Montgomery Bus Boycott and the MIA's victory in *Browder vs. Gale* made Dr. King's name commonly spoken with great reverence in black households throughout America's black community during that time.

And although Vice President Nixon stood by Eisenhower's side as he fought for the civil rights of blacks, Dr. King did not violate his strong belief in withholding public endorsements. Nixon knew that his chance of receiving support from the black community would greatly increase with Dr. King's support.

The media hounded Kennedy about his wavering on civil rights issues for months. He struggled to find a position that satisfied everyone—segregationists, civil rights leaders, and the media. And in May of 1960, Senator Kennedy made a spur-of-the-moment decision to seek advice from Harry Belafonte in New York.

Senator Kennedy stands with Dr. King as he tries to please both sides of the civil rights issue.

According to some reports, Kennedy did not call him before he arrived—he

---

[89] Senator John F. Kennedy, Profiles in Courage: Decisive Moments in the Lives of Celebrated Americans, the United States, Harper and Brothers, 1956, P. 140

[90] Bruce Bartlett, Wrong on Race: The Democratic Party's Buried Past. New York, St. Martin's Griffin, P. 161

simply showed up at Belafonte's doorstep and expected Belafonte to make time for him.

Belafonte met with Kennedy, and Kennedy asked him how to get support from blacks. Belafonte told him that he had to find a way to get Dr. King to endorse him.

Much to Belafonte's surprise, Senator Kennedy didn't know anything about Dr. King—not even his name.[91]

It was no secret that John F. Kennedy, and the entire Kennedy family, live lives of wealth, prestige, and privilege very few people get to experience. Some consider them American royalty even today. And their lifestyle keeps them sheltered and completely shielded from many events experienced by average Americans. But even so, considering the media attention given to the Montgomery Bus Boycott, it's hard to imagine that Senator Kennedy was so out of touch with mainstream America that he never heard of Dr. King before he visited Harry Belafonte. Nixon knew about Dr. King and knew him personally, so Senator Kennedy quickly realized that he had some catching up to do.

Other civil rights leaders, such as baseball star Jackie Robinson and Roy Wilkins, from the NAACP openly spoke against Kennedy. They remembered how he had supported segregationists throughout the years and believed Kennedy would turn his back on them if he became president.

Kennedy did meet with Dr. King and other civil rights leaders. But he also met with die-hard segregationists in Washington, DC, and throughout the South. When asked to declare is position on civil rights, he used carefully crafted rhetoric that did not place him firmly on either side. Several media outlets continued to strongly criticize Kennedy's refusal to commit to either side of the argument.

Nixon, however, made his position clear. He was completely in favor of civil rights and enjoyed considerable support from the black community essentially because he was Eisenhower's vice president. Nixon also enjoyed positive media coverage after the National

---

[91] Bruce Bartlett, Wrong on Race: The Democratic Party's Buried Past. New York, St. Martin's Griffin, P. 161

Republican Party strengthened its position on the issue in the 1960 Republican Platform during the convention. It appeared as if Nixon would garner greater support from the black community during the race.

Kennedy Exploits Dr. King's Misfortune

An unfortunate event, coupled with a costly misstep by Nixon, turned the tide in favor of Kennedy. College students in the Atlanta area contacted Dr. King and asked him to join them in a sit-in protest at a local department store. Dr. King agreed and participated as one of the followers and not the leader.

During October of 1960, Dr. King was arrested as he participated in a lunch counter sit-in at Rich's Department Store. Dr. King refused to post bail and remained in jail with the students for several days. During that time, however, a multitude of blacks from the Atlanta area protested in front of the jail and throughout the city. The store manager agreed to drop the charges and Dr. King and the students were released.

As the students returned to their schools, Dr. King was immediately arrested again for not paying the fine for a previous charge of operating a vehicle with an out-of-state license. The fine was supposed to have been paid by King's attorney. Dr. King discovered, later, that his attorney did not pay the fine and he was placed back in his cell.

At approximately 3:00 a.m. that morning, Dr. King was abruptly awakened by several prison guards and taken to the state prison in Reidsville, Georgia.

When Atlanta's black community became aware of the extremely uncommon prison transfer at 3:00 a.m., they feared for Dr. King's life.

Dr. King being released from jail.

And they became even more angry when they discovered it was over a traffic violation.

It was then that Senator Kennedy contacted Dr. King's wife, Coretta—who was pregnant at the time—and expressed his sympathy about the situation. Kennedy also offered his support. Senator Kennedy used his influence with Georgia's Democratic governor to secure Dr. King's release. And Kennedy's help was enough to cause many blacks to reconsider their support for Nixon.

Meanwhile, Nixon's campaign staff urged him to become involved, but he refused. Nixon knew that he was in a much better position on the civil rights issue than Kennedy. Additionally, the media was still talking about the strength of the GOP platform and criticizing Kennedy on his constant wavering. Clearly, Kennedy was pandering to the black community, and Nixon was sure everyone would see right through it.

But unfortunately, the strategy worked! Kennedy's expression of deep concern for Dr. King's family and his ability to get Dr. King out of jail was enough for a significant number of blacks to forget that Kennedy stood shoulder-to-shoulder with Southern segregationists. And Nixon's lack of empathy was enough to cause many to forget that he stood proudly in favor of civil rights and never wavered.

Senator Kennedy was another example of the Democrats' ability to connect emotionally with the public in such a profound manner that it caused many people to ignore his shortcomings and disregard what was most important to them. Senator Kennedy won the election with 68 percent of the black vote. And Vice President Nixon lost with 7 percent less support from black voters than President Eisenhower.[92]

It was a decision that many blacks—including Dr. King—later regretted. After he assumed office, neither President Kennedy nor Vice President Johnson nor anyone in the Kennedy Administration did anything to further the cause of civil rights.

---

[92] http://blackdemographics.com/culture/black-politics/

Kennedy's Solution: Tokenism

Throughout his presidency, Kennedy's civil rights rhetoric was insincere, and his tone was unenthusiastic. The actions of his administration told the true story about his position.

For example, the Department of Health, Education, and Welfare only issued construction grants to hospitals designated for whites only; the Department of Labor conducted training programs in 142 all-white schools and only 14 black schools; and although Kennedy banned housing discrimination in the Justice Department, his brother US Attorney General Robert Kennedy did nothing to enforce it.

Moreover, only an average of 8.3 percent of blacks were registered to vote from 100 Southern counties.[93] Unfortunately, a significant number of white southerners were still holding onto their discriminatory beliefs. US Attorney General Robert Kennedy was aware of this, but defending civil rights was very low on the list of priorities of the Kennedy Administration.

In March of 1963, *The Nation* published a scathing yet cautiously worded article "*A Bold Design for a New South*." The article written by Dr. King himself addressed the administration's poor performance on civil rights during their first two years in office.

In the article, Dr. King lamented about how, within his first few years in office, President Kennedy had backed away from the civil rights issue and showed little interest in making any progress. Dr. King also expressed his disappointment about how civil rights was no longer a primary domestic political issue.

Dr. King wrote, "*The President backed away from the Senate fight to amend Rule 22, the so-called filibuster rule; had he entered the fray, the amendment would probably have passed. Rule 22, the greatest obstacle to the passage of civil-rights legislation, would have been smashed. But the President again remained aloof.*"

---

[93] Bruce Bartlett, Wrong on Race: The Democratic Party's Buried Past. New York, St. Martin's Griffin, P. 166

Dr. King also criticized Kennedy's refusal to support the Supreme Court ruling in *Brown vs. the Board of Education*, pointing out that nothing was being done about black unemployment. He further warned the nation about the growing use of tokenism.

"Two thousand school districts remain segregated after nearly a decade of litigation based upon Supreme Court decisions. Hundreds of Southern communities continue to segregate public facilities, yet even after the immense efforts and sacrifices of the weary Negro citizens of Albany, Georgia, the government enters the fray only at the periphery, filing an amicus curiae brief. Negro unemployment has mounted to double the proportion of white unemployment, and government action produces a handful of jobs in industries possessing government contracts, and housing discrimination confines Negroes to slums, North and South," Dr. King said.

For years, President Kennedy strove for the approval of opposing forces for the sake of his presidential ambitions. He publicly met with civil rights leaders and joined in their outrage about societal injustices. But he also spent time socializing, backslapping, and expressing agreement among the country's hard-core segregationists.

Dr. King criticizes President Kennedy's inaction on civil rights and his support of tokenism.

Kennedy's solution for his dilemma only created a new monster for the civil rights movement to contend with—tokenism.

"Tokenism was the inevitable outgrowth of the Administration's design for dealing with discrimination," Dr. King wrote. *"The Administration sought to demonstrate to Negroes that it has concern for them, while at the same time it has striven to avoid inflaming the opposition. If tokenism were our goal, this Administration has adroitly moved us towards its accomplishment. But tokenism can now be seen as a genuine menace. It is a palliative which relieves emotional distress but leaves the disease and its ravages unaffected. It tends to*

demobilize and relax the militant spirit which alone drives us forward to real change."[94]

President Kennedy brought the deceptive practice of tokenism to the forefront of America society. Rather than fully desegregating public schools, most Southern schools allowed only enough blacks—perhaps two or three—to attend so that officials could claim the schools were desegregated.

State and local governments placed "token blacks" in visible positions so that they could claim that they honored the civil rights of blacks. Private businesses did the same thing.

One of the greatest dangers of tokenism was it deceived well-meaning whites, especially Southern whites, into believing that—at long last—they were giving blacks the respect that they demanded. They believed that if a handful of blacks were treated properly and respectfully, then all were treated properly.

Segregationists supported tokenism, believing that President Kennedy had created a real solution. But Kennedy only created another evil system for the civil rights movement to fight. A system that, in many ways, was more difficult to overcome.

Tokenism easily soothed the guilty conscious of whites across America. And a big part of Dr. King's strategy for social change was to employ the guilt, shame, and outrage of whites across America as leverage against whites in the South.

It became much more difficult to point out the inequalities in society when the segregationists responded by pointing to the few blacks they allowed into their schools and places of business, or to whom they sold homes.

The tokenism phenomenon came at the worst possible time, according to Dr. King. After decades of sowing the seeds for racial equality in the South and fighting for civil rights in the face of violence, threats, and economic hardship, Dr. King had begun to see the fruit of his labor, and very likely the labor of President Truman and President Eisenhower, spring from the hearts of white Southerners.

---

[94] https://www.thenation.com/article/archive-bold-design-new-south

About half of the Southern white population began to express genuine desire for true change. And tokenism threatened to uproot King's progress.

"*It (the South) is already split, fissured into two parts; one is ready for extensive change, the other adamantly opposed to any but the most trivial alterations. The Administration should not seek to fashion policies for the latter; it should place its weight behind the dynamic South, encouraging and facilitating its progressive development*," Dr. King said.

Dr. King also pointed out that 15 years after President Harry Truman released his 1947 Civil Rights Committee Report, many white Southerners began to see that President Truman was right. For Southerners to know why the South consistently fell behind the rest of the country economically, including high paying wages, job growth, the use of modern technology, population growth, and manufacturing, they did not have to look any further than their own Jim Crow laws. The South was holding itself back.

Dr. King continued: "*The simple and arresting truth that became clear in 1962 is that significant elements of the South have come to see that segregation has placed the whole region socially, educationally, and economically behind the rest of the nation. We have stopped justifying and begun rectifying racial wrongs. We have traded self-deception for self-respect. This is the South we are proud of—a land of gentlemen, plain-spoken, manly and respectful of their people. Not a swampland of the deceitful where weasels dodge and cavil and speak half-truths to the unknowing.*"[95]

It was the shocking and horrific attack by public safety officers against black demonstrators in Birmingham, Alabama, that forced the Kennedy Administration to take decisive action in early 1963. During the spring of that year, Dr. King and his supporters were brutally attacked by police officers and firefighters on direct orders from Police Commissioner Eugene "Bull" Conner. Bull Conner was also the national committeeman for the Alabama State Democratic Party and acted with the full support of Democratic Governor George Wallace.

---

[95] https://www.thenation.com/article/archive-bold-design-new-south

Hundreds of protesters were attacked with night sticks, police dogs, and fire hoses in full view of the national media. Images of

unarmed, peaceful black demonstrators being beaten to the ground, chased, scattered, and mauled by vicious dogs, or drenched and battered with water from the fire hoses of the Birmingham Fire Department filled the television screens of many Americans during the calamity.

Gov. George Wallace orders police to attack protestors

America saw resources intended for the protection of life and property turned into weapons of war—and they were outraged and rightfully disgusted.

Civil Rights leaders throughout the country held President Kennedy directly responsible for the incident. His refusal to stand firmly and publicly in favor of civil rights along with his continuous efforts to seek the approval of segregationists had actually emboldened them. Under the Kennedy Administration, they felt completely free to use public resources in a violent manner against blacks in ways that had not been seen since the 19th century.

Kennedy suffered politically and knew that he had to take a stand. So, in June of 1963, he offered a civil rights bill.

Dr. King delivers his historic "I Have a Dream" speech.

The bill provided equal access to hotels and restaurants, banned discrimination in the federal government and for companies that held federal contracts, and it increased the authority of the Justice Department to bring lawsuits against school districts that still refused to desegregate.

Kennedy's civil rights bill strongly resembled Eisenhower's civil rights bill of 1957. But Kennedy offered to include the original versions of Section 3 and Section 4, which he and Lyndon Johnson removed.

Dr. King and civil rights leaders across the nation began to organize a march on Washington, DC, in support of Kennedy's civil rights bill. On August 28, 1963, over 250,000 Americans of all races marched through the streets of the nation's capital and assembled at the Lincoln Memorial where Dr. King delivered his historic speech, "*I Have a Dream.*"

President Kennedy was assassinated before his civil rights bill reached Congress in November of 1963. Despite his shortcomings and obvious insincerity to their cause, black Americans and many civil rights leaders greatly mourned Kennedy's tragic death.

Vice President Lyndon Johnson was sworn in as president aboard Air Force One about an hour and a half after President Kennedy was declared dead.

Chapter 11: 1963–1965
Johnson Rides the Political Waves

Occupying the White House was always President Johnson's objective since his days in the Senate. During those years, Johnson did his best to appear to support civil rights for blacks when, in fact, he did not.

Johnson did not know he would ascend to the presidency so quickly and under such tragic circumstances. But he was there nonetheless, and all eyes were focused on him.

Unlike his years in the Senate, as the nation's chief executive, Johnson could not hide among 99 other faces. The White House provided no such anonymity. Furthermore, the nation was badly traumatized by Kennedy's public and very brutal assassination. America needed to heal, and its people needed to be comforted.

Vice President Johnson being sworn in as president.

Anyone with even the dullest political instincts knew that the weeks following Kennedy's death were not the time to take a firm stand in favor of segregation. The civil rights issue was extremely divisive, and Johnson's instincts were finely honed and razor sharp.

Not only were his political instincts extremely keen, his eyes were very clear. Johnson saw that the traditions of the old South he treasured his whole life were disintegrating before him.

A very significant number of white Southerners were now in favor of civil rights for blacks and the number of white supremacists Democrats was shrinking in Congress. It was only a matter of time before they were all crushed under the weight of true social progress.

During the last 10 years, Dr. Martin Luther King Jr. and his supporters had seized the moral high ground of the civil rights issue and held it firmly through nonviolent protests. His "*I Have a Dream*" speech brilliantly communicated what race relations would look like if the federal and state governments truly honored the Declaration of Independence and the US Constitution.

With great eloquence and passion, Dr. King painted a beautiful and glorious picture of a racially diverse American society that lived, worked, and worshipped God in fellowship and in peace.

Reasonable Americans could not disparage this vision of what America could become. Meanwhile, the outrageous and barbaric tactics of Bull Conner and other hard-core segregationists in Alabama completely backfired and likely helped place most Southerners, and all other Americans, firmly in Dr. King's camp.

Also, 1964 was presidential election year. Being the political opportunist he was, Johnson decided to kill two birds with one stone—so to speak.

Like a skilled surfer focused on navigating his way around powerful and perilous waves, President Johnson decided to get ahead of the changing political tide, stand in favor of Kennedy's civil rights bill, and embrace the popularity of President Kennedy to make it his own.

Johnson believed that standing in favor of civil rights would not only prevent him from being crushed by

President Johnson meets with Dr. King.

the oncoming tsunami, but the passage of the bill could help heal the nation of its tragic loss.

President Johnson made the passage of the bill his first order of business after taking office. During a joint session of Congress, five days after the death of Kennedy, Johnson announced that civil rights would be his top priority.

"We have talked long enough in this country about equal rights. We have talked for one hundred years or more. It is time now to write the next chapter and to write it in the books of law. I urge you again, as I did in 1957, and again in 1960, to enact a civil rights law so that we can move forward to eliminate from this nation every trace of discrimination and oppression that is based upon race or color. There could be no greater source of strength to this nation both at home and abroad," Johnson said.

The Hypocrisy of Lyndon Johnson

The situation created a depth of irony so profound and that it could not be overlooked by Washington insiders and those who knew President Johnson. Only seven years earlier Johnson, with the help of senate Democrats, maneuvered President Eisenhower into signing a powerless and ineffective civil rights bill by making the most outrageous claims conceivable.

Johnson and the Senate Democrats had claimed that the bill would destroy Southern law enforcement agencies and state courts; they said that federal judges would randomly throw Southerners in jail; and they claimed that the civil rights bill would force Southerners to commingle with blacks and have biracial children.

These lies were told by Democrats in the US Senate to gut Eisenhower's Civil Rights Act of 1957—and it worked. But now, President Johnson was publicly pressured to restore the enforcement provisions and sign the bill into law!

Despite the paradox and his overwhelming hypocrisy, President Johnson had the sympathy of the nation in his favor. Regardless of Kennedy's indifference toward blacks and his record on racial issues, the deep sympathies the people of America compelled them to memorialize President Kennedy by enshrining his proposed civil rights bill into law—thus making it a lasting part of his legacy.

The bill passed the House in February of 1964 and encountered tremendous opposition in the Senate, which was controlled by the Democrats. Despite the need for national healing, staunch segregationist Democrats Richard Russell, Strom Thurmond, Robert Byrd, William Fulbright, and Sam Ervin were determined to defeat the bill with another prolonged filibuster. This one lasted for weeks.

Senate Democrats Fight the Civil Rights Bill; Senator Dirksen Saves It

During the filibuster Democratic Senator Robert C. Byrd completed his address 14 hours and 13 minutes after it began. Senator Byrd's commitment to racial segregation led him to record the second-longest filibuster in the history of the US Senate. Historically, the filibuster had been a reliable weapon in the Democrat arsenal, which helped defeat many civil rights proposals in the past.

But now President Johnson found himself in opposition to the same Senate Democrats who helped him defeat Eisenhower's bill. This time, however, Johnson had a new ally—Republican-minority leader Everett Dirksen of Illinois.

Senator Dirksen worked closely with Democratic Senate whip, Hubert Humphrey, to get 67 votes to break the Democrat filibuster. On June 10, 1964, Senator Dirksen delivered a speech on the floor of the Senate that many historians believed persuaded most of his colleagues to break the filibuster.

Dirksen said, "*Today the Senate is stalemated in its efforts to enact a civil rights bill, one version of which has already been approved by the House by a vote of more than 2 to 1. That the Senate wishes to act on a civil rights bill can be divined from the fact that the motion to take up was adopted by a vote of 67-17. There are many reasons why cloture should be invoked, and a good civil rights measure enacted. First, it is said that on the night he died, Victor Hugo wrote in his diary, substantially this sentiment: 'Stronger than all the armies is an idea whose time has come.' The time has come for equality of opportunity in sharing in government, in education, and in employment. It will not be stayed or denied. It is here.*"[96]

When the clerk proceeded to call the roll for a cloture vote, it was Republican Senator John James Williams from Delaware who cast the critical 67th vote. And when the roll call ended, the Senate voted 71 to 29 to end the filibuster—a four-vote margin of victory.[97]

The final vote in the House was 290 in favor and 130 against, with 152 Democrats and 176 Republicans voting in support. Out of the 130 who opposed the bill, 104 were Democrats.

President Johnson signed the bill into law on July 2, 1964. The law prohibited discrimination in public places, provided for the integration of schools and other public facilities, and made employment discrimination illegal.

About 89 years before President Johnson signed the Civil Rights Act of 1964 into law, seven black Republican congressmen went to the floor of the House of Representatives and argued in favor of the passage of the Civil Rights Act of 1875. The bill passed and

Senator Everett Dirksen

was sign into law, but eventually it was struck down by the Supreme Court in 1883.

The two bills were virtually identical. But the prevailing racial sentiments during the 19th century would not allow the 1875 bill to survive.

The 1964 bill, in contrast, did survive. Although Congress did not wholeheartedly and enthusiastically take the step toward the goal of "*all men are created equal*," it took the step none the less.

---

[96] https://www.senate.gov/artandhistory/history/common/image/CivilRights_DirksenSpeechJune101964.htm

[97] https://www.senate.gov/artandhistory/history/minute/Civil_Rights_Filibuster_Ended.htm

Segregationist Response to Civil Rights Act

The reaction to the bill's passage among many segregationists was just as senseless and irrational as ever. Rather than accept the law, offer their products and services to blacks, and make a greater profit, a significant number of businesses throughout the South preferred to hurt themselves by either selling their businesses or closing their doors forever.

The greatest example was the Democratic Governor of Georgia, Lester Maddox. Governor Maddox was so committed to racial segregation that he closed his business, the Pickrick Family Restaurant, rather than serve black customers as equals to whites.[98]

But white Southerners were no longer united on the issue of racial segregation. When Johnson went along with the Southerners who wanted change in their society, he knew that he might be presiding over the loss of the Southern states to the Republican Party for the foreseeable future.

"I know the risks are great and it might cost us the South, but those sorts of states may be lost to us anyway," Johnson told former Kennedy aide Theodore Sorensen.[99]

During the same time Johnson was lamenting the possible loss of the South to the Republicans, his political maneuvering yielded a great harvest of votes for him on election day in 1964. President Johnson defeated Republican presidential nominee Barry Goldwater in a landslide victory.

Georgia Gov. Lester Maddox announces that he is closing his family business to fight racial integration.

---

98 The Digital Library of Georgia. https://dlg.usg.edu/record/geh_maddox_9
99 Bruce Bartlett, Wrong on Race: The Democratic Party's Buried Past. New York, St. Martin's Griffin, P. 168

There is no question that a big part of Johnson's victory was because he rode a wave of sympathy for President Kennedy. With that sympathy, Johnson carried 44 of 50 states and won with 486 electoral votes.

Johnson's prophecy about the Southern states began to come to true. Barry Goldwater won the states of South Carolina, Georgia, Alabama, Mississippi, and Louisiana. Historically, each of these states supported Democrat candidates. But this time, they demonstrated that they were now willing to support Republicans, and more Southern states would follow in future elections.

How did black America vote? About 94 percent of blacks supported Democrat Lyndon Johnson that year.[100] It was the greatest amount of black support for a Democrat at the time.

The Battle for Voting Rights

The civil rights movement had made great strides and accomplished many things by this point. But there was still one more obstacle, one more barrier to overcome, and one more wall to tear down before blacks could confidently say they stood equally with whites in the eyes of the law.

During the mid-1960s, many Southern states continued to block African Americans from exercising their Fifteenth Amendment right to vote. In Dallas County, Alabama—where blacks made up more than half the population, for example—only 2 percent of blacks were registered to vote. [101]

Dallas County was under the authority of militant segregationist Sheriff Jim Clark, who often wore a button that said "Never" which was possibly his automatic response to blacks registering to vote. Clark's deputies often used electric cattle prods in response to public demonstrations.

The use of poll taxes, literacy tests, multiple-paged voter registration forms, and other laws effectively blocked black Americans

[100] https://blackdemographics.com/culture/black-politics/
[101] https://www.britannica.com/event/Selma-March

from being able to vote despite voter registration drives conducted by the NAACP, the Student Nonviolent Coordinating Committee and the Southern Christian Leadership Council.

When they went to the polls, they were often told by elections officials they had to recite the entire US Constitution or explain complicated aspects of it before the officials would give them a ballot. Some blacks faced confusing voting regulations or were told they had insufficient reading skills.

Segregationist had lost their public schools to integration, and they had lost public transportation and public places to equal rights. They were determined to draw the line at voting rights. The extremists, which were found in the Democratic Party, believed that if Southern blacks could vote, whites would lose everything because of the strength of their numbers.

Even after many blacks migrated to the North and Midwest during the 1920s and 1930s, the black population in the South was always very high enough to make a difference in any statewide election. For example, the black population of Mississippi during the mid-1960s was 36.8 percent, in South Carolina 30.5 percent, in Louisiana 29.8 percent, in Alabama 26.2 percent, and in Georgia 25.9 percent.[102]

Although the Democrats were glad to have the presidency, they were always more concerned about keeping the South under Democrat control. Since the Compromise of 1877, the Democrats were willing to sacrifice their federal ambitions in return for control of Southern states. There they could maintain their way of life—which also trampled the rights of Southern blacks.

Historically, honoring the right of blacks to vote greatly threatened Democrat control over the South. When blacks voted during the late 19th century, they voted Republican and Southern states were under Republican control, which was completely unacceptable to them. It was only the use of terrorist tactics by the Ku Klux Klan

---

[102] Campbell Gibson and Kay Jung, "Historical Census Statistics of Population Totals by Race, 1790 to 1990"

and oppressive Jim Crow laws that enabled the Democrats to regain control of the Southern states.[103]

Now, 100 years later, they saw the South slipping away from them again. Barry Goldwater won five Southern states during the 1964 election. And the Democrats believed that if all blacks voted freely that year, they would join the white Southerners who voted for Goldwater and the entire South would be lost.

The Clash on Edmund Pettus Bridge

Dr. Martin Luther King Jr. and other civil rights leaders were determined to break through this final barrier and they purposed to use the same non-violent tactics that had served them so well in the past. Dr. King, who was chairman of the Southern Christian Leadership Conference during this time, and other civil rights leaders, organized a 50-mile march from Selma to Montgomery, Alabama. The march would culminate with Dr. King delivering a speech at the top of the steps of the state capitol building demanding Gov. Wallace to respect the right of blacks to vote.

Alabama State Troopers stop protestors as they reach the end of the bridge.

In March of 1965, Dr. King and about 600 protestors began their march. Among the them were black men, women, and children of all ages that decided that they were not going to cooperate with an evil system anymore.

---

[103] Benjamin Tillman, Speech: Their Own Hot-Headedness, Washington, D.C., http://historymatters.gmu.edu/d/55

The march was highly publicized and included many white people as well as members of the media who walked with them every step of the way.

The protestors marched through Selma with no trouble at all. But when they reached the Edmund Pettus Bridge, they encountered an army of Alabama state troopers blocking their path. Hundreds of troopers with helmets holding nightsticks were there with some on horseback. They, and their patrol cars, were lined up blocking the protestors' path as if they were protecting the final remnants of the old South.

The troopers were ordered by Governor Wallace to *"use whatever measures necessary to prevent the march"*[104] into Montgomery. The bridge itself was named after a Confederate general and grand dragon of the Ku Klux

Alabama State Troopers attack civil rights protestors.

Klan. So, it was likely not a coincidence that Governor Wallace had chosen the bridge as a stopping point.

The officer in charge ordered the protestors to disperse, and the protestors refused. The troopers then put on their gas masks, held their clubs in both hands, and attacked the protestors. The troopers beat the protestors to the ground and fired tear gas in their midst.

The officers on horseback charged at the protestors and forced many to run back across the bridge. Men and women held their children close as they fled.

Television cameras recorded and broadcasted the entire calamity. ABC News interrupted its scheduled telecast, which coincidentally was about Nazi war crimes, to broadcast the attack on protestors live. Millions of Americans saw the brutality of the Alabama state

---

[104] https://www.britannica.com/event/Selma-March

troopers under Governor George Wallace. Many people were injured and hospitalized. And the event became known as "Bloody Sunday."

The nation exploded with outrage toward Governor Wallace's— his actions had completely backfired. Support for Dr. King arose throughout the country with spontaneous demonstrations being held in about 80 cities. Later, Dr. King, determined and undaunted, began to organize another march on Alabama's state capitol with hundreds more protestors than he had when he made his first attempt. In the meantime, attorneys for the SCLC petitioned the court to stop Gov. Wallace from interfering with their demonstration. The petition was heard by US District Court Judge Frank Johnson Jr.

Additionally, President Johnson, who was very adept at staying ahead of the winds of political change, sent a legislative proposal to Congress to end black voter disenfranchisement and strike down all barriers to the ballot box in the South. On March 15, 1965, President Johnson addressed Congress urging them to take swift action to enact the legislation.

"What happened in Selma is part of a far larger movement which reaches into every section and State of America. It is the effort of American Negroes to secure for themselves the full blessings of American life. Their cause must be our cause too. Because it is not just Negroes, but really it is all of us, who must overcome the crippling legacy of bigotry and injustice. And we shall overcome," Johnson said.[105]

President Johnson received bipartisan praise for the proposal; however, many of his Democrat colleagues felt deeply betrayed.

"The President sold out to the Negroes 100 percent!" said Democratic Congressman George Andrews from Alabama.[106]

"I do not agree with the President. There is no constitutional issue involved," said Democratic Senator John L. McClellan from Arkansas.[107]

---

[105] h t t p s : / / w w w . b r i t a n n i c a . c o m / e v e n t / S e l m a - M a r c h / We-Shall-Overcome-LBJ-and-the-1965-Voting-Rights-Act
[106] The Post-Crescent, March 16, 1965, P. 1
[107] The Post-Crescent, March 16, 1965, P. 1

"*I shall filibuster against it,*" said Democratic Senator Allen J. Ellender from Louisiana.[108]

In mid-March of 1965, Judge Johnson ruled in favor of the protestors. In his decision the judge wrote: "*The law is clear that the right to petition one's government for the redress of grievances may be exercised in large groups…and these rights may be exercised by marching, even along public highways.*"[109]

Gov. Wallace began to buckle under the weight of public pressure and the court. Just before Dr. King made his next attempt to march into Montgomery, Gov. Wallace contacted President Johnson and told him he was willing to send the Alabama National Guard to protect the protestors. In the minds of many, it was a very confusing offer. Was Gov. Wallace going to send the National Guard to protect the marchers from his own state troopers?

As he addressed the Alabama State Assembly, the embattled governor announced that Alabama could not afford to provide protection for the protestors and any protection would have to be provided by the federal government.

Wallace's stubbornness forced President Johnson to take a page from Eisenhower's playbook. And days before the march, President Johnson federalized the Alabama National Guard and deployed about 2,000 soldiers from the US Army to protect over 25, 000 protestors. And just as the nine black children were escorted into Little Rock Central High School by armed soldiers, in 1957, thousands of protestors were given a military escort into Montgomery, Alabama

Protestors Arrive Triumphant in Montgomery

Governor Wallace's location was unknown on the day Dr. King, his supporters, and thousands of armed soldiers from the US military and Alabama's National Guard marched into the state capitol. It's very likely that he left town.

---

[108] The Post-Crescent, March 16, 1965, P. 1

[109] https://www.britannica.com/event/Selma-March/We-Shall-Overcome-LBJ-and-the-1965-Voting-Rights-Act

The protestors held a rally on the steps of the state capitol building and demanded the governor to honor the Fifteenth Amendment right of blacks to vote. On that day, March 25, 1965, Dr. King stood on the steps the Alabama State Capitol building and delivered the following speech:

"Our whole campaign in Alabama has been centered around the right to vote. In focusing the attention of the nation and the world today on the flagrant denial of the right to vote… Let us therefore continue our triumphant march to the realization of the American dream. Let us march on ballot boxes, march on ballot boxes until race-baiters disappear from the political arena. Let us march on ballot boxes until the salient misdeeds of bloodthirsty mobs will be transformed into the calculated good deeds of orderly citizens. Let us march on ballot boxes until the Wallace's of our nation tremble away in silence.

Dr. King speaks on the steps of the Alabama State Capitol building.

"Let us march on ballot boxes until we send to our city councils, state legislatures, and the United States Congress men who will not fear to do justly, love mercy, and walk humbly with thy God. Let us march on ballot boxes until brotherhood becomes more than a meaningless word in an opening prayer, but the order of the day on every legislative agenda.

"Let us march on ballot boxes until all over Alabama God's children will be able to walk the earth in decency and honor.

"I know you are asking today, 'How long will it take? When will wounded justice, lying prostrate on the streets of Selma and Birmingham and communities all over the South, be lifted from this dust of shame to reign supreme among the children of men? How long?' Not long, because no lie can live forever. How long? Not long."

Once again, Dr. King galvanized the entire nation to support his cause. He inspired, aroused, and invigorated millions of Americans to act and to stand in favor of the destruction of the walls and barriers placed between Southern blacks and the ballot box.

Dr. King was correct in that it did not take long to destroy the obstacles that prevented blacks from voting. On May 26, 1965, the US Senate passed the Voting Rights Act of 1965 with a vote of 77 to 19. The bill passed the House 333 to 85 on July 9, and President Johnson signed the bill into law on August 6, 1965.

Chapter 12: 1965–1968
Johnson Takes a Page from Roosevelt to Retain the South for Democrats

The political landscape in the South had drastically changed. Blacks now had the power to send elected officials to represent their best interests in city councils, school boards, county governments, state legislatures, the US Congress, as well as the White House. They also had the power to elect judges who would be fair in the court rooms. And because more blacks were registered voters, they had the power to run for political office.

President Johnson announces his "war on poverty."

For the Democratic Party, this was a living nightmare. They did not believe for one moment that the new bloc of black voters would ever support them given their history of segregation, lynching, and the brutal oppression of blacks during the last 10 decades. Many Southern Democrats believed, and rightly so, that Southern blacks would avenge themselves at the ballot box and join with white Southerners to vote Republicans. They believed that black and white Republicans would once again become allies and permanently remove Democrats from public office.

It had happened during the late 19th century, and they believed it was going to happen again.

President Johnson had the same concern. For months he heard constant criticism from fellow Democrats about how he had betrayed the South and virtually handed the entire region over to the blacks and the Republican Party.

But Johnson had a plan to mitigate the damage, if not strengthen the Democrats' hold on the South. Johnson saw a possible outcome that other Democrats failed to see because of their fear and anger.

Johnson was a good student of political history and he was aware of how blacks strongly supported Republicans after the passage of the Fifteenth Amendment. But he was also very familiar with how a segregationist Democratic President, Franklin D. Roosevelt, won the black vote during the Depression.

Thanks to the New Deal, President Roosevelt received an overwhelming majority of the black vote in 1936. It was the greatest black support for a Democrat since the passage of the Fifteenth Amendment. One source says that Roosevelt received as much as 71 percent of the black vote during the presidential election.[110]

Johnson planned to do the same thing: to provide black Americans ongoing and consistent government support so that blacks would support him and the Democratic Party for the foreseeable future.

On January 8, 1964, President Johnson introduced his "war on poverty" during the State of the Union address.

"This administration today here and now declares unconditional war on poverty in America. I urge this Congress and all Americans to join me in that effort. Poverty is a national problem, requiring improved national organization and support. But this attack, to be effective, must also be organized at the state and local levels. For the war against poverty will not be won here in Washington. It must be won in the field, in every private home, in every public office, from the courthouse to the White House. Very often, a lack of jobs and money is not the cause of poverty,

---

[110] https://www.factcheck.org/2008/04/blacks-and-the-democratic-party/

but the symptom. Our aim is not only to relieve the symptoms of poverty but to cure it—and above all, to prevent it."[111]

The war on poverty included the passage of the Economic Opportunity Act and established the Office of Economic Opportunity (OEO). The OEO's mission was to (a) expand the economic safety net for the poor and unemployed, (b) provide financial assistance and for the health needs of the nation's working poor and elderly, (c) expand educational opportunities, and (d) create new methods to eliminate poverty in America's cities.

What President Roosevelt started in 1936, President Johnson partially completed in 1964. And despite the Democrats' history of KKK attacks, lynching, oppressive Jim Crow laws, and complete control over every aspect of the lives of Southern blacks, Johnson's plan to lavish black Americans with government largess worked very well. And since 1964, the Democratic Party has enjoyed monolithic political support from black America.

In fact, President Johnson was famously quoted by biographer and historian Doris Kearns Goodwin as saying, "*I'll have those niggers voting Democrat for the next 200 years.*"

President Johnson's so-called war on poverty drew most black Americans into the Democrat camp, but no one knew how strong the hold would be. There was no way to know, at that time, how influential the party would be, especially when considering the Democrats' history of oppression of blacks.

It was at this time that the world witnessed an unfortunate repeat of tragic history.

Civil Rights Leaders Betray Blacks

The West African Slave Trade began in the 16th century when Western European countries authorized their fleets to go into countries along Africa's western coast to bring slaves to the Spanish colonies in Central and South America.

---

[111] State of the Union Address on January 8, 1964

When kidnapping raids became too dangerous for the Europeans, the slave traders established forts and trading stations along Africa's west coast. It was at these trading posts where African tribal leaders met with slave traders to negotiate the sale of captured prisoners after tribal wars.

Tribal wars were frequent in Africa and the slave traders realized that they could serve their own interests by working with the leadership on both sides of the wars. The tribal leaders delivered their prisoners to the white slave traders and the African leaders became very wealthy. The traders, meanwhile, had more than enough slaves to fill their ships without any risk to themselves.

Bayard Rustin, Civil Rights Leader and Socialist

The American Communist Movement during the 1930s planted a lot of ideological seeds in America, but especially in the black community. It also had a lot of financial support from Joseph Stalin and Communist International.

But the American Communists of the late 1960's did not need foreign support anymore. Their ideology sank deep into American minds, took root, sprang up, and began to flourish and thrive under their own power. And like the tribal leaders who sold their captured prisoners to white slavers, the Socialists and Communists, within the civil rights movement, saw an opportunity to advance their true agenda and they exploited it.

One of the first to see it was Bayard Rustin. Bayard Rustin was a well-known civil rights protestor who worked closely with Dr. King and the NAACP.

Rustin was very well respected and strongly urged NAACP as well as black America to support the Democratic Party's social agenda. He also argued that every organization that was involved in the March on Washington, DC, should now support the Democrats.

FBI director J. Edgar Hoover always suspected that the civil rights movement was infiltrated by Communists and Socialists, who were using the plight of black America to destroy the United States. The FBI strongly believed that American Communists were placed within the movement either by the Kremlin or by Fidel Castro of Cuba. From time to time, the FBI listened to phone conversations of many civil rights leaders, including Dr. King, to expose the Communists among them.

The question of Communist involvement in the civil rights movement followed Dr. King throughout the late 1950's and the 1960's. From time to time members of the media asked him if there were any Communists in the Montgomery Improvement Association, the NAACP, the SCLC, or any civil rights organization. During a speech in Jackson, Mississippi, in 1963, Dr. King responded to their questions once again and he famously said, "*There are as many Communists in this freedom movement as there are Eskimos in Florida.*"

Dr. King always denied Communist involvement in the civil rights movement when asked by the media. But the ugly truth is this: Looking back at that era with the benefit of books and articles published by the civil rights leaders themselves, there were Communists and Socialists working with them.

Their objective—at the least the goal of the Socialists among them—was to transform the relationship between America's government and the American people. They wanted the federal government, with its immense network of bureaucracy, regulators, and department heads, to take control of America's economy, its wealth, and redistribute it as the government saw fit.

The Communists, however, had something else in mind—they wanted to overthrow the American government through violence first and then redistribute the wealth. The Communists and Socialists completely blended in with the civil rights movement to make their true cause virtually indistinguishable from the civil rights movement.

There were clear distinctions between Communists and Socialists in Dr. King's mind. Dr. King, who spent the Christmas of 1949 reading the works of Karl Marx, *The Communist Manifesto* and *Das Kapital*, makes those distinctions clear in his autobiography.

"I reject the Communist materialistic interpretation of history. Communism, avowedly secularistic and materialistic, has no place for God. This I could never accept, for as a Christian I believe that there is a creative personal power in this universe who is the ground and the essence of all reality—a power that cannot be explained in materialistic terms. I disagree with Communism's ethical relativism. There is no absolute moral order, no immutable principles and consequently, almost anything—force, violence, murder, lying—is justifiable. And I oppose Communism's political totalitarianism. In Communism the individual ends up in subject to the state and man becomes hardly more than a depersonalized cog in the turning wheel of the state."[112]

Any educated Christian, random preacher, or minister would reject Communism for the same reasons cited by Dr. King. It's a form of government that forces God, church, and morality out of the lives of the people, strips them of their humanity, and robs them of what little personal assets they have. But as strong as his feelings were against Communism, Dr. King expressed a clear affinity for Socialism. *"From my early teen years, I was deeply concerned about the gulf between superfluous wealth and abject poverty, and my reading of Marx made me ever more conscious of this gulf. And although modern American capitalism had greatly reduced the gap through social reforms, there was still a need for a better distribution of wealth,"* Dr. King wrote.[113]

It was the Stock Market Crash of 1929 followed by the Great Depression of the 1930's that shaped Dr. King's beliefs about Capitalism and Socialism. As a young man he saw for himself the shelves in grocery stores, in Atlanta, Georgia, that once held food and provisions for his community completely barren. He saw his friends and neighbors evicted and living in the streets. And he saw the long breadlines, the desperation, the starvation, the complete humiliation

---

[112] Dr. Martin Luther King Jr, Edited by Clayborne Carson, The Autobiography of Martin Luther King, Jr., New York, Boston, Intellectual Properties Management, Inc. in association with Grand Central Publishing, 1998, P. 20

[113] Dr. Martin Luther King Jr, Edited by Clayborne Carson, The Autobiography of Martin Luther King, Jr., New York, Boston, Intellectual Properties Management, Inc. in association with Grand Central Publishing, 1998, P. 21

and indignities suffered by the poor. And King, like many in the black community during the Depression, was taught that the poor was suffering because of the actions of the rich.

And like most black families during that time, King's family depended upon Roosevelt's New Deal Program for food. And it was the socialistic New Deal Program that provided relief and offered assurances in the future for poor blacks during desperate times.

Bayard Rustin discusses the movement with Dr. King.

"Capitalism is always in danger of inspiring men to be more concerned about making a living than making a life. We are prone to judge success by the index of our salaries or the size of our automobiles, rather than by the quality of our service and relationship to humanity. Thus, capitalism can lead to a practical materialism that is as pernicious as the materialism taught by Communism."[114]

Like many blacks introduced to Communism during the 1930's, the concept of Socialism appealed to Dr. King. No one will ever know if members of the media ever asked Dr. King if there were any Socialists within the civil rights movement. If they had, we could speculate how Dr. King would have answered them. But regardless, Socialism was the common ground upon which he stood alongside Baynard Rustin.

But Rustin was also a Communist. He was also gay and an outspoken chairman of the A. Philip Randolph Institute. Rustin also served as Dr. King's secretary and was very active in Socialist and Communist organizations such as the Young Communist League and Social Democrats, USA. He was a member of the Congress of

[114] Dr. Martin Luther King Jr, Edited by Clayborne Carson, The Autobiography of Martin Luther King, Jr., New York, Boston, Intellectual Properties Management, Inc. in association with Grand Central Publishing, 1998, P. 21

Racial Equality, the Southern Christian Leadership Conference, and the War Resisters League.

Rustin was also a prolific writer and great communicator. Dr. King consulted with him often and Rustin played a vital role in organizing the March on Washington, DC. He was a very important part of Dr. King's inner circle.

During the 1950's and 1960's, America had even less tolerance for gays than it did for minorities. So, the fact that Rustin was gay made him a liability for the civil rights movement, so he stayed in the background. And the fact that he was a Communist made him an even greater liability because J. Edgar Hoover and the FBI were watching him and anyone else they suspected was working for the Communist Party.

In February of 1965, Rustin wrote the article "*From Protest to Politics: The Future of the Civil Rights Movement*"[115] in which he claimed the only way for blacks to enjoy life in America was to transform its economy from being driven by the private sector to being governed by the public sector.

"*I believe that the Negro's struggle for equality in America is essentially revolutionary,*" Rustin wrote. "*While most Negroes—in their hearts—unquestionably seek only to enjoy the fruits of American society as it now exists, their quest cannot objectively be satisfied within the framework of existing political and economic relations. The young Negro who would demonstrate his way into the labor market may be motivated by a thoroughly bourgeois ambition and thoroughly 'capitalist' considerations, but he will end up having to favor a great expansion of the public sector of the economy. At any rate, that is the position the movement will be forced to take as it looks at the number of jobs being generated by the private economy, and if it is to remain true to the masses of Negroes.*"

Rustin also said that the only way blacks could achieve the America dream and equality with whites was through massive government intervention in every important aspect of life.

---

[115] https://www.commentarymagazine.com/articles/
from-protest-to-politics-the-future-of-the-civil-rights-movement/

"Let me sum up what I have thus far been trying to say: the civil rights movement is evolving from a protest movement into a full-fledged social movement—an evolution calling its very name into question. It is now concerned not merely with removing the barriers to full opportunity but with achieving the fact of equality," Rustin wrote. *"I fail to see how the movement can be victorious in the absence of radical programs for full employment, abolition of slums, the reconstruction of our educational system and new definitions of work and leisure."*[116]

Johnson Makes a Faustian Deal to Retain the South

President Johnson discusses the "war on poverty" with R. Sargent Shriver.

Rustin's influence reached into every corner of the civil rights movement. The NAACP and other organizations took his recommendations to heart and began considering giving their full support to the Democratic Party. Rustin continued to publish articles, traveled, and spoke at meetings, urging blacks to support the Democratic Party and Johnson's so-called war on poverty.

President Johnson appointed R. Sargent Shriver as director of the Office of Economic Opportunity and Shriver hired Michael Harrington as a consultant. Harrington was also a close friend of Rustin's.

Harrington, another Socialist, authored the books, *The Other America* and *Voluntary Socialism.* Harrington was also the chairman of the League for Industrial Democracy, which was dedicated to the abolition of capitalism.[117] He was also the chairman of the Democratic Socialist of America from 1982 until 1989. Furthermore, his writ-

---

[116] https://www.commentarymagazine.com/articles/
from-protest-to-politics-the-future-of-the-civil-rights-movement/

[117] Alan Stang, It's Very Simple: The True Story of Civil Rights. United States, The Western Islands, Belmont, Ma., January 1, 1965, P. 165.

ings also often appeared in socialist publications such as *The Worker*, which was the leading socialist newspaper in the country at the time.

Harrington advised Shriver on how to spend billions of dollars in federal money. Shortly after Harrington began his work, Rustin contacted him and requested a grant for the Leadership Training Institute for Civil Rights Activists, which was created by Rustin himself.

In his letter to Harrington, Rustin said that the funds would be used to create jobs not only for young blacks but poor whites, thereby helping to fulfill the mission of the president's war on poverty.

Rustin's request was approved, and his organization received hundreds of thousands of dollars to create jobs for blacks and poor whites throughout the years.

And flood gates of federal money opened wide. It was not long before the NAACP and many other civil rights organizations followed Rustin's lead and cashed in at the expense of the black community. For example, on November 6, 1964, NAACP executive director Roy Wilkins made a stunning announcement. Wilkins announced that the NAACP would no longer focus on racial equality but from this point forward only focus its energy on fighting poverty in America.[118]

Michael Harrington, Johnson Administration Official and Socialist

To this day, the NAACP continues to receive the greatest amount of its funding, 59 percent, from the federal government in the form of grants.[119]

Other organizations did the same thing. Immediately after the NAACP began taking federal funds, William Strickland, the execu-

---

[118] Alan Stang, It's Very Simple: The True Story of Civil Rights. United States, The Western Islands, Belmont, Ma., January 1, 1965, P. 166.

[119] https://www.influencewatch.org/non-profit/naacp/

tive director of the Northern Student Movement, which was a branch of the Student Nonviolent Coordinating Committee, announced the organization was abandoning the fight for desegregation to join in the fight against poverty.

"Integration in no longer the issue," he said. *"The issue is poverty,"* Strickland said.[120]

The list of organizations receiving federal grants continued to grow until they were joined by a new organization, Operation Breadbasket. The goal of Operation Breadbasket was the same as the others, to fight poverty in urban areas with the use of federal funds. The organization was founded by Dr. Martin L. King Jr. in 1966. Dr. King appointed the Reverend Jesse L. Jackson Sr. to serve as the organization's first director in Chicago, Illinois.

When Dr. King joined the procession of civil rights leaders lined up for federal grants, President Johnson knew he had succeeded in winning support from the leadership of black community for the Democrats. And Johnson hoped that like the 16th-century tribal leaders led their prisoners into the hands of the slave traders, the civil rights leaders would persuade black Americans to support the Democrat Party.

After he established Operation Breadbasket and eight months before his assassination, there were clear signs that Dr. Martin Luther King Jr. was having a change of heart about Socialism. He spoke against the philosophy as he delivered a speech to the Southern Christian Leadership Conference, in Atlanta, Georgia, on August 16, 1967.

Throughout the speech, Dr. King promoted the principles of hard work, education, and determination. He encouraged all blacks not to depend of the government for their success and happiness, but to rely individually on God and their own inner strength.

"As long as the mind is enslaved, the body can never be free. And no Lincolnian Emancipation Proclamation can do this for us. No civil rights bill can bring us this kind of freedom. The Negro must reach into

---

[120] Alan Stang; It's Very Simple: The True Story of Civil Rights. United States, The Western Islands, Belmont, Ma., January 1, 1965, P. 166.

the depths of his soul and write with the pen and ink of assertive manhood his own Emancipation Proclamation," King said.

Jesse Jackson Sr., Director of
Operation Breadbasket in Chicago

But the die was cast and there was no turning back as each organization succumbed to personal ambition and the misguided thinking of their leadership. And each organization eventually bowed at the feet of President Johnson and the Democratic Party.

President Johnson's war on poverty secured the support from civil rights leaders for Democrats. But what about the rest of black America? At that time, black Americans still knew who their enemies were. They remembered that it was the Democrats who had denied them a good education, lynched them, falsely accused black men and sent them to prison—and it was the Democrats who refused to allow them to vote.

Throughout the mid to late 1960s, civil rights leaders embraced the Socialist philosophy of Bayard Rustin. They urged black voters nationwide to support the Democratic Party. They said that blacks had to forget about the Democrats' racism of the past. They lectured and argued that the Democratic Party understood that black Americans could not rise from poverty with only education, hard work, and determination—they needed all the help they could get from the federal government.

Communists and Socialists Gain Political Influence

Rustin was not alone in his effort to persuade black voters to fully support the Democrats. He was joined by individuals such as Reverend Fred Shuttlesworth, the vice president of Dr. King's

Southern Christian Leadership Conference. Shuttlesworth later became president of the Southern Conference of Human Welfare.[121]

Carl and Anne Braden were also among those who persuaded

many blacks to support the Democrats. Carl Braden was the national sponsor of the Fair Play for Cuba Committee, a Communist organization. Ann Braden, a radical Communist, was also the editor of the *Southern Patriot*,

Communists Carl and Anne Braden in Kentucky.

which was published by the Southern Conference of Human Welfare.

In several articles, Ann Braden advocated for the violent overthrow of the Kentucky state government during the mid-1960s.[122]

The process took some time. But within a decade, with persistence and considerable help from the media, the Socialist wing of the civil rights movement persuaded black Americans to support and defend their own oppressors—the Democratic Party. Black Americans were led to believe that supporting Democrats would lead to the elimination of poverty as well as equality for all.

Whether or not it was Johnson's intention, the programs he created as political tools to leverage black votes for the Democratic Party were being used as a platform to promote Socialism.

There is no doubt that Johnson was fully aware of the communist infiltration of the civil rights movement. But he was not as concerned about it like J. Edgar Hoover. And although most government officials did not believe there was any difference between Socialists and Communists, Johnson made a very clear distinction just as Dr. King did. Communism was a threat to America, and

---

[121] Alan Stang, It's Very Simple: The True Story of Civil Rights. United States, The Western Islands, Belmont, Ma., January 1, 1965, P. 115.

[122] Alan Stang, It's Very Simple: The True Story of Civil Rights. United States, The Western Islands, Belmont, Ma. January 1, 1965, P. 114

Communists were enemies who had to be defeated. Johnson's expansion of America's role in Vietnam proved that.

But Johnson's actions clearly demonstrated that he did not view Socialism as a threat to America—and neither did Roosevelt for that matter.

The Democratic Party during that time believed the same thing. Johnson and the Democrats viewed Socialists as useful tools to help secure political power for themselves—nothing more.

They also believed the Socialists could help remake the Democrats' public image, from being the party of racism, segregation, and Jim Crow to becoming the party of equality and justice for all. And for those reasons, President Johnson pulled out a chair to give Socialists a seat at the table of American politics within the Democrat Party. Individuals such as R. Sargent Shriver, Michael Harrington, and Baynard Rustin were no longer on the outside looking in. Other Democrat leaders throughout the country followed Johnson's lead and did the same thing. And now, the Socialists had access to resources and infrastructure, such as local volunteers and meeting places, and fundraising capabilities, that they've never had before.

As the Democrats and Socialists advanced their war on poverty, they pronounced themselves to be champions of minorities and the poor. And as the Democrats worked in American's urban areas, they publicly embraced the Socialists as friends and allies.

But that would backfire on the Democrats in a very big way!

President Johnson greatly miscalculated. What he did not realize at the time, what no one realized, was that the America's political landscape was still changing. America was at the beginning stages of a political realignment the outcome of which no one would see for about a decade.

In that picture, whites in Southern states abandoned the Democratic Party and began to vote Republican. But why? Why the change?

Since 1876, the eleven Southern states were known as "the Solid South." The South earned that nickname because the people within that region stubbornly voted for Democrats for every public office from President of the United States to the local dog catcher. The Democrats held a firm grip on every political position and all the economy. And the Republicans had little to no hope of breaking the Democrats' hold.

The Democrats hoped that an alliance with the Socialists would help them continue to hold onto their political power. And their alliance still exists to this day.

Most Americans agreed that Communism was a clear threat to America. And although the Democrat leadership made a distinction between Communists and Socialists, most of the American people did not—especially the people of the South.

Chapter 13: 1965–1968

Socialist Revolutionaries Try to Overthrow America

To fully understand America's political realignment and the decisions made by black America in modern times, we not only have to study their path since the Reconstruction era, we must closely study the events of the 1960s.

The 1960s were a pivotal time in black political history. It was a point when black Americans, after decades of traveling a road of hardship and struggle for civil rights, truly arrived at a fork in that road that led to two different destinations.

The Communist Party is revived during the 1960s with support from many in the black community.

One path led to true freedom and equality. They were equipped with equality in education, equality in the law, and the right to vote. The black community had everything they fought for and everything they needed to forge a better future for themselves and their children.

The other path led them back into bondage. Unfortunately, most blacks in America did not consider who their allies were—and perhaps they didn't care. They did not consider the fact that the civil rights leadership had joined with Socialists and Communists. Perhaps it didn't matter to them because they believed the most immediate threat to their future was America's tolerance of Jim Crow laws and racial discrimination.

Or maybe some blacks believed that they were only using the Communists and Socialists to get what they wanted. Unlike the moderate Republicans in Congress during the first half of the 20th century, the Communists and Socialists did not care about the unpopularity of the civil rights issue. They forged ahead regardless of how uncomfortable the issue made white Americans feel. They also had energy, enthusiasm and financing. And black Americans needed an ally with all these things and more because they weren't getting it from moderate Republicans. So, perhaps some blacks believed that once they achieved their goals, they would abandon the Communists.

We can speculate forever about what most blacks were thinking during that time. If we believe the statements made by individuals such as Muhammad Ali and Dr. King, we can conclude that blacks only cared about issues close to home such as racial injustice within their own country. They cared nothing about Communist encroachment.

Aside from showing little concern about the Communist threat, most people can agree that blacks were never educated about Communism and Socialism or why Capitalists and Socialists are locked in an ongoing global battle—a conflict that still exists today.

Communism is the most destructive form of government in the history of the world. And Socialism, essentially, is the first step into Communism. Like holding fire to the corner of a sheet of paper, the very nature of Communism is to spread itself and destroy everything it touches. And if it is not resisted and fought, it will continue to destroy nation after nation.

Since the early 20th century, black Americans have rightly engaged in their own battle for civil rights. Unfortunately, the civil rights struggle completely distracted and blinded them to the global struggle against Communism. It was this lack of education coupled with the experience of American segregation and racial discrimination that made blacks the perfect, unwitting, political pawns of Socialists in a high-stakes geopolitical game.

Let us stop any further speculation and talk about what we do know. We know, from studying history and the civil rights movement, that the leadership of the civil rights movement played an important role in leading blacks back into the control of their oppressors—the Democratic Party.

Why? Because the Socialists among them wanted to support the Democrats' socialist agenda.

The Socialists cared much more about their political agenda than the future of blacks in America. They did not care about the Democrats' historic oppression of blacks. Otherwise, they would have urged black voters to stay away from the Democrats.

Blacks were led back to the Democrats during an era in which American Communists and Socialists, unlike any other time in history, made their presence known to all Americans.

The 1960s were one of the most turbulent and violent periods in America. The entire decade was characterized by riots, bombings, protests, assassinations, and shouts of political, social, and cultural revolution on almost every college campus. America saw a resurgence of rebellion that made the Communist movement of the 1930s look very tame by comparison.

Between 1964 and 1971, there were about 750 riots in urban areas. Approximately 228 people were killed with 12,741 people injured, and there were over 15,000 separate incidents of arson.[123]

Day after day, year after year, Americans heard about more senseless and unjustifiable violence in their streets and colleges for the sake of "the revolution." Police officers were ambushed and killed across America as well judges and various state and local government officials. The most notable assassinations were President John F. Kennedy, Dr. Martin Luther King Jr., and presidential candidate Robert Kennedy.

During the early to mid-1960s, UC Berkley was ground zero for multiple protests, political activism, and countercultural events. The leaders of the UC Berkley movement were close associates of the Black Panthers during that time, and they seized control of campus buildings, completely disrupting classes and academic activity to advance their agenda.

---

[123] The Consequences of the 1960's Race Riots Come into View. NY Times, Dec. 30, 2004, By Virginia Postrel

On April 19, 1969, several black students armed with rifles and shotguns and some dressed in military uniforms seized Willard Straight Hall at Cornell University, holding their professors hostage. The "students" demanded that the school establish race-based education with racially pure teachers and professors.[124]

Black socialist revolutionaries conduct an armed takeover of Willard Straight Hall.

The nationwide chaos was committed openly by individuals who embraced Communism and wanted to overthrow the American government. The American people got a good look at the Communists on the nightly news and in their own streets. And the American people knew exactly what the Communists wanted to do.

American was, indeed, faced with a revolution from within. Individuals from multiple organizations wanted to change its politics, the economic system, the country's traditions, its culture, and everything that made America distinct from the rest of the world.

All the Socialist revolutionaries agreed that they wanted America to change, but they could not agree on how to achieve this goal. They often clashed with each other, stumbled over one another, and competed for additional support.

There were basically two types of revolutionaries during this era, the radical Communists and the Socialists. The radical Communists, such as the Black Panthers, the Students for a Democratic Society, the Congress of Racial Equality, the Vietnam Day Committee (which openly discussed the assassination of politicians), SLATE, a student activist organization at UC Berkley, and the Weather Underground all wanted to overthrow the American government quickly with war in the streets and bombings.

---

[124] Jonah Goldberg, Liberal Fascism: The Secret History of the American Left from Mussolini to the Politics of Meaning, the United States, Doubleday, 2007, P. 163

These were people who believed they could achieve their objectives the same way Vladimir Lenin and the Bolsheviks overthrew the Russian czars and established Communist Russia.

The Socialists, however, wanted to change America slowly and gradually from positions of power from within the country. They believed they could infiltrate and take control of America's educational institutions, every level of government, every form of entertainment, and the media.

They wanted to teach Socialism at every school while undermining America's capitalistic system at the same time. Furthermore, they wanted to use Hollywood and the national media to create positive views of life under Socialism, and, through legislation and policy decisions, give American's small doses of Socialism until they became hooked on it so that future generations of Americans would demand a Socialist form of government.

During a speech and at the height of the Cold War, in 1961, Russian leader Nikita Khrushchev openly and brazenly declared his strategy and how the United States would eventually fall to socialism.

"We can't expect the American people to jump from capitalism to communism. But we can assist their elected leaders in giving them small doses of socialism until one day they will awaken to find they have communism."

"Give them small doses of socialism...."—Nikita Khrushchev

Many like-minded individuals throughout America's colleges and universities agreed with the Russian leader. From the prestigious Ivy League colleges in New England to Midwestern schools surrounding the Great Lakes to the sunny and fun-loving universities throughout California, America's colleges taught and promoted Socialism.

In 1966, two professors from Columbia University developed and promoted a strategy they strongly believed would equally distribute America's wealth. But the Marxist plan could only succeed after the destruction of America's capitalist economy.

Professors Richard Cloward and Frances Fox Piven wrote an article published in *The Nation* entitled *"The Weight of the Poor: A Strategy to End Poverty."* In it, the two professors advocated overwhelming and collapsing the federal government and the US economic system by forcing millions of people into the welfare system until the government could no longer sustain them.

Then the US government would collapse upon itself.

Cloward and Piven's plan was implemented in New York City during the early 1970s. With promises of meeting their families' every need and expressions of concern for their future, the Democrats and Socialists within the state and local governments encouraged blacks to sign up for every government welfare program available. But not because they cared about their future of the black community. They needed massive numbers of people to carry out their Socialist plan, and blacks, as always, were readily available.

New York city's welfare recipients skyrocketed to over a million people and New York was faced with bankruptcy.

The city's government could not pay for everyday services such as sanitation, transportation, and public safety. New York saved itself from collapse with help from the federal government and by making some very difficult budget choices.

Today, radical socialist professors still embrace and teach this philosophy with the belief that it is the path to economic equality for the masses. However, instead of encouraging blacks to sign up for welfare, they support placing innumerable illegal immigrants into America's welfare system.

Professor Richard Cloward

The Democrats Embrace Socialist Revolutionary Saul Alinsky

One of the most notable and influential individuals who embraced and taught the beliefs of the Socialist revolutionaries was Saul Alinsky.

Saul Alinsky was a Chicago-born political activist, socialist, and professional community organizer. Throughout the 1960s, Alinsky organized blacks in urban areas, college students, and union workers to protest various political issues in Chicago, New York, California, Michigan, and many other large cities throughout the country.

Alinsky, who graduated from the University of Chicago, also provided training for radical organizations and taught them how to use what he believed to be the most effective tactics to achieve their goals.

Saul Alinsky provides the guidelines for Democrat Socialists radicals.

Alinsky's tactics included mobilizing mass numbers of people and encouraging them to either intimidate their opponents into silence, bully them until they submitted to their demands, provoke them into physical altercations and fights, or shock the sensibilities of the general public with the most vulgar and indecent behavior imaginable.

Alinsky's methods are still being practiced by radicals in the 21st century. One of the most memorable incidents was during the fall of 2011, when members of the protest group Occupy Wall Street publicly defecated in Zuccotti Park in New York.[125]

There is no doubt that Alinsky had Khrushchev's comments in mind when he wrote his book *Rules for Radicals: A Pragmatic Primer*

---

[125] https://nypost.com/2011/10/10/sex-drugs-and-hiding-from-the-law-at-wall-street-protests/

for Realistic Radicals. Alinsky and his radical followers were getting nowhere with the use of radical and extreme methods. So Alinsky offered his book as a guide to help "realistic radicals" to slowly gain social, political, judicial, and economic power. After they gained this power, they could change America from within.

In a nutshell, Alinsky wrote that radicals must hide their true beliefs and intentions behind concepts that no reasonable person can argue against, such as equality and justice. But once the policy is established and their positions secure, the mask comes off and they reveal their true intentions.

The only good thing a reasonable person can say about Alinsky's book was that it helped calm the radical Communists. It helped them to realize that they would never achieve their goals with bombings, riots, and assassinations. It helped many of them to accept that the only way to reach their goal was through slow and progressive change, which mitigated their acts of violence.

Rules for Radicals was very popular reading in Democrat circles during the 1960s and 1970s. It was taught in colleges and studied in private groups. The information given by Saul Alinsky was not only embraced by Socialists and Communists but also wholly and completely adopted by the Democratic Party.

Alinsky's book became more than a model and guide to radical Socialists and Democrats—it became their doctrine, their creed and foundation. *Rules for Radicals* became the standard to which all Socialists and Democrats conformed and supported.

Alinsky himself was embraced as somewhat of a messianic figure who could do no wrong. Labor unions and other groups working for "economic and social change" sought his advice and counsel across the country.

The contents of Alinsky's book were never seriously challenged from within the Democratic Party and no one has ever offered to replace them. During a CBS television interview with John H. Bunzel, Alinsky shocked the American people when he candidly and unashamedly admitted that the source of his inspiration was the devil. Many within Democrat circles dismiss this fact, but Alinsky was serious. In fact, Alinsky dedicated his book to Lucifer.

"Lest we forget at least an over-the-shoulder acknowledgment to the very first radical: from all our legends, mythology, and history, the first radical known to man who rebelled against the establishment so effectively that he at least won his own kingdom—Lucifer."[126]

Alinsky continued to use "devilish" metaphors when he explained why he preferred to divide people along economic, social, and racial lines. He said the focus of his work is always to mobilize the "have-nots" against the "haves" because he believed the "have nots" were always, somehow, morally superior.

"If given a choice, I'd pick Hell because that's where the have-nots are," Alinsky said. *"Once I got into Hell, I'd start organizing, just like I do here. The have-nots are my kind of people."*

Apparently, Alinsky believed that the Devil was morally superior to God. And it is hard to believe that any serious-minded adult would embrace the thoughts and beliefs of an individual who gives honor to Satan and turns to him for inspiration as he tries to change America. But many honored Alinsky back then and Alinsky's model is still embraced by Democrats today.

Hillary Rodham Clinton studied and supports the Alinsky model.

One individual on whom Alinsky's book made a deep and lasting impression was former first lady and two-time Democratic Presidential candidate Hillary Rodham Clinton.

As a student at Wellesley College in Wellesley, Massachusetts, in 1969, Hillary Rodham wrote her 92-page senior thesis about Saul Alinsky: *"There's Only the Fight: An Analysis of the Alinsky Model.* In the document, Hillary Rodham expressed great sympathy and support of his efforts to change America.

---

[126] Saul Alinsky, Rules for Radicals: A Pragmatic Primer for Realistic Radicals. United States, Random House, 1971, P. 4

Another modern-era Democratic leader whom embraced Alinsky was former President Barak Obama. President Obama was a community organizer himself, just like Saul Alinsky. And during his career as an organizer, Obama taught the Alinsky model to other community organizers.

Johnson Knows Democrats Lost the South and Bows Out

During the months leading up to the 1968 presidential election, the American people continued to endure wave after wave of violence in their streets and on college campuses. Demonstrations against the Vietnam War were frequent, chaotic, and often ended in violence against police officers.

Emboldened by the clear and deepening divisions within America, radical Communists gathered publicly and spoke out against capitalism on many street corners as well as in colleges and universities.

The mounting tumult and anarchy, along with the growing dissatisfaction with the Vietnam War, became too much for President Johnson. On March 31, 1968, Johnson announced that he was not going to run for reelection for president of the United States.

President Johnson announces he will not run for reelection.

That day Johnson said, "*I do not believe that I should devote an hour or a day of my time to any persona, or partisan cause or to any duties other than the awesome duties of this office. Accordingly, I will not seek nor will I accept the nomination of my party for another term as president.*"

What a difference a decade can make! During the late 1950s, Johnson had done everything in his power as a US senator to position himself as a national leader. He created the illusion of being in favor of the Civil Rights Act of 1957 as he stripped the law of its enforcement provisions.

He deceived civil rights leaders and the general public to believe he was a true champion of civil rights.

And he helped to establish an alliance between Socialists and Democrats to help secure the black vote for the Democratic Party.

Clearly Johnson was committed to ambitious, partisan politics. But in March of 1968, he told the American people he would not devote any time to any partisan cause.

Could it be that after years of riots, demonstrations, and violence, Johnson realized he had made a huge mistake by joining the Democratic Party with the Socialists? Could it be that Johnson realized he never should have made a distinction between Socialists and Communists? Could it be that Johnson realized that providing a political home for Socialists also placed America on a divisive and destructive path?

Prior to the 1960s, American Socialists and Communists worked on the periphery and the extreme fringes of American politics. They did not have resources like Republicans or Democrats, and they were not nationally organized like the two major parties.

The 1960s changed everything for them after they merged with the Democrats. As time moved forward, the Socialists and Communists not only persuaded many Democrats to embrace their beliefs but also imposed their beliefs upon them.

President Johnson was always good at forecasting political change in America. When he saw that the South was changing and

Detroit erupts into five days of rioting leaving 43 people dead and over 450 people injured.

that America would no longer tolerate Jim Crow segregation and discrimination, he positioned himself ahead of the changing political tide.

It is likely that Johnson saw the tide changing again. But this time, there was nothing he could do. So, it is possible that Johnson decided to get out of politics before the next massive political wave hit the shoreline.

I think that the unpopularity of the Vietnam War was a big factor in Johnson's decision. But I also believe that Johnson was equally concerned about the chaos and anarchy breaking out across America. Johnson knew that it was not going to end anytime soon, and he knew that America would not tolerate any more Alinsky-style radicalism.

To help keep control over the black vote during the post-Jim Crow era, President Johnson led the Democratic Party to make a deal with the devil: radical Communists and Socialists. And at the same time, he gave radicals a strong foothold in America's government and American politics. He gave them resources and a foundation to build upon. And the Democrats, as well as the American people, would pay for it.

America blamed the Democrats for the surge of radical behavior in their streets and college campuses—and President Johnson saw it coming.

Socialists Inflict Chaos on the 1968 Democrat National Convention

The straw that broke the camel's back was very likely the tumult and chaos that engulfed the Democratic National Convention in Chicago during late August of 1968 at the International Amphitheatre.

The people of Chicago not only hosted thousands of Democratic delegates from across the country but thousands more radical Socialists, Communists, Vietnam demonstrators, and anti-poverty activists converged on the city.

They laid siege to the convention—and the entire city of Chicago.

The Democrats knew they were coming and prepared for them. The main doors leading into the building were made bulletproof, the convention hall was encircled by a steel fence with barbed wire carefully weaved along the top, and groups of well-armed police officers, security guards, and secret service agents were near every entrance and exit and walking the aisles of the meeting hall.[127]

Many of the demonstrators were not there to have their voices

Protestors attempt to storm the convention hall during the 1968 Democratic National Convention.

heard, but to provoke a confrontation with the Chicago Police and draw attention to themselves and their specific causes. Protestors stopped traffic, fought with police officers, and lashed out against capitalism by destroying private property and small businesses.

Mayor Richard Daley sent 12,000 police officers to respond to the riots. Shortly afterward, Daley requested more boots on the ground from the state and federal governments. Before it was over, an additional 5,000 national guardsmen and 7,500 federal troops fought and grappled with the demonstrators who had come from across the country.

Much of the violence was broadcast live on television, and the event became known as the Battle on Michigan Avenue. Fighting spilled over into the meeting hall itself. Throughout the gathering, delegates began to fight on the convention floor for unknown reasons. Several brawls erupted throughout the Amphitheatre and Chicago Police had to deal with violence inside as well as outside the convention hall.

The chaos and confusion was a bitter reminder of another Democratic event that ended in violence: the 1924 Democratic National Convention at Madison Square Garden in New York.

Most of the delegates of that convention were active members of the Ku Klux Klan who attended the convention wearing white

---

[127] https://www.smithsonianmag.com/history/1968-democratic-convention-931079/

hoods and robes. The Klan delegates attended in large numbers in support of William McAdoo for president of the United States. They also attended in support of their members on the Democratic Platform Committee.[128]

Democrats welcome the KKK to the National Democrat Convention at Madison Square Garden in 1924.

When the convention was over, about 5,000 Klan members gathered Elwood Park in Long Branch, New Jersey, to celebrate their victory during the convention. They wore their hoods and robes, made speeches, and burned crosses. But the Klan members did not like being observed by residents within the area. So, they attacked six people who were watching them and frightened the others away.[129]

The American people watched the events in Chicago in shock and stunned disbelief. For years they had witnessed extremist Communists and Socialist tear their country apart through rioting, assassinations, assassination attempts, and the Socialist indoctrination of their children on colleges campuses.

The people saw that the extremists wanted to establish another form of government that not only conflicted with their values but completely undermined the US Constitution. And they saw that this radicalism was coming from the Democratic Party!

Former Vice President Richard Nixon was the Republican nominee for president in 1968. Despite the chaos at the Democratic National Convention, the Democrats were able to nominate Vice President Hubert Humphrey. And joining them on the ballot was

---

[128] The New York Times, June 24, 1924, P.1
[129] The New York Times, July 6, 1924

former Alabama Democratic Governor George Wallace, who ran for president as an independent candidate.

Governor Wallace was a committed segregationist throughout his political career. He fought the civil rights movement in Alabama with all the resources at his disposal. He was nationally known for sending Alabama state troopers to attack Dr. King and other civil rights protestors on the Edmund Pettus Bridge in Alabama.

Wallace was furious at the Democratic Party for weakening itself on the racial segregation. So, he campaigned on defending segregation in the South. He also blamed President Johnson for the dramatic social changes that occurred during the 1960s. Wallace wanted the South to remain the way it was and he was willing to fight for it.

Wallace did not see Johnson's support of civil rights as part of a political calculation to save the South for the Democratic Party. He saw it as unconditional surrender.

But when it came to keeping the Southern white vote for the Democrats, Wallace's opinion did

Segregationist Gov. George Wallace runs for president in 1968.

not matter to a majority of Southerners and neither did his campaign. The people of the South also decided that they wanted nothing to do with Socialist and Communists extremists. The Southern voters, without question, rejected the politics of the extremists and—by extension—the Democratic Party.

Most of the American people throughout the rest of the country felt the same way. On election day, November 5, 1968, the American people elected Republican candidate Richard Nixon as president of the United States.

The Solid South Is Broken; States Turn Republican Red

Nixon won all Southern states except for Georgia, Alabama, Mississippi, Louisiana, Arkansas, and Texas, which were split between George Wallace and Hubert Humphrey.[130]

Within the next decade, those states drifted into the Republican column and remain supportive of Republican national candidates to this day.

All of Johnson's plotting and scheming, not only to ascend to the presidency but to retain the Solid South for Democrats, blew up in his face. To his credit, he had enough political foresight to see it coming. But it all came into focus, however, much too late for him.

He saw that America on whole favored civil rights for blacks, so he brought the bitter, reluctant Democrats onboard. But he had also feared a backlash from Southern black voters, which caused him to seek an alliance with extremist Socialists to secure black votes for the Democratic Party.

Richard Nixon wins the South to become president in 1968.

Johnson had no idea that their extremism would chase white Southern voters away from the Democrats into the waiting arms of the Republicans. In this regard, Johnson's foresight failed him.

But the change may have happened anyway because, as Dr. King pointed out during the Kennedy Administration, Southern whites were demonstrating a change of heart about racial discrimination. The radicalism embraced by the Democrats possibly served only to speed up the process of Southern white voters leaving the Democrats.

Johnson was right about one thing. His adoption of Socialist policies along with help from Socialist extremists within the civil rights movement firmly secured the black vote for the Democrats.

---

[130] https://www.270towin.com/1968_Election

During the 1968 election, Hubert Humphry received 85 percent of the black vote.[131]

Despite the Democrat's horrific history of tyranny, domination, and oppression of blacks, Johnson secured support from them overwhelmingly for decades to come. That support, however, came at the expense of the Southern white vote in all Southern states.

Moreover, the outrageous conduct of the extremists did not matter to black Americans. Blacks never questioned why the Democrats promoted the teachings of Saul Alinsky, a man who publicly honored the devil.

The chaos that consumed the 1968 Democrat Convention did not matter to blacks and neither did the radicals' continual advocation of the overthrow of the US government. Additionally, the Democrats never apologized to black America for hundreds of years of oppression, yet blacks embraced them as their champions.

Today, the extremist rhetoric from American Socialists and Communists still does not matter to black Americans. Mainly because today, just as during the 1960's black voters are completely uninformed and were never educated about the dangers of Socialism and Communist encroachment.

---

[131] https://blackdemographics.com/culture/black-politics

Chapter 14: 1970–1982
Socialist Democrats Use Communist Tactics to Secure Black Support Indefinitely

By the 1970s, the black vote was firmly in the hands of the Democratic Party. Throughout the country and at every level of government for every political office, blacks directed their collective political strength toward the Democrat candidates.

But how long would it last? Of course, President Johnson was quoted boasting that he would *have those niggers voting Democrat for 200 years.*

With the memory of Democrat oppression still fresh in their minds, it was not hard for anyone to envision at least a split in the black vote between the Republicans and the Democrats.

It was not hard to imagine black families talking with their children in their homes about the hardships they suffered at the hands of the Democrats. It was not hard to imagine black families gathered in their living rooms or at dinner tables sharing

"I'll have those niggers voting Democrat for 200 years."—Lyndon Johnson

stories about the days when Democrat lynch mobs were sent against them.

It was not hard to image black fathers and grandfathers talking about the days when the Southern justice system arbitrarily arrested black men, produced false witnesses in court, and filled their prisons with blacks for the purposes of free labor. And it was not hard to imagine these black men talking about the days when they had to keep their heads down in public for fear they may be accused of looking at a white woman and becoming the next Emmitt Till.

And it was not hard to image black mothers and grandmothers sharing stories with their daughters about the days when they did not dare resist the sexual advances of white men for the sake of feeding their families.

The memory of these atrocities fresh in the minds of black Americans was cause for concern for the Democrats and Socialist extremists. Future generations of blacks could no doubt decide to oppose Democrat candidates for these reasons. No one was certain if the newly established social programs were strong enough to hold onto black support.

But one thing was certain: After centuries of controlling blacks in America, the Democrats were not going to let them go now. They had to find a way to control them that was more socially acceptable.

For the sake of their agenda and its future, these conversations within the homes of black Americans had to change. The Democrats' Socialist allies knew exactly what to do because their historic leadership in Russia had the same problem.

And the Communists dealt with it successfully.

One of over 1,300 statues that honored Vladimir Lenin in the Soviet Union during the 1970s.

Throughout the 20th century, Communism caused unparalleled human suffering around the world. About 70 million Chinese were killed in China by their Communist government, about 20 million people in Russia, five million in the Ukraine, and millions in Cambodia.

They also enslaved millions of people throughout the African continent, Central Asia, Vietnam, and North Korea.

Between 1917 and 1924, Vladimir Lenin, the recognized father of Communism, killed millions of Russians with the starvation and famine created by his government. In many cases, Lenin did not wait for the people to starve—he simply executed them.

But by the early 1970s there were over 1,300 statues of Lenin placed throughout the Soviet Union in honor of his "legacy." There were also numerous buildings, streets, and squares named after him.

Despite Lenin's bloody and murderous history in Russia, the generations that followed truly honored him. But how? How did the Communists leadership steer the opinions and the feelings of the masses in favor Lenin and Communism when history was against them?

Here's how: Communists had control of the news media, the entertainment industry, and the educational system. All three institutions were filled with loyal Communists who benefitted from the oppressive system and wanted it to continue.

It was through these same institutions that the Communists in the media, entertainment, and education influenced the Russian masses and future generations to view Communism in a favorable light. In fact, in Joseph Stalin's biography, the Communist leader famously said, "*Education is a weapon, whose effect depends on who holds it in his hands and at whom it is aimed.*"

Following Lenin's death, the Russian people and children were continuously fed a steady diet of misinformation and lies about the regime of Vladimir Lenin. Russian theaters presented him as being heroic and kind. Russian schools taught their students that Lenin was a benevolent leader and blamed his enemies for Russia's problems, while the Russian news media ignored the lasting effects of his tyranny.

They lied and covered up his brutality, his cruelty, and his evil treatment of the Russian people. As a result of their consistent and persistent efforts, they produced a new generation of Russian citizens the held Lenin in high esteem. And to many Russians, Lenin was deemed flawless and unquestionable.

The Democrat Socialists had to do the same thing. So, they began to follow the Russian playbook on how to deceive massive numbers of people, including future generations. With the help of like-minded individuals in media, entertainment, and education, they fed blacks a constant diet of misinformation that would confuse and deceive not only them but also their children.

The Big Switch

Two of the biggest parts of the Democrats' misinformation campaign are known today as the (a) the "*big switch*" and (b) "*the Southern strategy*" or "*Nixon's Southern strategy.*" Both rely heavily on placing the blame for black oppression upon Republicans.

In the big switch, college professors, historians, media elites, and university professors from America's most prestigious schools teach, promote, and cultivate the belief that Democrats and Republicans actually "switched" positions on the issue of race in America.

That certainly is convenient for the Democrats, is it not?

They teach that after fighting in the Civil War to end slavery; enshrining the Thirteenth, Fourteenth, and Fifteenth Amendments into the US Constitution; fighting the Ku Klux Klan; fighting to stop the legal lynching of blacks; and opposing Jim Crow laws and segregation, the Republican Party made an 180-degree turn and decided to oppress blacks, exchanging their policy of freedom for the Democrats' policy of oppression.

To support this ridiculous claim, Socialist teachers, professors, and media elites say that all members of the former Dixiecrat Party became Republican after the 1948 Democratic National Convention in Philadelphia.

Remember, the Dixiecrat Party only existed for about one year. They were a group of Democrat leaders who were very angry with President Harry Truman after Truman successfully altered the Democrats' platform on segregation.

Among the 26 known members of the Dixiecrat Party, 21 were senators and five were governors, and they nominated South Carolina Governor Strom Thurmond as their candidate for president.

For a lie to have any hope of survival for any length of time, there must be a fragment of truth in it. The sliver of truth Socialist extremists attach their lie to is this: After losing the 1948 election, the Dixiecrat Party dissolved. And, in 1964, Strom Thurmond left the Democrats and became a Republican. And Democrats claim that Strom Thurmond contaminated the entire Republican Party with his racist position.

In fact, Thurmond was one of three former Dixiecrats who became Republican. The other 23 former Dixiecrats returned to the Democratic Party and renewed their fight against desegregation.

If Strom Thurmond had infected the Republican Party with racism, would not 23 Dixiecrats infect the already racist-minded Democrats even more?

This is what the professors at Harvard, Yale, Princeton, Cornell, and the University of California teach today. The notion that three out of 26 members of the Dixiecrat Party changed their political affiliation to Republican 16 years after the Dixiecrats dissolved, causing a seismic shift in their position on civil rights, is beyond absurd.

Let's imagine, for a moment, what a real switch would look like. Both political parties would have to agree to exchange planks in their political platforms. That would require a National Joint Convention of the Republican and Democratic Parties with delegates from both in attendance.

The Republican delegates would have to vote to remove the racial equality plank in their platform and offer it to the Democrats. The Democrat delegates would have to vote remove their racial discrimination plank in their platform and give it to the Republicans.

Then we would have a real "switch."

Obviously, this scenario never happened. The Republican Party may be many things, but it is not foolish enough to insert the deadly poison of racism into its platform, especially considering that the party itself was created to fight racism.

The second part of the misinformation campaign is more well known than the big switch. I must admit, the fragment of truth is much harder to find in it, which makes it hard to understand how the campaign has survived for this long.

Nixon's Southern Strategy

Like many deeply intrenched lies, the promotion of Nixon's Southern strategy was created and driven by the news media during the 1970 midterm congressional elections.

During that year, national and many local media outlets used the congressional elections to revise Nixon's 1968 victory in the South, much in the way the 21st-century media tried to revise Donald Trump's victory in 2016 by claiming that

1968 Electoral Collage Map

Trump secretly colluded with the Russian government to steal the presidency.

Nixon's victory in the South came as just as big shock to the national media back then.

The "Solid South" had been solidly Democrat since the Reconstruction. So, in their minds of media experts, Hubert Humphrey should have easily won in that region.

But even though the truth was in front of them, they refused to accept it. They refused to believe that Democrats' alliance with the Socialists chased away the white Southern vote.

Media Revises Nixon's Presidential Victory

The national media used the occasion of the 1970 midterm elections to offer explanations of how Nixon won in the South.

Throughout that year, over 31,300 news articles and headlines appeared across America using term "Nixon's Southern strategy."

Each story defined and redefined the term, and each writer offered a new reason for how Nixon won the South in 1968. A close examination of the media political coverage in 1970 shows there was just as many stories, if not more, about the 1968 presidential race as there were about the 1970 congressional elections.

Eventually, the media concluded that Nixon won the South by appealing to Southern racists. Of course, they ignored the fact that it was George Wallace, not Richard Nixon, who operated a racist campaign.

Additionally, news analysts appeared on talk shows, throughout 1970, to convince the public that Nixon made an appeal to Southern segregationists to win the South.

Some stories in the print media used misleading headlines, which is tactic still used today. The purpose of an incorrect headline is to cause readers to think and believe that the headline is true, because media executives know that most readers hardly ever read an entire printed story.

Knowing this, the editors will write a headline that says one thing, even if it conflicts with the information in the story. If the conflict is discovered, then the editors would simply chalk it up to human error.

An example of this is found in a story by James Boyd that was published in *The New York Times* on May 17, 1970. In fact, it is a perfect example.

The headline in this story reads "*Nixon's Southern Strategy: It's All in the Charts.*" The story is about a very controversial political analyst named Kevin Phillips. Phillips believed that absolutely everyone voted according to their ethnic background and not according to individual beliefs.

Phillips believed strongly in what today we call identity politics. He worked with various political circles to promote this theory. He also believed that the only thing a candidate had to do to win votes was to frame his message according to whatever emotionally moves the ethnic group with the greatest number of voters.

Hidden deep within the very lengthy article, Boyd goes on to say that Phillips offered his services to the Nixon campaign in 1968. Boyd writes, "*Though Phillip's ideas for an aggressive, racist campaign strategy that would hasten defection of the working-class white Democrats to the Republicans, his ideas did not prevail with Nixon's 1968 campaign*"[132]

In truth, Phillips tried to persuade Nixon to operate a racist campaign to capture votes from Southern Democrats. But Nixon rejected him. The headline implies that not only did Nixon embrace Phillips's idea, but that it worked for him.

Senator Al Gore Sr. redefines "Nixon's Southern strategy."

Media, Democrats, and Civil Rights Leaders Revise Black Political History

The media relentlessly imposed their flawed version of Nixon's victory upon the American people during the 1970 midterm elections. And they did it with help from congressional Democrats and civil rights leaders.

For example, in an article headline, "*As No. 1 Target of Nixon's Southern Strategy: Gore's Survival Battle in the National Spotlight,*" Tennessee Democratic Senator Al Gore Sr. defined the Southern strategy as an

NAACP Director Roy Wilkins helps Democrats redefine the political party's position about race issues.

---

[132] The New York Times. "Nixon's Southern Strategy: It's All in the Charts." By James Boyd May 17, 1970.

alliance between Richard Nixon and George Wallace to undermine the Democrats in the South.

That story conflicted with an article published in the *Vancouver Sun*, which claimed that long-time political strategist John Mitchell developed the Southern strategy.

The deceptive headlines and the misrepresentations, along with cooperation from civil rights organizations, was enough material for Socialist teachers and professors to push the idea that the reason Southern voters supported Republicans was because the Republicans were now the racists.

Additionally, they began to teach future generations that the Democrats were now the champions of civil rights, justice, and equality.

They also used every opportunity that presented itself to accuse Republicans of being racist. Other news outlets that participated in the Socialist propaganda campaign were *The Arizona Republic*, *The Courier*, *Atlanta Journal-Constitution*, *Dayton Daily News*, *Santa Fe New Mexican*, *The Town Talk*; *LA Times*; *Pittsburg Press*, *The Ithaca Journal*, and many others.

More news outlets joined in the deception throughout the country. In an editorial published in *The Fresno Bee* and *The Republican* with the headline "*The Cost of the Southern Strategy is too High*" on March 6, 1970, C.K. McClatchy accused Strom Thurmond of being the "mastermind" behind the Southern strategy and defined it as a Republican plan to curtail the civil rights of blacks in the South.[133]

In a United Press International wire story headlined "*Nixon's Southern Strategy Failed*," we see the leadership of the once-noble NAACP help the Socialist effort to deceive black America into believing that the Republicans were now their enemies and the Democrats stood as their champions.

In the story, Executive Director Roy Wilkins defined the Southern strategy as a rallying cry for Southern segregationists. Wilkins, who also said that America does not tolerate segregation

---

[133] The Fresno Bee The Republican. "The Cost of the Southern Strategy is too High" By C.K. McClathy. P. 11

anymore, used the Republican loss of 11 seats in the House of Representatives to help promote the idea that Republicans were the racist. [134]

During a speech at the NAACP annual convention in Cincinnati, NAACP Chairman of the Board of Directors Stephen G. Spottswold told convention delegates that the Nixon administration "*can rightly be characterized as anti-Negro.*"[135]

But without question, the loudest voice of deception from among the civil rights leaders came from Reverend Ralph Abernathy of the Southern Christian Leadership Conference (SCLC).

Reverend Abernathy had stood shoulder-to-shoulder with Dr. King during the civil rights movement and became an outspoken leader of the SCLC after Dr. King's assassination. We should also not forget that the Reverend Abernathy and the NAACP worked closely with Nixon when he and President Eisenhower passed the Civil Rights Bill of 1957 against Democratic opposition.

Rev. Abernathy leads blacks back into the hands of the Democrats while accusing Nixon of racism.

Abernathy's participation in the deception helped not only lead the black community back into the hands of the Democrats but also remake their public image by continuously accusing the Republican Party of being the enemy of the poor and the reason for the troubles of black America.

During a news conference on April 25, 1970, Reverend Abernathy compared Richard Nixon to Adolf Hitler.[136] During a

---

[134] Kingsport News. "Nixon's Southern Strategy Failed" UPI, November 12, 1970, P. 18

[135] Florence Morning News, July 3, 1970, P. 4

[136] The Bennington Banner, April 25, 1970, P. 1

speech before an audience of about 1,000 at Central Washington State College in Ellensburg Washington, Reverend Abernathy told students that the Nixon Administration wanted to bring black America to "*the brink of political repression.*"[137]

During a speech in Atlanta, Georgia, Abernathy placed President Nixon on a list of 10 most unwanted politicians.[138] And while speaking to students at the University of Massachusetts in Amherst, the Reverend Abernathy again blamed President Nixon for the "*cancer of racism*" in America.[139]

Only 13 years earlier, Abernathy worked side by side with Nixon and the Eisenhower administration. But in return for federal grants for the "war of poverty" from the Democrats, Abernathy turned on Nixon and the Republicans. And he led black America to do the same.

The Reverend Abernathy, Roy Wilkins, Bishop Spottswood, and other civil rights leaders were unfailingly at the beck and call of the Democrats to help defeat Republicans. In the 21st century, the NAACP continues to serve the Democrats, even when it is clearly against the best interest of the black community.

Today the NAACP focuses its resources in support of the militant gay, lesbian and transsexual agenda supported by those who do not tolerate or accept any disagreement from others and imposes their views them they like it or not. The NAACP also focuses its resources in support of illegal immigration, increased abortions, and any issue the Democrats believe will help defeat Republicans.

As a whole and as a group of people, none of these issues are in the best interests of the black community. In fact, the NAACP of today is actively working against the interests of the black community as we will see more clearly in Chapter 16.

The participation of these civil rights leaders is the most outrageous aspect of Socialist propaganda campaign. Seeing individuals who truly fought for civil rights engaged in such profound treachery

---

[137] The Daily Chronicle, May 15, 1970, P. 16
[138] The Beckley post-Herald The Raleigh Register, May 24, 1970
[139] The Berkshire Eagle, April 23, 1970, P. 10

by bowing their knees to the segregationists, selling out the people they fought for, and turning against their long-time political allies generates feelings beyond disappointment.

In fact, there are truly no words that can accurately express the feelings of sorrow, grief, and anger this betrayal has created among people who clearly see what they have done.

Additionally, they helped inspire hatred for Republicans. Like a cattleman who leads herds of cows into a slaughterhouse, they led millions of trusting black people back into bondage and into the hands of their oppressors.

The Most Important Investigation that Did Not Happen

For decades, civil rights leaders such as Reverend Ralph Abernathy of the Southern Christian Leadership Conference (SCLC) and Roy Wilkins of the NAACP held a very special place in black America.

They were on the front lines of the civil rights battle fighting for the dignity of blacks throughout the country. During the early and middle of the 20th century, who could argue whether or not the SCLC and NAACP did an excellent job? They held the banner of civil rights high during perilous times and performed a great service for the black community.

Because the SCLC and the NAACP proved they had the black community's best interest at heart, we must ask why they did not investigate the Democrats' claim about the big switch? Why did the SCLC or the NAACP fail to investigate the media's claim about Nixon's Southern strategy?

There are no records of any such investigation to be found and no news reports quoting civil rights leaders that express doubt about the media's assertions. The Democrats and the media were making an incredible claim. These charges certainly merited an investigation—especially if a group is concerned about the future of black America, which the NAACP claimed to be.

If the charges were true, then the black community should abandon the Republican Party—and rightly so. But if the charges were not true, then the leaders of the civil rights organizations were misleading black America.

After all the fighting, the protest marches, the court battles, the hardship, and all the legal and legislative victories, the black community would end up back on a new type of plantation mired in a new form of slavery.

To avoid this nightmare, a true civil rights leader who truly cared for future generations of blacks would have launched an investigation into the media assertion of the big switch and the claims about Nixon's Southern strategy and publish the findings.

But there was no investigation—and no one questioned the Democrats or the media. The NAACP as well as the other civil rights organizations simply got onboard without question.

A thorough search of news articles published throughout the 1970s on a variety of media databases clearly does shows that Abernathy and Wilkins and other civil rights leaders were quoted many times supporting the claim that the Democratic Party was now the Party of Civil Rights and the Republicans were the enemies of blacks.

It was this historic betrayal that helped the Democratic Party secure political support from the black community for one of the most committed segregationists in the South, Governor George Wallace.

Alabama Blacks Vote for George Wallace in 1982

It is interesting to note that the propagandists ignore the fact that former Alabama Governor George Wallace ran for president in 1968. And it was George Wallace, a long-time product of the Democratic Party, who truly campaigned on a racist platform in 1968. And he's conveniently excluded from public discussions about the 1968 presidential race.

Wallace's campaign for governor of Alabama in 1982 removed all doubt about the success of the Socialist misinformation cam-

225

paign. The loyalty of Southern black voters to the Democratic Party was about to be tested like never before.

George Wallace stood as the perfect symbol of the Democrats' racist history. He was a notorious segregationist who fought desperately to keep public schools and public places segregated. And no one could forget that it was Governor Wallace who sent state troopers and police officers to the Edmund Pettus Bridge to attack Martin Luther King Jr. and his supporters.

It was also Wallace with support from public safety superintendent Bull Connor, who sent firefighters and police officers to continue the attack. Wallace was the living symbol of a true Democrat.

There were many black residents within the state of Alabama in 1982 who remembered this. But now, the nation would see if blacks would vote for him.

And they did! On November 2, 1982, George Wallace defeated Republican Emory Folmar with about 57 percent of the total vote, including over 90 percent of the black vote.[140]

About 90 percent of Alabama blacks vote for segregationist George Wallace for governor in 1982.

The election of George Wallace with 90 percent of the black vote in Alabama proved that the Democrat propaganda machine was just as effective as the Communist machine that operated in Russia throughout the mid to late 20th century.

After the Alabama election, Democrats nervous about their control over blacks could relax. Their miseducation had taken hold. They knew that if blacks would vote for George Wallace, they would loyally support the Democrats going forward regardless of the horrors of the party's past.

---

[140] https://www.ourcampaigns.com/RaceDetail.html?RaceID=7393

The Fall of the NAACP

Today, the NAACP is less than a shadow of its former self.

Today's NAACP bears no resemblance to the organization that fought bravely against lynching, segregation, and Jim Crow laws during the early to mid-20th century.

It cannot be compared to the organization that defeated segregationist lawyers in the US Supreme Court and drove the state of Oklahoma and six Southern states to repeal state laws that disenfranchised black voters in 1915.

Today's NAACP is nothing compared to the organization that compelled President Woodrow Wilson to publicly denounce the Ku Klux Klan and used full-page ads to expose Democrat support and involvement in lynching throughout the South.

Today's NAACP cannot hold a candle to the organization that fought to pass the Dyer Anti-Lynching Bill and it cannot be compared to the organization that defeated segregationists in the Supreme Court in 1953 and ended Jim Crow laws in Washington D.C.

Today's NAACP is nothing like the organization that triumphed over Democrat Mayor William Gayle in the Supreme Court in 1956, stopped segregation on public transportation, and ended the Montgomery Bus Boycott with a glorious victory.

And today's NAACP cannot be compared to the organization that argued in favor of immediate desegregation of public schools in the face of threats from rabid Democrat white supremacists.

During that time, the NAACP nobly fought for the dignity of blacks to live their lives with honor and respect from their fellow Americans and their government.

But today, the NAACP surrenders the dignity of black Americans in court rooms throughout the country to advance the agenda of American Socialists and increase the political power of the Democratic Party.

One of the biggest examples of how the organization sacrifices blacks on the Democrats' alter is seen the NAACP's response to voter identification laws.

Between 2010 and 2013, state governments established laws that required voters to present identification to election officials to help ensure the integrity of the election process. Among these states were North Carolina, Alabama, Texas, Missouri, Tennessee and many others.

Republicans are in favor of Voter ID laws, but Democrats are strongly against them.

On August 12, 2013, North Carolina Republican Governor Pat McCrory signed Voter ID into law, but the North Carolina NAACP quickly challenged it in federal court, arguing that the presentation of identification, at the polls, is too cumbersome for African Americans.

"*The state shouldn't make it more burdensome for black voters to cast their ballots,*" said NAACP Chairman William Barber.[141]

Barber was one among a long list of NAACP officials who portrayed blacks as so weak and feebleminded that they cannot reach into their wallets or purses and produce identification for the purpose of voting. One NAACP member after another declared the same thing in federal

court, sacrificing the dignity of black Americans to help the Democrats.

The same insulting, condescending, and extremely disparaging argument was repeated by many state-level NAACP organizations in courtrooms throughout the country to help Democrats defeat voter ID laws.

Under the guise of protecting their voting rights, the NAACP adopted the same arguments used by 19th-century Democrats claiming that blacks were to weak-minded to vote. According to the NAACP, if blacks had to present ID at the polls, they would become lost and overwhelmed.

But let us be clear about this: Blacks have no problem presenting ID at airports, hotels, financial institutions, and shopping malls. The organization of the 1950s would never present blacks as being so weak and helpless—that organization would have provided an image

---

[141] Michael Hewlett, "Blacks Are Twice as Likely Not to Have Photo ID, *Winston-Salem Journal* (Winston-Salem, NC) Jan. 26, 2016.

of a strong and capable group of people that is more than able to meet the requirements of the law.

But not the organization of today.

Furthermore, NAACP members and supporters also testified that blacks lacked the life skills, the desire, and the wherewithal to acquire and maintain proper identification. Charles Stewart, a professor of political science at the Massachusetts Institute of Technology, said that blacks were twice as likely to lack proper ID because they did not have proper education, did not have transportation, and remain in a state of continual poverty.[142]

In January of 2020, US District Court Judge Lorretta C. Biggs ruled in favor the NC NAACP which prevented the implementation of the state's new Constitutional Amendment that required photographic identification to vote. On page 32 of the ruling Judge Biggs wrote, *"For those struggling to navigate daily life making a trip to the county board or the DMV during open hours can be prohibitively costly. Both options for acquiring free ID makes demands on the person's time and transportation costs because the individual must present themselves to apply in person."*[143]

Another provision within the Voter ID law was that voters had to vote at their proper voting precinct on election day. The NAACP, however, saw this as another opportunity to ingratiate themselves with the Democrats.

To ensure they did everything they could to defeat the law and destroy what little respect remained for the black community, NAACP officials testified that the law had to be overturned because it was very difficult for blacks to determine where their correct voting precincts were located.

In their zeal to serve and support the Democrats and their Socialist agenda, the NAACP also surrendered the black commu-

---

[142] Hewlett, "Blacks Are Twice as Likely Not to Have Photo ID."

[143] NC State Conference of the NAACP, Chapel Hill, Carrboro NAACP, Greensboro NAACP, High Point NAACP, Moore County NAACP, Stokes County NAACP, Forsyth County NAACP v. Gov. Roy Cooper, NC State Board of Elections, 18CV1034, US District Court for the Middle District of North Carolina. P. 32

nity on issues such as education, abortion, illegal immigration, and fatherhood, which is made more clear in chapter 16.

Whenever an issue is addressed in court, whether it is about charter school education or abortion, the NAACP is there to provide the most demeaning testimony to make the black community appear to be as hapless and helpless as possible.

Today's NAACP has fallen from a high pedestal and its special place in black political history to land at the feet of the Democratic Party. Now the organization, once admired and esteemed during the 1950s, exists only to kiss the Democrats' feet at the expense of blacks, who they once truly defended.

Chapter 15: 1982-Present Day
Democrats Retain Black Support But Cannot Regain the South

President Bill Clinton convinced Southern voters that he was not a radical Democrat Socialist.

The Democrats still had a problem regaining the Southern white vote. Throughout the rest of the 20th century, the Democratic Party desperately tried to hide its radicalism. The party members cast themselves as "moderates" or "progressives" in an attempt to regain people's support.

With the exception of the 1976 election of Democratic President Jimmy Carter, the South remained firmly in the hands of the Republicans until the election of Democratic President Bill Clinton in 1992. President Clinton won six out of eleven Southern states, in 1992 and 1996.

President Clinton successfully persuaded enough Southern white voters that he was not a radical Socialist, communist-sympathizing Democrat. Clinton's public confrontation with political activist and hip-hop star Sister Souljah, in 1992, mitigated the concerns of white southern voters about him. During an interview with *The Washington Post* about the 1992 Los Angeles riots, published May 13, 1992, Sister Soulja supported the actions of the rioters and advocated in favor of a killing spree of white people. Clinton publicly denounced the hip hop star and was deemed, by the media, as unsympathetic to militant Socialists.[144]

All Americans, particularly in the South, branded Socialist radicals as extremely dangerous forever. They were responsible for the chaos of the 1960s and would never get the support of white Southern voters.

But Clinton convinced the public that he was not a radical, which helped him win a second term, unlike the previous Democratic President Jimmy Carter.

Democrats Embrace Radical Socialism

The radicals, however, would not stay hidden forever. They were reinvigorated by the election of President Barak Obama.

With this breath of new life, the radicals began to remake the Democratic Party in their own image and likeness. As they did, America saw things it has not seen since the 1960s.

President Barak Obama supported by radical Socialists and promised to "fundamentally change America."

During his first four years in office, President Obama inserted himself into a series of local incidents in which he took a position against the police, while also elevating known opponents of law enforcement. In 2009, President Obama accused the Cambridge Police Department of *"acting stupidly"* following the arrest of a Harvard professor. In 2011, Obama invited a rapper known as Common to the White House for an event to celebrate poets. The president knew that Common was an outspoken supporter of Assata Shakur, who

---

[144] David Mills, Sister Souljah's Call to Arms: The rapper says the riots were payback. Are you paying attention? *The Washington Post*, May 13, 1992

was convicted for killing a police officer and fled to Cuba. But the president invited him anyway.

In 2013, Obama supported Debo Adegbile for a position within the Department of Justice knowing that Adegbile filed a petition on behalf of Mumia Abu-Jamal, who was convicted of killing a Philadelphia police officer in 1982.

Also in 2013, President Obama turned public sentiment against the Sanford Police Department, in Sanford, Florida, over the death of Trayvon Martin. During a speech in the White House press briefing room he said, *"When Trayvon Martin was first shot, I said that this could have been my son. Trayvon Martin could've been me 35 years ago."*[145]

Obama also involved the White House in the police-related deaths of Michael Brown in Ferguson, Missouri, and Eric Garner on Staten Island in 2014.

Obama's comments inspired radicals to organize public demonstrations and marches in which the participants openly called for the death of police officers. In New York, hundreds of protestors marched through the streets and chanted, *"What do we want? Dead cops! When do we want it? Now!"*

Similar protests arose in large cities throughout the country. It was just a matter of time before someone acted upon their chants. On November 29, 2009, four police officers were ambushed and killed in a coffee shop in Lakewood, Washington. And on December 20, 2014, two New York City police officers were ambushed and killed by Ismaaiyl Abdullah Brinsley to avenge Michael Brown and Eric Garner.

Beginning in 2016, the American people witness the rise of Antifa, an organization that sends mobs of masked individuals to violently disrupt public events by attacking the attendees. Every event targeted by Antifa features individuals and speakers who disagree with the agenda of the Democratic Socialist and Communists. And the goal of Antifa is to intimidate their opposition into silence.

---

[145] https://obamawhitehouse.archives.gov/the-press-office/2013/07/19/remarks-president-trayvon-martin

Although Democrat leaders publicly denounce Antifa and its terrorist tactics, it is no secret that the traveling attack mobs work to help Democrats.

One clear example of the connection is Joseph Alcoff. In February of 2019, Joseph Alcoff, Thomas Massey, and Tom Keenan were charged with aggravated assault and ethnic intimidation of two Hispanic Marines as part of an Antifa mob attack in Philadelphia.

The two marines, Alejandro Godinez and Luis Torres, were in Philadelphia to attend a marine event at a nearby hotel at the same time a gathering called the "We the People" rally was in progress. The rally was organized to support pro-life issues, the Second Amendment, local law enforcement, ICE and enforcement of federal laws on illegal immigrants.

Antifa attacks anyone that disagrees with radical Socialists.

Alcoff and the other assailants assumed that Godinez and Torres, who were wearing plain clothes, were part of the rally and attacked them.

Alcoff was well connected in Democratic political circles in Washington, DC. He worked as a campaign manager for a Democratic policy group known as Americans for Financial Reform and his work was supported by Senator Dianne Feinstein (D-Ca), Senator Jeff Merkley (D-Ore), Congressman Elijah Cummings (D-Md), and Congresswoman Suzanne Bonamici (D-Ore).

There also several pictures of Alcoff on social media standing proudly with Congresswoman Maxine Waters (D-Ca).[146]

It is hard to accept the idea that Alcoff worked so closely with congressional Democrats, while they were unaware he was one of the

---

[146] https://www.foxnews.com/politics/
antifa-activist-facing-assault-charges-was-tied-to-democratic-policymakers

anarchists who supported them by attacking and intimidating their opponents.

Another glaring example of burgeoning Communist boldness occurred during the spring of 2019, when the North Carolina Association of Educators formerly adopted the historical, easily recognizable Communist fist as its logo and openly displayed it as thousands of North Carolina teachers marched on Raleigh wearing communist-red T-shirts for a rally on May 1st. May 1st is a date recognized by Communists, throughout the world, during which Communism is celebrated.

For a long time, the Democrats concealed the presence of radicals within their ranks because, despite the propaganda promoted in 1970 about why they lost the South to Nixon, they knew the truth. They knew that white southern voters supported Republicans, in 1968, because of the Democrat's relationship with Socialists. And they knew that the American people would never support them if they continued to be the party of Socialist extremism. So, the Socialist revolutionaries among them had to keep quiet and stay hidden.

Democratic Congresswoman Maxine Waters standing to the right of Antifa leader Joseph Alcoff.

But that is no longer true. The Democratic Party leadership has embraced what they tried to push away and hide—Socialist and Communist beliefs within their ranks. And more Democrats have accepted the Socialist and Communist agenda regardless of what the American people think.

It also appears as if the radicals have taken over the leadership of the Democratic Party. For example, 2016 and 2020 Democratic Presidential Candidate Bernie Sanders proudly declares himself as a Socialist and openly declares that, if elected, he would lead America down a path of Socialism.

Another proud Socialist Democrat that has quickly taken the reigns of leadership is Congresswoman Alexandria Ocasio-Cortez from New York's Fourteenth District. Ocasio-Cortez is a member of the Democrat Socialists of America and has drafted a plan for America she calls the Green New Deal.

The plan calls for free college tuition for every American, a 70 percent tax rate for the wealthy, Medicare for everyone, the abolition of combustion engines, and the refitting the heating and air conditioning systems of all homes and buildings to make them all friendly to the environment. The plan also calls for the abolishment of US Immigration and Customs

Congresswoman Alexandria Ocasio Cortez

The Green New Deal is, without question, the most radical Communist proposal ever offered in the history of the United States. And the most shocking fact is that every 2020 Democratic presidential candidate supports it or some version of it.

Additionally, on June 14, 2017, Socialist revolutionary James Hodgkinson, armed with an assault rifle, opened fire upon several Republican congressmen at Eugene Simpson Park in Alexandria, Virginia.

The congressmen were practicing for an annual Congressional baseball game for charity. According to reports, Hodgkinson asked South Carolina Congressman Jeff Duncan about the party affiliation of the members on the field. When Duncan said they were Republicans, Hodgkinson produced his weapon and fired about 60 rounds at the congressmen.

Five members of Congress were shot, including House GOP Whip Steve Scalise, who was critically injured but survived his wounds along with the other victims of the attack.[147]

America has not seen such blatant attempt to murder public officials since the 1960s when Socialist revolutionaries attacked state and local politicians, police officers, and judges on a more frequent basis.

Black Democrats Ignore the Dangerous, Socialist Agenda

Despite the obvious presence of radical Socialists and Communists within the Democratic Party and its dangerous agenda, America's black community overwhelmingly supports the Democrats.

Like the generations that participated in the civil rights movement during the 1950s and 1960s, blacks in the 21st-century were never educated about the dangers of Socialism and Communism.

Since 1965, they voted consistently and blindly for the Democratic Party regardless of the exploitation of their fears and the destruction, seen daily in the black community, caused by their policies.

Within the minds of most blacks, the Democratic Party is infallible. It is perfect and cannot make mistakes. And if a flaw in any Democrat is discovered, it is ignored. Other blacks might believe they do not have any choice but to vote Democrat because they've supported Democrats for so long it's become a cultural tradition. And to those blacks that believe that supporting Democrats is part of the black culture, they simply don't want to betray the culture.

Many blacks do believe that the Democratic Party knows what is best for them better than they know themselves, which leads many of them to despise, or even hate, other blacks who support or cooperate with Republicans.

---

[147] https://www.history.com/this-day-in-history/
james-hodgkinson-shooting-republicans-baseball-game

For example, in January of 2017, comedian, actor, and author Steve Harvey met with Republican President Donald Trump. Not only is Harvey known in the entertainment industry, he is known for his philanthropy and support of low-income blacks across the country. For decades, Harvey has been a long-time supporter of educational initiatives, black colleges, and black-owned businesses.

Steve Harvey is well-established as a consistent supporter of black America and has been for a long time.

During a meeting with President Trump, Harvey discussed the possibility of working with Dr. Ben Carson and the Department of Housing and Urban Development to create community centers in cities across the country

Actor, Comedian, and Author Steve Harvey

where inner city children and adults can learn life skills, improve literacy, receive financial education, and build low-income homes. President Trump was very receptive to the idea.

But days after the meeting, Harvey was severely criticized and berated by blacks across the county through social media for working with a Republican president. Blacks from every corner of the country called Harvey "*a sellout,*" "*coon,*" or "*Uncle Tom*" for working with Trump.

The fact that Harvey was trying to improve the lives of blacks across the country did not matter, and Harvey's history of supporting black America did not matter. The only thing that mattered, to many blacks across the country, was being slavishly faithful to the Democratic Party.

If other blacks do not fall in line in full public support of the Democratic Party, they receive the same treatment. Rather than consider them as independent, those blacks are vilified, criticized, castigated, and punished for not following the group mind-set of most blacks in America.

Most black Democrats never challenge any of the most questionable and controversial Democrat proposals—they simply accept them. For example, in February of 2016, the Democrat-led Charlotte City Council passed a law that allowed transgendered individuals to choose whichever public bathroom that corresponded with their chosen sexual identity.[148] This opened a debate to consider if transgender high school students to share the same locker rooms and bathrooms.

Despite the affect these proposals may have black children, they were not questioned or challenged by the NAACP nor was it challenged by prominent black Democrats. And, as a whole, the black community remained silent about it.

Most blacks do not consider what can happen to their community, economically, with a flood of illegal immigrants. All they know is that they must support it because its supported by Democrats. And many generations have turned a blind eye to the fact that a large percentage of black children graduate from high school functionally illiterate.

During the 19th century, several prominent and successful black men took the time to consider the future of blacks in America. These men did very well for themselves and their families. They escaped slavery and despite the severe violence and racism of their day, they became wealthy and successful businessmen, politicians, writers, and public speakers.

These prominent black men and former slaves were able see into the future of their people and accurately prophesize what would happen to them. One of these individuals was Frederick Douglass. It was with somber tones, a broken spirit, and great heaviness of heart that Douglass foretold exactly what we see in black America today.

---

[148] https://www.nydailynews.com/news/national/n-city-transgender-choice-public-bathroom-article-1.2540757

Chapter 16: The Mouth of the Lion:

The Prophetic Warning from Frederick Douglass

During his lifetime, Frederick Douglass was many things. He was born a slave and became very wealthy, successful, and known throughout the United States and Western Europe.

There is no doubt that one of the things that led him down his path of success was his insatiable curiosity.

Douglass was born in in Talbot County, Eastern Shore, Maryland, near Easton in 1818, on the plantation of Captain Thomas Auld and Edward Lloyd. He had a very sharp and inquisitive mind, and, at a very young age, he became aware that not all blacks were slaves.

He saw that some blacks in America were free.

As an adolescent, Douglass did not understand why this was so. Why

Frederick Douglass

were he and his family being kept as slaves, while the black men he saw riding through Easton or the black men serving as sailors along Maryland's ports were not?

He agonized over this question and it tormented him day and night. He tried to get answers from his fellow slaves, but most of them did not dare address the subject. They were fearful and did not want to be heard participating in a discussion about freedom. They knew that if the slave master heard them, they would be punished or sold away from their families.

But Douglass was fearless and undaunted. He continued to ask questions and refused to be denied. He would not rest until he knew the truth.

He learned nothing from the other slaves, so he set out to find the answers himself. But he knew he had to learn how to read, if he wanted to find those answers. Douglass used sharp rocks and discarded pieces of wood to teach himself how to read and write. As an adolescent, Frederick Douglass did not have the resources teenagers have today. He did not have books or any printed materials. He did not have a pen, pencils, or paper. They were all denied to him.

And he did not have a school filled with teachers eager to help him. And he certainly did not have the internet. All he had was his own inner strength, the power of his own will, self-discipline, a few friends, and a determination that proved to be unstoppable.

As he scratched out the letters of the alphabet on pieces of wood, who knew that, eventually, his words would help stir the hearts of Americans to end slavery? Who could imagine that a self-educated former slave would become such a powerful writer and thoroughly versed in US law, the Constitution, the Bible, and world history?

Douglass's burning curiosity and determination not only started him down a path of freedom and answered all his questions about slavery, it led him to being immortalized in the pages of American history. On September 3, 1838, after two unsuccessful attempts, he finally escaped slavery and eventually made New Bedford, Massachusetts, his home.

In 1846, Douglass started his own anti-slavery newspaper called *The North Star*. Its slogan was *"Right is of no sex—Truth is of No Color—God is Father to us all, and we are all brethren."*[149]

---

[149] https://www.loc.gov/exhibits/treasures/trr085.html

The North Star was so successful it helped launch Douglass's career as a public speaker. In fact, Douglass became one of the most powerful speakers of the 19th-century Abolitionist Movement. He traveled throughout the Northern states and the Midwest, delivering compelling speeches and urging America to end slavery.

Frederick Douglass was also an active Republican, which is something else you will never hear during black history month. He supported Republican candidates and encouraged everyone, especially former slaves, to do the same.

Douglass also knew the Democrats better than most Republican elected officials, including President Abraham Lincoln. In 1861, President Lincoln offered to compensate slave owners with federal funds if they set them free. As advisor to the president, Douglass told him in polite but strong terms that his plan would fail because the Democrats were too proud and that they were faithful to the concept of slavery.

Frederick Douglass was right. The Democrats refused Lincoln's offer and chose war.

Douglass also traveled throughout Western Europe to speak against slavery. And during the Civil War, he recruited black soldiers to fight. Douglass also worked as a US ambassador to Haiti.

Frederick Douglass began his life under the oppression of slavery and achieved a level of greatness no one dreamed a former slave could attain.

Yes, Frederick Douglass was many things. But if you look deeper into his life and his writings, it appears he was also a prophet.

After the Civil War, Douglass was very concerned about the condition and the future of former slaves. On December 7, 1869, he delivered a speech in Boston, Massachusetts entitled, "*Our Composite Nation.*"

In the speech Douglass said that the future of America will be "*the perfect national illustration of unity and dignity of the human family the world has ever seen.*"[150]

---

[150] https://www.blackpast.org/african-american-history/1869-frederick-douglass-describes-composite-nation/

Douglas also said, during a speech in 1883 following a Supreme Court ruling declaring Civil Rights Act of 1875 unconstitutional, that the future of both blacks and whites in America is linked.

"*The lesson of all the ages is that a wrong, done to one man, is a wrong done to all men. No man can put a chain about the ankle of his fellow man without finding the other end fastened about his own neck.*"[151]

Douglass issued a prophetic warning to blacks who support Democrats.

But in a private communication to a good friend, Douglass said something else. Douglass knew the Democrats and how tireless, ruthless, and relentless they could be. He knew they held firmly to the misguided belief that black people were inferior and were much better off submitting themselves to white people.

And unfortunately, too many blacks believed the same thing about themselves.

Since the ratification of the Fifteenth Amendment in February of 1870, some Democrats believed they could easily persuade blacks to support the Democratic Party if the Democrats offered to take care of their personal needs. Most blacks refused, knowing very well that the Democrats did not have their best interests at heart.

But some did and they voted for them. By 1888, a presidential election year, the numbers of black Democrats grew strong enough to hold a Black Democratic Convention in Indianapolis, Indiana.

Incidentally, the black Democrats had to have their own national convention because the white Democrats did not want them at their convention.

---

[151] Edited by Philip S. Foner, Frederick Douglass: Selected Speeches and Writings, Chicago, Illinois, Lawrence Hill Books, P. 685

When Frederick Douglass heard about the meeting, he wrote a letter to a friend D.A. Shaker, who shared Douglass's concern for blacks voting for Democrats. Mr. Shaker added Douglass's words to his own as he tried to convince black Democrats to forsake the Democratic Party and support Republican candidate, Benjamin Harris, for president.

America's black population would be 48 percent higher today, if not for targeted abortions.

In his letter Douglass wrote: "*Few things pain me more than to hear of any colored man voting the Democratic ticket. Such talk, in my mind, is high treason against the best interests of the colored race.*"

"*Do they think the best way to gain their rights is to support the party that has distinguished itself by stomping on them? Do they think that true independence is found only in perfect reliance and dependence upon the Democratic Party?*"

Do they think the safest place for the lamb, is in the mouth of the lion?"[152]

In his letter to Mr. Shaker, Douglass used a very graphic metaphor to illustrate what would happen to blacks in America.

Douglass prophetically described future generations of blacks as a thoughtless lamb that voluntarily places its neck between the jaws of a lion.

Douglass said that some blacks wanted to support the party that had historically "stomped" on them and wanted to rely on the Democratic Party to manage their affairs.

Douglass said that many blacks would be more than willing to surrender their freedom in exchange for free food, clothing, and shelter.

---

[152] The Frederick Douglass Papers, https://www.loc.gov/item/mfd.07005/

Douglass saw this phenomenon as a great threat to the future of black Americans. He decided to take on the issue himself and spoke before large groups of black voters, some of which argued in favor of supporting the Democratic Party.

He traveled the country and publicly endorsed Benjamin Harris, urging black voters to support him. And on the eve of the election, Douglass tried desperately, again, to convince black Democratic voters that the Democrats had not changed, and that they never would.

During his speech, Douglass said, "*Men die, but parties live on… they change their representatives, but they retain their character with steady uniformity and stability. Their tactics change, but their character never does…and the Democrats kill the Negro!*"[153]

Let us look at how the black community's continual submission to the Democrats has literally cost blacks their lives.

Abortion Reduces the Black Population

It is no secret that the Democrats use their political power, wealth, and influence to keep abortions frequent and legally possible during all stages of pregnancy. They even use their power to continue the abortions even when a newborn baby survives the procedure.

A majority of abortion clinics are established within walking distances of black neighborhoods in large cities.

How has this position affected the black community? The Democrats' abortion policy has stopped blacks from becoming 48 percent of the US population and continues to hold them at 13 percent.

---

[153] Frederick Douglass Papers at the Library of Congress. https://www.loc.gov/collections/frederick-douglass-papers/about-this-collection/

About 19 million black babies have been aborted since the *Roe v. Wade* Supreme Court decision in 1973. Almost 1,000 black babies are aborted every day in the United States, and the abortion rate for black women is four times the rate of White or Hispanic women.

Furthermore, about 36 percent of all abortions are performed on black women. Considering that the total current black American population is about 42 million, the 20.35 million black American abortions are equal to about 48.45 percent of the total Black American population.

We can reasonably conclude that if not for abortion, the total Black American population would be approximately 62.35 million, or 48 percent greater than it is today.[154]

According to BlackDemographics.com, the American black population was at its highest between 1790 and 1810, at 19 percent of the total US population.[155]

But how is that possible? As a percentage of the total US population, how could the American black population during the early 19th century be six points higher than the black population of the 21st century?

Perhaps 18th-century blacks were more prosperous and more capable of establishing and building families. Perhaps they had better jobs and a comfortable lifestyle that made it possible for them to raise more children.

We know that is not true. But today's so-called "black leadership" never asked the question: Why is the population of black America consistently the lowest percentage of the total US population? When you consider that blacks have been in America since the 16th century, the question demands an answer.

The answer can found in a study conducted by the Life Issues Institute in Cincinnati, Ohio. The Life Issues Institute completed an analysis of 2010 Census data that concludes that Planned Parenthood

---

[154] http://www.urbancure.org/blog/post/abortion-is-the-biggest-single-negative-force-on-black-american-growth

[155] https://blackdemographics.com/population/

strategically builds and operates most of its abortion facilities in locations that target black Americans for abortions.

And they have done it for decades. Planned Parenthood is an historic ally of the Democratic Party as far back to the 1920s. The organization's founder, Margaret Sanger, was a staunch advocate of population control of the black race, which was in complete agreement with Democrats views.

Ever since, both organizations have worked together to keep the black population as low as possible. Since the *Roe v. Wade* Supreme Court decision, they have been more successful than they could ever dream.

Life Issues Institute's research shows that about 62 percent of Planned Parenthood's abortion centers are within walking distance of black neighborhoods in cities with a high black population.[156] Additionally, the research reveals that Planned Parenthood uses census property section maps to determine where to place their abortion centers.

For example, in Cincinnati, Planned Parenthood established an abortion center within a two-mile walking distance of land sections that make up communities heavily occupied by blacks. The minority population of these neighborhoods is between 43 and 95 percent.

In Houston, Texas, Planned Parenthood placed a facility within a two-mile walking distance of neighborhoods with black occupancy between 31 and 94 percent.

The same is found in large cities—including Detroit, Chicago, Philadelphia, Los Angeles, and Pittsburg—throughout the entire country. The study shows that 102 out of 165 of all Planned Parenthood abortion facilities purposefully target the black community. The result makes black women four times more likely to abort their babies than white women.

Do you think the abortion numbers would be the same if Planned Parenthood targeted white communities with abortion facilities for decades? No, it would not. In fact, the numbers would be very different.

---

[156] https://www.protectingblacklife.org/pdf/PP-Targets-10-2012.pdf

Frederick Douglass's assessment about the Democrats in 1888 appears to still be true today. But Douglass was not the only 19th-century civil rights champion to issue a stern warning to future generations of blacks about the Democrats.

Two others were North Carolina Republican State Senator Abraham Galloway and US Senator Hiram Rhodes Revels.

A Prophetic Warning from Abraham Galloway

Galloway, one of the cofounders of the North Carolina Republican Party, was the first known high-profile former slave to desperately warn former slaves about the Democrats' deception.

Abraham Galloway

Galloway was born in slavery in 1837 and lived near the Cape Fear River in Smithville, which is known today as Southport, North Carolina.

When he was 18 or 19 years old, he successfully escaped slavery. In May of 1863, he was recruited by the Abolitionist Movement to be a spy for the Union Army.

After the Civil War, Galloway returned to North Carolina and helped establish and build the Republican Party in North Carolina. Later, he became one of the state's first black senators.

After the ratification of the Fifteenth Amendment, some Democrats immediately tried to entice newly enfranchised black voters to support the Democratic Party.

This effort did not escape Galloway's notice. On November 14, 1867, Senator Galloway spoke at a meeting in Wilmington, North Carolina in which he responded to the Democratic efforts to persuade blacks to vote for Democrats.

During his speech Galloway said, "*They call us to sustain them as they are our best friends. But what friends are those that propose to re-enslave us?*"[157]

It was a warning issued to a people newly freed from bondage, who had little or no confidence in their own ability to take care of themselves. And some of their former masters tried to take advantage of their insecurities.

Senator Galloway encouraged them to be their own masters, to be independent and strong, and to beware of the trap that was laid for them by individuals who now claimed to be their friends.

A Prophetic Warning from Hiram Revels

Unlike Frederick Douglass and Abraham Galloway, Hiram Revels was not born a slave. He lived as a free black man and grew up in Fayetteville, North Carolina. His father was a Baptist preacher, and Revels eventually became a minister himself, serving as a chaplain for the Union Army during the Civil War.

On January 20, 1870, the Republican-controlled Mississippi State legislature voted to send Revels to the US Senate to take the

Senator Hiram Revels

seat once held by Jefferson Davis, who had been the president of the Confederate States.

The irony was not lost to the political elites in Washington, DC, or the American public when they saw President Jefferson Davis replaced by a black man.

---

[157] David Cecelski, The Fire of Freedom: Abraham Galloway and the Slaves' Civil War. North Carolina, University of North Carolina Press, September 2012

Revels was the first black man to serve in the US Senate. He traveled throughout the South and gave speeches before large crowds of former slaves. He spoke words of encouragement, hope, and inspired many to build a better future for themselves and their children.

But like Douglass and Galloway, Revels encountered a few timid and cautious former slaves who did not want to antagonize their former masters by voting Republican. And although most blacks voted for the GOP during that time, Revels felt the need to issue a warning to his audience. During a speech before a large crowd of former slaves, Senator Revels said,

"If ever influenced by the friendship of your Democratic neighbor, you desert the Republican flag, desert the Republican standard, desert the Republican Party that has freed you, you will be voting away your last liberties. Would the Democrats rescind those rights if they are returned to power? They will do it as certainly as the sun shines in the heavens."[158]

Frederick Douglass, Abraham Galloway, and Hiram Revels warned that if black Americans supported the Democratic Party, they would lose their freedoms. Today, blacks certainly do support the Democrats, so let us look at the liberties lost within black America throughout the decades. And although they knew this would happen, I doubt that either Douglass, Galloway, or Revels could have imagined the degree of devastation we see today.

Social Programs Quench the Fires of Freedom

Throughout the civil rights era, white Americans saw thousands of black men and women marching through the streets of cities across the country, demanding their freedom year after year. It was clear to all that freedom was their desire and they would not go another day without it.

But Lyndon Johnson's "war of poverty" effectively doused the flames of freedom that burned within their hearts.

---

[158] Phillip Dray, The Epic Story of Reconstruction through the lives of the first Black Congressmen. New York, Mariner Books, 2008, P. 61

Additionally, the will of many blacks to improve themselves and strive for better lives was destroyed.

According to Blackdemographics.com, about 41.6 percent of black Americans received at least one form of public assistance during 2012.[159] During President Obama's first term in office, enrollment into the food stamp program rose by 70 percent.[160]

According to the US Census Bureau's 2014 American Community Survey, about 30.1 percent of blacks participated in Food Assistance or the Supplemental Nutrition Assistance Program (SNAP). About 29.3 percent received Medicaid and 14.5 percent participated in Section 8 Public Housing Programs.

Since 1965, about 15 trillion dollars have been spent on various social programs in support of the "war on poverty." For blacks who receive these benefits, their upward economic progress was exchanged for guaranteed food, housing, and medical benefits.

To hold onto these guarantees, they and their families must remain near the poverty level. These programs have produced a group of people who are content with a low standard of living.

Unfortunately, living on the government dole for years

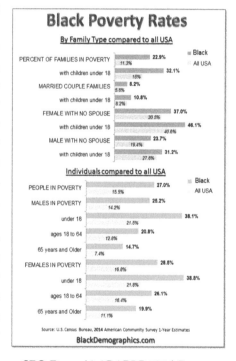

SEQ Figure * ARABIC 1014 Poverty Chart by BlackDemographics.com

has twisted the thinking of many blacks. For too many, learning how

---

[159] https://blackdemographics.com/households/poverty

[160] https://www.washingtontimes.com/news/2013/mar/28/ food-stamp-president-enrollment-70-percent-under-o/

to take full advantage of the social programs has more value than anything they could learn in school.

Generation after generation of black families have taught their children how to be placed on lists for public housing, how to remain qualified for welfare checks, and how to remain qualified for medical benefits. Therefore, many public housing communities in cities across the country see multiple generations of the same family occupying public housing facilities.

These distorted priorities have led to a devaluing of education within the black community, which is the one thing that virtually guarantees freedom. The educational condition of black students has been an ongoing crisis for decades. In 2015, the National Assessment of Education Progress as well as many other independent studies revealed that the performance of black students in US schools is significantly and consistently much lower than white students.

The study showed that only 18 percent of black fourth graders nationwide had proficient reading skills, and only 19 percent were proficient in math.[161] Additionally, black high school students drop out of school at a much higher rate than whites. Between 2011–2012, only 69 percent of black high school students graduated, while whites graduated at 86 percent.[162]

Epidemic of Fatherless Homes in the Black Community

Without question, the greatest problem that faces the black community, second only to abortion, is single-parent homes.

According to the US Census Bureau's 2013 American Community Survey, about 78 percent of black families in poverty are headed by single mothers. And about 75 percent of all black children, in America, are raised in fatherless homes.[163]

---

[161] https://www.usnews.com/news/articles/2015/12/11/african-american-students-lagging-far-behind

[162] https://www.governing.com/gov-data/education-data/state-high-school-graduation-rates-by-race-ethnicity.html

[163] US Census Bureau 2013 ACS

No one can deny that it was Lyndon Johnson's war on poverty programs that caused an explosion of single-parent homes and fatherlessness within the black community. Before 1965, only 7 percent of all children were born to unmarried women in the United States.

By 1970, the numbers skyrocketed largely due to the federal government providing unrestricted financial help to single pregnant women or to single women with children no matter how many children they had. Many of these women reached the unfortunate conclusion there was no need to get married and no

About 75 percent of all black children in America are raised in fatherless homes.

need for a father in the lives of their children because the federal government provided support for each child.

The liberal social policy also encouraged black young men to engage in extremely irresponsible behavior as they embraced the notion that the federal government would provide for any children that they produce. After living in this manner for several generations, many blacks have embraced this lifestyle and view it as "normal" within the black community.

The disproportionate number of fatherless homes has also caused black America to lead in many of the social problems facing the country. Research shows that children raised in fatherless homes are much more likely to engage in antisocial behavior that places them on a path that leads to inevitable encounters with law enforcement.

Children raised in fatherless homes are four times more likely to fall into poverty, and girls without fathers are seven times more likely to become pregnant as a teenager. Fatherless children are also more likely to abuse drugs and alcohol, more likely to have behavioral problems, more likely to go to prison, more likely to commit a crime, and twice as likely to drop out of high school.[164] These social problems, triggered by fatherlessness, have led to nearly 43 percent of the country's prison population consisting of black Americans.[165]

Urban areas within cities such as Los Angeles, Baltimore, St. Louis, Philadelphia, Detroit, Chicago, Boston, and New York are in ruins and suffer daily from the blight of decay, violent crimes, and drugs—all of which primarily occur within the black communities led by Democrat mayors and city council members.

It is a very grim and sobering picture of a people who have suffered great oppression and affliction—and fought, clawed, and struggled to earn their freedom—only to be led back into bondage.

But I do not believe this is the end of their story. Because even as black Americans were being misled by the NAACP and civil rights leaders committed to the Socialist agenda—and even as they were being misled by the Democrats, there were points of light along the path for them to turn toward.

As the years have unfolded, these lights became brighter and brighter. I believe, in the very near future, the lights will be bright enough for all black Americans to clearly see that they have been misled.

And black America will take corrective measures—in earnest.

---

[164] https://www.fatherhood.org/fatherhood-data-statistics
[165] https://www.urbancure.org

Chapter 17
Hope for the Future

Dr. Thomas Sowell

Even as so-called civil rights leaders such as Roy Wilkins covered up for Democrat segregationists; purposely, maliciously, and wrongly accused the Republican Party of the historic oppression of blacks; and helped the media rewrite history, there were black teachers, authors, writers, and intellectual giants who were desperately directing black American's toward the truth.

They wrote numerous articles and books and lectured at many institutions declaring that the civil rights leaders had betrayed the black community and were using them as pawns to advance the Socialist agenda.

They also appeared on various television and radio talk shows and discussed the dangers of Socialism and Communism to help open the eyes of black America to the destruction they unwittingly embraced.

The Early Black Intellectual Giants
Dr. Thomas Sowell

Two of the greatest minds among these champions of freedom during the 1970s were Dr. Thomas Sowell and Dr. Walter Williams.

Dr. Sowell is an economist and sociologist. He was born in Gastonia, North Carolina, in 1930, but grew up in Harlem, New York. After he was honorably discharged from the US Marines, he earned a bachelor's degree from Harvard University, a master's degree from Columbia University, and currently serves as a Senior Fellow at the Hoover Institution and Stanford University.

Dr. Sowell, who is also a syndicated columnist, has written 51 books and lectured at colleges and universities across the nation to help educate black America about the menace of Socialism and Communism and teach them about the principles of good economics. Among his published works are *Marxism: Philosophy and Economics*, *Education: Assumption versus History*, *Race and Economics*, and *Wealth, Poverty, and Politics*.

During his years in the intellectual arena, Dr. Sowell became known for short, pithy, but extremely accurate comments that struck at the heart of whatever issue he addressed. One of Dr. Sowell's most notable comments was "*The black family survived centuries of slavery and generations of Jim Crow, but has been disintegrated by the expansion of the welfare state.*"

Dr. Walter Williams

Dr. Walter. E. Williams is another black intellectual who during the 1970s made courageous efforts to correct the path of black America. Dr. Williams was born and raised in Philadelphia, Pennsylvania. After he was discharged from the US military, Williams earned a bachelor's degree in economics from California State College in 1965 and a master's degree and PhD in economics from UCLA.

In 1980, Dr. Williams began working as a professor of economics

Dr. Walter Williams

for George Masson University and served as chairman of the school's Economics Department until 2001.

Dr. Williams is also a syndicated columnist and his articles are published in hundreds of newspapers across the country every week. Williams has also traveled, given speeches, and authored many books that speak directly to the problems in black America. Among his written works are *Liberty versus the Tyranny of Socialism*, *Race and Economics: How Much can be Blamed on Discrimination*, *The State Against Blacks*, and *All It Takes is Guts: A Minority View*.

Dr. Williams has also made many radio and television appearances to debate with other scholars on the superiority of Capitalism over Socialism. Williams has appeared on shows such as *Nightline*, *Firing Line*, *Face the Nation*, *MacNeil/Lehrer*, and *Wall Street Week*. He also appeared in a PBS documentary in 2015 entitled *Suffer No Fools*.

For decades and to this day, Dr. Williams fights against the Democrats' Socialist agenda, which has broken the will of many blacks to strive for freedom and kept them in a continuous cycle of poverty. In recent years, Dr. Williams provided a description of "social justice" that the black community should embrace, rather than its current definition.

"Let me offer my definition of social justice: I keep what I earn, and you keep what you earn. If you disagree, then tell me how much of what I earn belongs to you and why."

Dr. Sowell and Dr. Williams were the two primary national voices within black America who tried to respond to the deception of the so-called "civil rights" leaders and correct the path of blacks during the 1970s and 1980s. Throughout that time, the media dismissed them as anomalies and not representative of "true black America."

Modern-Day Free-Thinking Blacks

For many years, it seemed like Sowell and Williams would be the only voices from within the black community to speak against the community's monolithic support of the Democratic Party.

But they were later joined by others who wanted to see the black community correct itself. Among them is Larry Elder, or *"the sage of South Central."*

Larry Elder was raised the son of a janitor and became an attorney, author, syndicated columnist, and radio program host. He earned a bachelor of arts in political science from Brown University in 1974, and a Juris Doctor from the University of Michigan Law School in 1977.

Elder began a career in media during the late 1980s on *WVIZ*, which later became known as the *Larry Elder Show* in 2004. His show became nationally syndicated by ABC Radio Networks.

Larry Elder

Elder consistently challenges the Democrat Socialist agenda during his broadcasts and has written several books to help loosen their hold on black America. Elder is the author of the bestselling book, *The 10 Things You Can't Say in America* as well as *What's Race Got to Do with It? Why it's Time to Stop the Stupidest Argument in America*, and *Stupid Black Men: How to Play the Race Card and Lose*.

Deneen Borelli and Star Parker are two more powerful national voices from within black America who are calling for blacks to abandon the Socialist agenda that has kept many of them in poverty. Borelli is a Fox News contributor and appears on finance shows. She is also the author of *Blacklash: How Obama and the Left are Driving Americans to the Government Plantation*.

Star Parker is a syndicated columnist and the founder and president of the Center for Urban Renewal and Education (CURE). CURE, a Washington, DC-based Public Policy Institute, was founded in 1995 to fight poverty and restore the dignity of the black community.

Parker is uniquely qualified to address single black young women raising children alone. Parker grew up in East St. Louis, Illinois, and fell into a life of drug and welfare abuse. Parker has also had four abortions.

In other words, Star Parker was trapped in the cycle of poverty created for her and other black Americans by the Socialist Democrats. Parker is the author of several books including *Pimps, Whores, and Welfare Brats: From Welfare Cheat to Conservative Messenger*, *Uncle Sam's Plantation: How Big Government Enslaves America's Poor and What We Can Do About It*, and *More Freedom—Good for Blacks, Bad for Black Politicians*.

Two other organizations dedicated to the restoration of dignity and free thinking in black America is LeaveThePlantation.org, founded by Mason Weaver, and the Frederick Douglass Foundation.

Weaver is a motivational speaker, a businessman, and the author of *It's OK to Leave the Plantation*, *The Rope*, *Diamond in the Rough*, and *Polishing the Diamond in the Rough*. Weaver has traveled the country extensively and challenges black Americans to think independently. He also continues to point out that individual blacks do not have to continue to support the Democrats because it is the path most blacks follow.

The Frederick Douglass Foundation, based in Washington, DC, teaches and promotes the principles embraced by Frederick Douglass himself to young black men and women throughout the country. The organization helps them understand the principles that took Douglass from slavery to freedom and uses Douglass's life as an example. The organization also helps them understand that those principles will do the same for them.

Today, each of these organizations has stepped into the role that was abandoned by the NAACP. They are determined to see black America free from the grip of Socialist Democrat deception. And the advent of social media and the explosion of its popularity may make that happen much sooner than anyone suspected.

The Brave, the Bold, the Fearless Free-Thinking Blacks on Social Media

The unexpected, unpredicted growth and expansion of social media has brought with it an explosion of more voices from within the black community who are ready and willing to join the fight.

And these groups of advocates are very appealing to young people and others who spend a lot of time on the internet and demand their attention. They are very well informed, hard-hitting, educated, unintimidated, relentless, courageous, and uncompromising.

They speak with boldness and their rhetoric is very blunt, yet sharp. They are not concerned about politeness or hurt feelings and their only concern is the unfiltered truth.

Unlike their predecessors, Drs. Thomas Sowell and Walter Williams, this new generation of free-thinking blacks adds a great deal of comedy, humor, wit, and sarcasm to their intellectual arguments. It appears that knowledge mixed with entertainment is an effective formula to reach 21st-century black America.

Although not all online and public responses to them have been positive, it appears that their message is penetrating the minds of the masses.

Alonzo Rachel and Apostle Claver T. Kamau-Imani

Among the first to appear was musician, entertainer, and political commentator Alonzo "Zo" Rachel, host of *Zo Nation*, and Apostle Claver T. Kamau-Imani, founder and chairman of Raging

Alonzo Rachel, host of "Zo Nation."

Elephants.org and Raging Elephants Radio.

Rachel first became known by posting numerous videos on YouTube directly challenging black Americans to explain why they vote consistently for Democrats. Later, Rachel included educational aspects to his video that exposed the racist history of the Democratic Party.

Rachel's videos were not only informative and educational, but very entertaining. Rachel captured the attention of blacks across the country with a unique blend of comedy, history, and education in each of his videos. Rachel worked for PJTV for several years and is still seen and heard on social media.

When Apostle Claver T. Kamau-Imani began in 2007 as a radio talk show host, he first directed his energy against Planned Parenthood and the disproportionate number of abortions of black babies in the United States. As his organization expanded into social media, Kamau-Imani's audience expanded, and he promotes the benefits of personal responsibility and freedom.

Kevin Jackson and the Blacksphere

One of the most courageous, unapologetic, and unfiltered voices among these champions of freedom is Kevin Jackson, founder of the *Kevin Jackson Show* and the Blacksphere.net. Jackson started on radio in 2009 and is now nationally syndicated. He blends pop culture with political commentary in his own unique way and has been a guest commentator for several news outlets. Jackson is also the author of *Race-Pimping: The Multi-Trillion Dollar Business of Liberalism*, *The Big Black Lie*, and *Sexy Brilliance and Other Political Lies*.

Diamond and Silk and the Hodge Twins

Attacking Socialism in pairs through social media and using comedy as a major part of their arsenal are former committed Democrats Lynnette Hardaway and Rochelle Richardson, otherwise known as Diamond and Silk and the Hodge Twins.

Diamond and Silk

Diamond and Silk first started with live streaming video blogs about their support for Donald Trump in 2016. Not only did their videos become very popular, but they got the attention of President Trump. Their videos were funny and communicated their belief in a cultural fashion familiar and commonly used among black Americans. The videos were humorous, yet strong and unapologetic in their support of Trump. Diamond and Silk also produced a political documentary entitled *Dummycrats* and appeared on several news outlets as guest commentators.

The Hodge Twins not only use social media as their platform, they appear in comedy clubs across the country, delivering edgy, no-holds barred comedy and sarcasm at the expense of Democrat politicians.

The Hodge Twins are, without question, the most fearless comedy duo in the entertainment industry and likely one of the greatest sources of offense for the Democrats.

Although they may deeply offend the sensibilities of the Democrat politicians, including many black Democrats, there is no doubt that they are good at what they do. They communicate effectively in an urban style that blacks easily connect with. And they make many black Democrats laugh at themselves, which causes them to reconsider their political choices.

Jon Miller and Candace Owens

Certainly among the boldest of this generation's independent thinkers are Jon Miller and Candace Owens.

Jon Miller is a White House correspondent for *CRTV* and the host of "*The White House Brief.*" He formerly worked as a journalist for Fox News, the Blaze, and Mercury Radio Arts.

Miller brilliantly uses his social media platforms to highlight the foolishness of the Socialist agenda. Like Alonzo Rachel, Kevin Jackson, and many others, Miller wraps complex news and information in easily digestible humor. Miller does not pull any punches, especially when the news deeply concerns the black community. And Miller appears to give equal, if not slightly greater, priority to entertainment over the news—which certainly works well in the black America.

Candace Owens hosts her own podcast for Prager University "*The Candace Owens Show.*" She was also the communications director for Turning Point USA, a nonprofit organization that works to educate and train college students about the benefits of capitalism, free markets, and limited government. Owens is also the founder of the *BLEXIT* movement, which encourages blacks to exit the Democratic Party.

Owens began by posting a series of videos on YouTube and Twitter under the title *Red Pill Black*, inspired by *the Matrix* movie series, in which the main character is required to swallow a red pill to see the reality of his situation.

Candace Owens testifies before the Democrat-controlled congressional committee.

In the early videos, Owens speaks directly and candidly to the black community about the misery inflicted upon them by the socialist agenda of the Democratic Party. She also confronts the continuous hatred and racism many blacks have for whites, which is inspired by the Socialists in America.

Additionally, her videos address the exploitation of the black community's fear of racism for socialist political gain. Owens effectively explains that, throughout the years, the black community has been conditioned to see racism where it is not present causing many black American's to turn to Socialists for help again and again. Owens also produced videos that address the "white guilt" phenomenon and misinformation about police brutality.

As communications director for Turning Point, USA, Owens traveled throughout the country and spoke on colleges campuses about the threat of Socialism, the racist history of the Democratic Party, and the benefits of a capitalist economy. She was often greeted with extreme hostility from Democrats, supporters of Socialism, and Antifa. But she persevered regardless at their attempts at intimidation.

Owens has also appeared on many cable news and talk shows and debated several Democrat members of Congress and leaders of liberal causes about the effects of their policies on the black community. During an interview on Fox News, Owens debated with civil rights attorney Leo Terrell and boldly claimed that the Democratic Party has always wanted blacks to fail in America.

In April of 2018, rapper, singer, and songwriter Kanye West posted on social media that he likes how Candace Owens thinks.[166] West, also an outspoken Trump supporter, used his considerable influence throughout the black community to support Owens.

During a congressional hearing about nationalism in 2019, Owens boldly confronted Democrat committee members about the racist history of the Democratic Party and the suffering and anguish blacks have endured because of them. Democratic Congressman Ted Lieu tried to discredit Owens by playing a recording of a statement made by Owens about Adolph Hitler. But Owens quickly responded to Congressman Lieu by revealing the full context of the recording.

"I think it's pretty apparent that Mr. Lieu thinks that black people are stupid and will not pursue the full clip in its entirety. He purposefully extracted the clip he cut off and you didn't hear the question that was asked of me," Owens said.

In less than 24 hours, the video of Owens's confrontation with Congressman Lieu and other Democrat committee members went viral and was seen almost 4.5 million times more than any other C-Span Twitter video or any other congressional hearing video.[167] According to Jeremy Art, C-SPAN's social media senior specialist, the video is the most watched C-SPAN Twitter recording of any House hearing.[168]

Owens's confidence and courage has also caught the attention of President Donald Trump, who praised her on social media as the latest of "*an ever-expanding group of smart thinkers.*"[169]

Owens has connected with young men and women of all races, between the ages of 18 and 35, across the country and receives a lot of

---

[166] http://www.thefader.com/2018/04/21/kanye-west-far-right-candace-owens

[167] https://www.marketwatch.com/story/that-clip-of-candace-owens-scrapping-with-ted-lieu-is-about-to-set-a-record-2019-04-11

[168] https://www.foxnews.com/politics/candace-owens-ted-lieu-cspan-twitter-record

[169] https://www.theguardian.com/us-news/2018/may/09/trump-candace-owens-very-smart-thinker

their public support. Some have even duplicated the BLEXIT movement by establishing their own social media campaigns encouraging blacks to abandon the Democratic Party such as *#RedPillBlackMan*, *#BlackButNotDemocrat*, and *#Walkaway*.

There is evidence to support that the combined efforts of these independent black thinkers along with Donald Trump's success as president are beginning to loosen the grip of the Democrats' hold on black Americans. In the spring of 2018, Rasmussen Reports released a new poll that says the president's approval rating among African Americans was at 36 percent, which has doubled since 2017.[170]

President Trump also can take credit himself for his improved popularity among blacks. According to the Bureau of Labor Statistics, the unemployment rate for African Americans dropped to 6.2 percent in May of 2019.[171] During the Obama years, between 2009 and 2014, black unemployment continued to bounce between and 12.7 and 16.8 percent.

President Trump has also aggressively engaged Congress about the illegal immigration issue, which is very important to black America. For decades, the Democratic Party has turned a blind eye and deaf ear regarding this issue not only to blacks but to all Americans. And President Trump is the first president in the modern era whose position on illegal immigration reflects their own.

So, there is hope for the future of black America. In 1970, the Democrats and their allies in the national media and universities across the country constructed elaborate lies about the big switch and Nixon's Southern strategy.

But Martin Luther King Jr. once said, "*A lie can live for a long time, but a lie can't live forever.*"

Enough time has passed since 1970 for blacks to look back with clear 20/20 vision and see that for the last 50 years, the Socialist Democratic Party has only exploited and used them. And will only continue to do so.

---

[170] https://www.usatoday.com/story/news/politics/onpolitics/2018/08/16/trump-approval-rating-african-americans-rasmussen-poll/1013212002/

[171] https://data.bls.gov/timeseries/LNS14000006

About the Author

Ken Raymond is an independent writer, researcher, and author who lives in Winston-Salem, North Carolina. He graduated from Winston-Salem State University in 1987 with a bachelor of art's degree in English.

Raymond is originally from Boston, Massachusetts, and he graduated from Cathedral High School where he developed a passion for writing and research. After college, Raymond focused on the research and study of black political history and published his work on various websites and on social media.

In 2011, Raymond founded Frederick Douglass University, a former nonprofit organization whose mission was to produce educational materials, CDs, DVDs, books, and videos and make them available to high schools and colleges nationwide.

The organization disbanded in 2013, but Raymond, a former member of the board of trustees at Winston-Salem State University, has continued to research, write, and publish black historical information that is generally disregarded by high schools and colleges.

As a young man who grew up in Mattapan, an African American neighborhood about eight miles south of downtown Boston, Raymond experienced and witnessed the hardship and struggles within America's black community.

Raymond is not only motivated by his life-long passion for writing and research but a genuine belief that African Americans today would live much better lives if they had full and complete understanding of their own history.

He is also motivated by a desire to see African Americans correct the unfortunate paths they have taken that led to poverty, violence, and despair in urban areas throughout America. Raymond believes that most African Americans would gladly and easily make these corrections if they were more informed about their own history.

For this reason, Raymond will continue research, write, and publish the black historical information that many educational institutions have chosen to ignore.